Approaches to Literature through Subject

The Oryx Reading Motivation Series

by Paula Kay Montgomery

ORYX PRESS
1993

The rare Arabian Oryx is believed to have inspired the myth of the unicorn. This desert antelope became virtually extinct in the early 1960s. At that time several groups of international conservationists arranged to have 9 animals sent to the Phoenix Zoo to be the nucleus of a captive breeding herd. Today the Oryx population is nearly 800, and over 400 have been returned to reserves in the Middle East.

Copyright © 1993 by Paula Kay Montgomery
Published by The Oryx Press
4041 North Central at Indian School Road
Phoenix, Arizona 85012-3397

Published simultaneously in Canada

Printed and Bound in the United States of America

∞ The paper used in this publication meets the minimum requirements of American National Standard for Information Science—Permanence of Paper for Printed Library Materials, ANSI Z39.48, 1984.

Library of Congress Cataloging-in-Publication Data
Montgomery, Paula Kay.
    Approaches to literature through subject / Paula Kay
Montgomery.
        p.   cm. —(The Oryx reading motivation series)
    Includes bibliographical references and index.
    ISBN 0-89774-774-7
    1. Literature—Study and teaching (Elementary) 2. Literature-
-Study and teaching (Secondary) 3. Children—Books and reading.
I. Title. II. Series
LB1575.M66   1993
820'.71'2—dc20   93-967
                                                    CIP

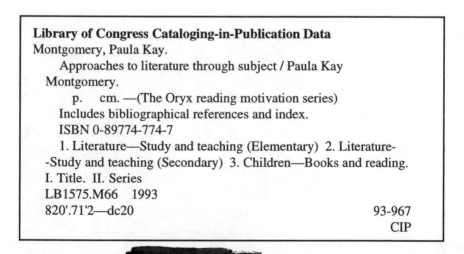

Contents

Series Statement

What makes an individual want to turn the page and read more? That question has puzzled many in the field of education. The answer is not always forthcoming. And, the answer is not the same for every individual. However, that is the question that prompted this series of books about getting students to read. The Oryx Reading Motivation Series focuses on the materials and approaches that seem to be prominent for grouping literature. The prime purpose for the investigation is to identify promising methods, techniques, and strategies that might motivate students or get students in grades five through nine to turn the page.

Each book in the series examines a particular approach to grouping literature: thematic, subject, genre, literary form, chronological, author, and comprehension skills. In each case, the literature is grouped for presentation in a different way to meet a specific purpose. For example, the comprehension-skills approach groups literature useful for teaching the same skill. That skill might be comparison: literature of all types that might be grouped together to exemplify the pattern of comparison. Literary form examines the structure of the literary work, such as the diary, novel, short story, and so forth, with an emphasis on the elements of those structures, including plot, characterization, etc. An author approach provides a study of the works of one author that might allow students to examine style, growth, and changes a writer has undergone. Works written over a given period of time or at the same time might be grouped for a chronological approach. Such an approach allows the reader to examine interrelationships between writers and their society. The interest of students in a particular subject makes the subject approach useful for grouping different literary formats and forms about the same subject. The genre approach capitalizes on particular student interests or skills, such as problem solving or history, and combines this with works of similar literary form and subject patterns. And, finally, the thematic approach groups materials around a common theme that may be investigated in depth by students.

Each book in the series is written for the classroom teacher and library media specialist. This partnership offers rich possibilities for combining the knowledge of teaching and literary content with the multiple resources of two professions that have long studied literature and searched for ways to make students want to turn the pages. Although the approaches, methods, strategies, and techniques may be used at any level, the materials have been selected for use by students in grades five through nine and are so noted in interest and reading levels. The titles may, in fact, be appropriate for older readers as well. Grades five through nine represent a period of development during which many students become lost and begin to lose faith in reading as a way of finding answers and gaining satisfaction.

Each book in the series is meant to provide one method for beginning an exploration with students. One would not expect every approach to work with every individual. Nor would one expect every teacher and library media specialist to enjoy or feel comfortable with every approach. Each approach is an option.

Finally, the sources and materials suggested in the series were selected given a number of criteria:

- General literary quality and accuracy;
- Availability;
- Readability and interest levels;
- Ethnic, racial, and sex-role representation;
- Availability of media support materials; and
- Recommendations in selected journals and guides.

It is the hope of the author that the suggested books and materials will serve as stimuli for grouping literature in attractive packages. Perhaps each package will tempt some reader to open the book and turn the page.

—Paula Kay Montgomery

Preface

How can we move from the testing and evaluation mode in reading and education to a more intellectually relaxed and stimulating way of modeling the rewards of learning? Perhaps if, as adults, we moved toward more subtle approaches that include doing more reading ourselves, we might instill that value in those younger. This notion is part of what motivated the present look at a subject approach to reading. Most adults who read for pleasure, as opposed to work, select materials related to their own interests. Isn't this equally important for young people? Isn't it important to let young people know that learning about what interests them is part of a quality of life that would be wished for all? Among all of the many subject area pursuits, there is room for students to find those they prefer.

With so many topics available that they might find interesting, how can it be possible that students might be turned off by reading? A subject approach can allow students the freedom to read without feeling pressure or fearing they will be penalized if a particular topic does not appeal. This book represents a concerted effort to look at available literature in combination with students' interests. By structuring opportunities, teachers may help students become aware of the many nurturing subjects they can read about. Students may then move from an awareness level to a position in which they develop their own abilities to select what will become their own preferences. In the process of practicing reading, they may become better readers and more involved citizens.

There are other approaches available; for example, a classroom teacher or library media specialist might try thematic, genre, author, chronological, literary forms and elements, or comprehension skills approaches as well. It would be a mistake to try only the subject approach with students. However, the advantage of this approach is that it emphasizes self-selection in many different areas, including practice reading in quantity, and the freedom to be in control of reading choices. In a well-rounded reading program, the subject approach would be used in connection with all of the others. It would also be hoped that parents and other reading volunteers might be called upon to help in this endeavor.

Several terms are used throughout this book that should be clarified for the reader. In the professional education literature, the terms *approaches, methods, strategies,* and *techniques* often are used interchangeably. Rather than further confusing the reader, for the purposes of this book, *approach* is defined as a categorization of the literature itself. Of the seven approaches to literature outlined previously (thematic, genre, author, chronological, literary forms and elements, comprehension skills, and subject), the subject approach offers one of the most enjoyable for motivating reading in quantity. Perhaps it is the satisfaction students feel when they find an interesting subject with which they are familiar or comfortable. It is a common experience for many library media specialists to have students request more materials about monsters, dinosaurs, motorcycles, stars, drawing, baseball, and so forth, because their imagination or their curiosity has been snared by encounters with these topics.

The term *method,* in the context of motivating literature appreciation, differs from the term *approach* in that it concentrates on the behavior of the individual using the literature. In the classroom situation, methods are most often seen as ways that teachers introduce information or instruction. However, methods are actually those behaviors of students and teachers that are generalizable for structured learning. They are represented by the general term *method* and refer to the application of principles, practices, and procedures that can be transferred, often to more than one area of interest or study. Methods discussed in this book, such as lecture, discussion, and brainstorming, are identified in the master chart presented in Chapter 1.

Techniques are more specific ways of presenting instructional material or conducting instructional activities. For example, there may be generalized ways of leading a discussion, but there are more detailed techniques for setting up and developing a panel discussion. *Techniques,* then, refers to the specific skills embedded within a method, such as pacing.

Finally, a *strategy* is the plan or the means by which a method might be used. The strategy includes the many considerations necessary for successful use of a method. For example, how students might be grouped, the arrangement of the learning area for using the method, or the use of specific behaviors to elicit response might be included in the strategy for using a method to motivate reading. A discussion technique might be used with a plan to provide plenty of "wait time" during certain types of discussions involving open-ended questions. This might be part of a strategy designed to help students think about the material they read.

The hope in a subject approach is that emphasis on variety and quantity will help some students to "click" with a particular topic and devour anything and everything they can get their hands on related to that topic. Therefore, the lists presented in the chapters of this volume encompass television programs, films, videotapes, books, articles, and so on. These lists may include topics generally considered outside the realm of educational materials, but they are suggested because, in fact, students are learning outside the "educational setting." Movies and television are at least as powerful motivators as what students see and hear in classrooms. Many films and television programs form the basis of conversations among peers at this age.

Therefore, the book is organized around the subject approach. The first two chapters offer some advice on investigating the approach and locating materials in certain subject areas. The following four chapters are devoted to subjects classified traditionally as people, places, things, and events. In each of these chapters, sample topics are investigated, providing sample methods and strategies and lists of materials or resources related to those topics and methods. These samples do not represent all possible methods, of course; they are presented only as examples.

Before I invite readers to browse these chapters, some special thanks are in order. First, thanks go to the professionals in libraries and library media centers in Maryland. Under the leadership of Maurice Travillian, assistant state superintendent for library development and services, Maryland's libraries have amassed accessible holdings connected through the Maryland Interlibrary Loan Agency. Titles and materials were located using the computerized tool of the network, Microcat. Also, a special thank you goes to H. Thomas Walker, Joseph Duckworth, Ron Martin, and Debbie

Chambers of the Howard County Public Schools, for their help in obtaining professional resources and hints about other resources.

Approaches to Literature
through Subject

1

What Is a Subject Approach?

Samuel Johnson stated, "Knowledge is of two kinds. We know a subject ourselves, or we know where we can find information upon it." The subject approach to motivating students to love and share literature incorporates both of these kinds of knowledge. A student may know or have an interest in a topic as well as want to find out more about that topic. The subject is the center of the approach, with reading a means to obtaining more knowledge about it.

A major assumption of many educators and teachers is that interests are primary sources of motivation. Cooper and Burger (1980) noted in their studies of causes of students' and teachers' academic success that interest in the subject matter is a major category of causes for success. Students who believe their efforts influence their achievements are more likely to learn than are students who believe that learning depends on teachers or other people (Wang and Stiles, 1976). This suggests that students who select their own subjects of interest may feel more control over learning, or that the learning locus of control is with the students rather than the teachers or adults.

An approach that takes advantage of the interests of students inherently will motivate students to read more. Such an approach would require the classroom teacher to balance students' pursuits of their present interests while stimulating new ones. The subject approach is one in which the interest of the student is of primary importance. A student identifies his or her interests and explores those areas of interest in order to satiate curiosity. In many instances, it may be the quantity of materials rather than their depth that interests a student. For example, the student interested in racing cars may not require all materials to be completely different. He or she may just want more and more about races. In other instances the student may want more in-depth information and knowledge about a topic, such as how a given car was developed. In that case, the student looks for more detailed, accurate, and specific information. The purpose for reading and the literary form of materials are different, but the main topic stays the same. Such an approach allows for both breadth and depth in reading.

The subject approach is slightly different from the thematic approach because a student might or might not delve into the deeper meaning of the subject. Nor are students necessarily required to make comparisons, synthesize, analyze, judge, or find the "true meaning of life." The subject is of value in and of itself. It is legitimate to read as much as possible about dinosaurs, stars, automobiles, UFOs, or whatever. Thus, it is likely that the subject approach may cause less pressure for the student than the thematic approach. There is an ease to the reading and, one hopes, a sense of plain fun.

This is not to say that critical thinking skills are not required. Although the student may not be *required* to think critically, often the amount of information absorbed about a subject combined with the motivation to find out more will cause the student to develop his or her own questions, which require higher-order thinking skills. The student capitalizes on those innate learning abilities and begins to practice control over what he or she remembers or chooses to synthesize, analyze, and so forth.

The subject approach provides practice, with the emphasis on quantity and variety of literary forms. The subject approach differs from the genre approach in that the subject alone rather than the literary pattern combined with the subject is dominant.

Given the many ages and levels of students, obviously their interests vary. Also, students' sex, maturity, and intelligence levels affect their interests (Gray, 1955). One might not expect female sixth graders to have the same interests as male eighth graders. Equally, young adults mature at different rates, and the varying levels of maturity within groups of young people result in many different interests among them. When maturity level is combined with level of intelligence, one might expect differences not only in interests, but also in the level of interest in any given subject.

ADVANTAGES AND DISADVANTAGES OF A SUBJECT APPROACH

A subject approach is cognitively and affectively advantageous for introducing adolescents to the multitude of possible reading topics. By providing students with global overviews of subject areas and opportunities to discover how much there is to assimilate when looking into any particular subject, teachers can help students to begin to appreciate the enormity of our knowledge base. Students' realization of the vast number of subjects that can be read about and explored reinforces their understanding of how comparatively short is any one human being's investigation time on earth.

Appreciation

Perhaps one of the greatest advantages to working with a subject approach is the actual practice time invested in reading. When a student finds a subject of interest, he or she has a built-in motivation to pursue that interest without thinking much about the reading act. Reading is the means to the end. It is almost recreational, in the sense that it provides a form of mental play. Reading can be considered a normal solution to finding out about a topic.

Such practice and exploration of subjects allows for self-selection. Students begin to exercise some needed control over what they want to know. They may feel the compulsion or drive to use reading as a method for creative problem solving. The satisfaction to be found in answering a question or learning something one never knew before should not be undervalued.

Other positive attitudes may be developed from a subject approach. Given the opportunity for self-selection of topics and materials, students incorporate the value of reading books and other materials and the information that may be gained from them. The relationship of reading to other media formats also is reinforced; it may no longer be enough to see a videotape about a topic. There are so many options for finding out that the student's "mental bag of tools" expands significantly. Reading comes to be considered a normal, routine activity that everyone can and must do.

By reading, a student learns that communication occurs between the reader and the author. Sustained thought while reading often brings a sense of satisfaction. And, for some, being a reader can lead to becoming a writer also.

Students involved in self-selection usually experience on their own the many ways to read books. For example, they may not need to be taught that it is as legitimate to read large or small sections before laying a book aside as it is to read a book all the way through. Books, or the print medium in general, become a way of extending their own thought. The book is not so sacrosanct that its value is greater than what it contains. Students may even discover that they can become experts on topics that others they come in contact with know little about. For some, such expertise brings prestige and the enjoyment of knowing stuff that adults—parents and teachers— might not know. Such power for the young adult becomes another motivator.

Skills

While use of a subject approach may instill positive attitudes toward reading within students, it also can allow development and practice of reading skills. Most subjects have been written about in many different literary patterns. Therefore, students could gain information about a topic such as dinosaurs from novels of different genres, from poetry, and from exposition. Making connections and experiencing different forms of literature become secondary to the act of finding out about the topic.

Exploration of topics of interest allows students to expand their vocabularies, especially related to those topics. As a student learns the vocabulary connected to the topic of interest, he or she learns and understands the words in relation to this context. Thus, the student can develop a schema about the information he or she gathers. The student is likely to arrange and rearrange this schema as he or she gathers more information about the topic. Eventually, a larger context understanding is established.

The student's experiential background might also be expected to expand. By reading many works about the same or similar topics, students become more fluent in reading about these topics because the vocabularies become more familiar and the schemata are more fully developed. Students experience continued success in learning or gathering information from context clues.

There are some disadvantages to using the subject approach. Because students are encouraged to read as much as they can about their topics of interest, they may feel the emphasis on quantity rather than quality. Although this does not have to be the case, the danger is there. Using the subject approach does not necessarily allow students in-depth study. Readers may consider quality, but judgment and critical reading are not the primary focus. Rather, the approach focuses on quantity rather than quality. This disadvantage can be overcome. A subject approach may be used before or after other approaches. In fact, the subject approach prepares students for more critical approaches, such as a genre or thematic approach and later an author or chronological approach.

RELATION TO OTHER APPROACHES TO LITERATURE

Classroom teachers and library media specialists may consider three components in motivating reading: the readers, the literature, and the tasks or strategies that will assist or enable students to enter or participate in the reading experience. These three major components may be seen in Figure 1.

The complex interplay is noted by many researchers (Pearson and Johnson, 1978; Heber, 1978) as essential for teachers to recognize as they work with students. When these three components are skillfully and competently managed, student motivation to read can be generated or improved.

This model can be defined and used in developing units of instruction, identifying methods for executing lessons, and identifying methods for grouping literature and students. In considering literature, there appear to be seven major ways of grouping the material for study, which can be categorized under the following approaches: subject, thematic, genre, literary forms and their elements, author, chronological, and comprehension skills. The tasks required of students include listening and reading/viewing as input and speaking and writing/producing as output. Finally, students may participate in these activities with their own learning

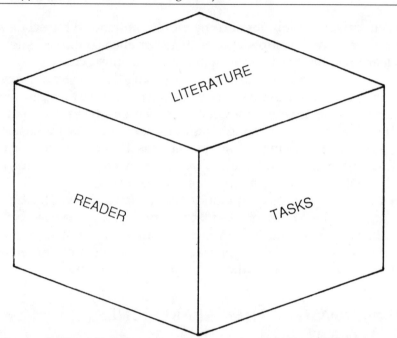

Figure 1. Three Primary Components for Reading Motivation

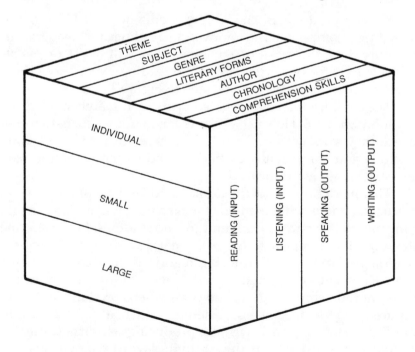

Figure 2. Interactive Components Contributing to Reading Motivation

styles and abilities in the following ways: individually, in small groups of two to eight or nine, and in large groups of nine or more. The three major components may be seen in an interactive model in which various components work together in a learning environment or situation. The components may be wielded to help establish motivating experiences for students. These interactive components are shown in Figure 2.

SAMPLE SUBJECT GROUPINGS

If a subject approach is taken, it might be useful to think about subjects in terms of nouns: persons, places, things, and events. These can be named and identified as more concrete subjects. While some topics can become thematic, this book suggests ways in which the readers can investigate them as subjects.

USEFUL ATTITUDES AND SKILLS FOR TEACHERS AND LIBRARY MEDIA SPECIALISTS

What helps the classroom teacher and library media specialist implement a subject approach? A combination of particular attitudes and skills is useful.

Attitudes

For the classroom teacher or library media specialist who loves to read, the first requirement is an easy one. A teacher or library media specialist who reads and is seen reading is a model. If that adult also talks about what he or she sees and reads as a routine matter, that is further reinforcement. This is especially true if he or she voices opinions about shared reading or viewing during conversations. For example, if after seeing a television movie such as *Sarah Plain and Tall* and reading the book, the classroom teacher talks with students about what they thought and truly listens to their opinions, questions them about reasons for their opinions, and offers his or her own ideas, the respect shown for viewing and reading is likely to register.

The belief that reading is valuable is likely to be transmitted, especially if students see this habit in force. Students may observe this valuing when classroom teachers or library media specialists talk about what they have read and listen to students talk about what they have read. Each time there is a conversation about a book or film read or viewed, students understand that reading is part of the expected "norm." When students express their own opinions about what they have read, they will know from the instructor's reaction whether or not the freedom to select and read is considered one of their rights and responsibilities.

Skills

Because the use of a subject approach relies on knowing what subjects are interesting to students, the classroom teacher or library media specialist who listens to students, values their opinions, and sensitively suggests materials related to those interests is most likely to succeed with the approach. There are other skills that may also be of use; these are discussed in turn below.

Questioning Techniques

Fluency in asking questions may be one of the more valuable skills available in the instructor's "teaching/learning basket." For example, the classroom teacher might ask as many questions as possible during a conversation to find out what is on a student's mind or of special interest on a particular day. Probing questions that require the listener to go beyond superficial one-word answers will give the library media specialist an edge in identifying an interest and a set of materials that would satisfy that interest. This means that the library media specialist who asks for more information, requests justification of an answer, responds with refocusing questions, and even prompts new questions in return from the student is more likely to gather information that will be helpful. Those higher-order questions that cannot be answered from memory or simple sensory descriptions often lead to special insights on the part of the questioner and the responder. Divergent questions that have no obvious correct answers leave the field open and allow the student to respond by going beyond known answers and proceeding toward exploring the unknown.

Organization and Structure

Called set induction, the practice of preparing a student for an upcoming activity is a very powerful skill for use in the subject approach. While many of the activities suggest freedom for students to explore on their own, the manner in which students are "set up" for the exploration makes a significant difference. When there are several students involved, the common frames of reference must be established so that students may interact and eventually form preferences. Advance organizers to help the students prepare for the material they may encounter can be so successful that it would be a disservice not to make use of them. Organizing the activity so that the students can explore interests with leisurely independence is enhanced when the experience is previously structured. And that exploration is further enhanced if the students understand the structure.

Within a well-organized structure students should receive stimulus variation. That is, varying behaviors on the part of the classroom teacher or library media specialist are likely to preclude boredom and apathy. The structure is not enough. The classroom teacher or library media specialist who can make the "same old thing" look new or different has a true gift. Sometimes varying the method from one activity to another is enough. At other times, the materials, methods, and possibility of student self-selection in the specific techniques set up an experience that may ignite an interest in a subject that will last a lifetime.

Finally, the ability of the classroom teacher or library media specialist to bring closure to an event is extremely helpful. There is a sense of well-being or completeness when there is an end to things. It does not mean the end of the interest, but an end to a particular interaction with the subject. The classroom teacher or library media specialist who can behave in a way that helps students see the logical progression of main ideas with subordinate ideas, and who can pull it all together, adds a sense of accomplishment for the student.

Reinforcement

It is easy to take reinforcement for granted or to forget what would be most reinforcing to a student. When a student shows an interest in a subject, the classroom teacher or library media special-ist should be aware enough to reward that student appropriately and to give him or her time to investigate. After all, that is a part of natural learning. The student does not necessarily have to be rewarded with a jelly bean, carrot, or high praise, although that kind of reward may appeal to some. Rather, the reward can take the form of the silent approval of letting go, so that the student can take control of his or her own learning and find out more. Not everything that a student learns has to have flowed directly from the expert classroom teacher or library media specialist. Rewards may come in a variety of formats.

In order to provide reinforcement, the classroom teacher should recognize attending behavior. Observation of facial expressions, body postures, activity or nonactivity, and conversations can pro-vide clues about students' high or low interest levels. Silence and nonverbal cues are powerful indicators that teachers can use to understand what directions students might like to take. When given the opportunity, students' bodies often show what they are reluctant to say. A shrug related to one topic or a meaningful raised eyebrow to a friend when a certain topic comes into the conversa-tion can provide instant clues to interests. In turn, the classroom teacher and library media specialist should be conscious of the cues that they give regarding interests or topics—their own and possibly those of students. Some cues may suggest areas that students might find they want to pursue. The classroom teacher who smiles on those with certain interests and frowns on those with others does influence, positively or negatively.

Practice and Repetition

Often it is difficult for students to move among new ideas without some help. The use of examples is extremely valuable. A classroom teacher or library media specialist who can find concrete examples, whether presenting information inductively or deduc-tively, may make new topics simple and relevant to students' experiences. Planned repetition—whether simple repetition, literal repetition, spaced repetition, cumulative repetition, or massed repe-tition—can help focus a student long enough for him or her to decide whether or not a topic challenges. Some topics that make little impression at one time may have great impact when presented in a slightly different way at a different time. Not all students are ready to hear about some topics at the same time. What might be of interest today can be overlooked tomorrow.

Teaching Methods

Knowledge of teaching methods and techniques available for use in introducing and exploring topics is a major tool category for a classroom teacher or library media specialist. The more methods that can be used successfully, the more likely it is the classroom teacher or library media specialist can vary the way topics can be explored.

Figure 3 shows many of the methods and techniques available to the classroom teacher and library media specialist. In this book, examples will be given for using art methods (papier mache and bulletin boards), audiovisual methods (microfilm, videotape, and simulations), directed learning (language experience), general discussion, drama (role play, reenactment, and story theater), field trips, inquiry methods (scientific investigation and individual study), reading (sustained silent reading and free reading), and writing methods (word processing).

FURTHER RESOURCES

Although the subject approach is not commonly discussed in literature, there are several articles that may help identify how to use subjects to interest students in reading. The subject approach is represented in many commercial materials and may fall under the term *thematic unit.*

Articles and Dissertations

Allington, R. "If They Don't Read Much, How They Ever Gonna Get Good?" *Journal of Reading* 21:1 (1977), pp. 57–61.

Bissett, D. J. "The Amount and Effect of Recreational Reading in Selected Fifth Grade Classes." Doctoral Dissertation, Syracuse University, 1969. *Dissertation Abstracts International* 30, 5157-A (1969). (University Microfilms No. 7010316)

Art Methods
  Illustration
    (various media formats)
  Modelmaking
    Models
    Dioramas
    Mock Ups
  Sculpture
    Clay
    Stone
    Papier Mache
  Textiles
    Fabrics
    Tapestries
  Bulletin Boards/Displays
  Crafts
Audiovisual Methods
(Production and Use)
  Sound
    Listening Activities
    Taped Radio Programs
  Visual
    Charts
    Graphics
    Flannelboard
    Microfilm
    Visual Activities
    Posters
    Animation
  Sound/Visual
    Film
    Sound Filmstrip
    Videotape
    Slidetape
  Interactive
    Computer Drills
    Simulations
    Databases
  Sound/Visual/Interactive
  Tactile

  Manipulative
  Sound/Visual/Interactive/Tactile
Brainstorming
Conversation
Dance
  Dance Forms (e.g., modern, ballet, folkdancing)
Debate
Demonstration
Directed Learning
  Learning Activity Package
  Directed Reading Activity
  Concept Guides
  Structured Overviews
  Guided Reading
  Paired Reading/Learning
  Contracts
  Learning Centers
  Language Experience Approach
  Behavior Modification
  Programmed Learning
  Graphic Organizers
Discussion
  Guided Discussion
  Exploratory Discussion
  Panel Discussion
  General Discussion
Drama
  Sociodrama
  Role Play
  Play
  Costuming
  Creative Dramatics
  Puppetry (e.g., marionettes, hand puppets, shadow puppets)
  Mime
  Storytelling

Figure 3. Methods and Techniques

Drama—Cont'd.	Book Talk
Reading Aloud	Book Report
Choral Reading	***Music***
Reenactment	Song Writing
Readers Theater	Listening to Music
Story Theater	Musical Drama
Field Trip	***Questioning***
Game	Question/Discussion/Eval-
Gaming	uation
Simulations	Interview
Inquiry Method (discovery)	Oral History
Scientific Method (investiga-	Author
tion)	Survey
Puzzles	***Reading***
Research Methods/Strategies	Sustained Silent Reading
Simulation	Free Reading
Individual Study	Browsing
Laboratory Experiment	Cooperative Reading
Do-Look-and-Learn	***Writing Methods***
Problem Solving	Diary/Journal Writing
Lecture	Writing in Literary Forms
Speech Making	Word Processing

Figure 3. Methods and Techniques—cont'd.

Connor, D. "The Relationship between Reading Achievement and Voluntary Reading of Children." *Educational Review* 6 (1954), pp. 221–227.

Cooper, H. M., and J. M. Burger. "How Teachers Explain Students' Academic Performance: A Categorization of Free Response Academic Attributions." *American Educational Research Journal* 17 (1980), pp. 95–109.

Gray, W. S. "A Summary of Reading Investigations, July 1 1953–June 30 1954." *Journal of Educational Research* 48 (1955), pp. 401–442.

Greaney, V., and J. Quinn. *Factors Related to Amount and Type of Leisure Time Reading.* Paper presented at the Seventh International Reading Association World Congress on Reading, Hamburg, Germany, 1978. ED 163402.

Hummel, Jeffrey W., and Fisher, Peter J. L. "Reading Attitudes and Reading Interests of Urban Intermediate Grade Students." *Psychology in the Schools* 22:4 (October 1985), pp. 470–472.

Mathison, Carla. "Stimulating and Sustaining Student Interest in Content Area Reading." *Reading Research and Instruction* 28:3 (Spring 1989), pp. 76–83.

Paratore, Jeanne R. "The Influence of Reader Interest and Reader Prior Knowledge in the Reading Performance of Unskilled Readers in the Center for Clinical Assessment." Doctoral Dissertation, Boston University, 1983.

Pfau, D. W. "An Investigation of the Effects of Planned Recreational Reading Programs in First and Second Grade." Doctoral Dissertation, State University of New York at Buffalo, 1966. *Dissertation Abstracts International* 27, 1719-A (1966). (University Microfilms No. 6613086)

Robinson, Helen M. "What Research Says to the Teacher of Reading: Reading Interests." *Reading Teacher* 8 (1955), pp. 173–177.

Shirey, Larry L., and Reynolds, Ralph E. "Effect of Interest on Attention and Learning." *Journal of Educational Psychology* 80:2 (June 1988), pp. 159–166.

Thompson, Mark E. *What Does Research Literature Say about Active Readers?* Paper presented at Annual Meeting of North Central Reading Association, Notre Dame, IN, 1984. ED250665.

Wang, M. C., and B. Stiles. "An Investigation of Children's Concept of Self-Responsibility for Their School Learning." *American Educational Research Journal* 13 (1976), pp. 159–179.

Williams, Carolyn. *A Study of the Reading Interests, Habits, and Attitudes of Third, Fourth, and Fifth Graders: A Class Action Research Project.* Paper presented at Annual Meeting of Mid-South Educational Research Association, Little Rock, AR, 1989. ED312612.

Books

Heber, Harold L. *Teaching Reading in the Content Areas.* Englewood Cliffs, New Jersey: Prentice-Hall, 1978.

Norvell, G. W. *The Reading Responses of Adolescents.* Boston: Heath, 1950.

Pearson, P. David, Jane Hansen, and Christine Gordon. *The Effect of Background Knowledge on Young Children's Comprehension of Explicit and Implicit Information.* Technical Report No. 116. Urbana: Center for the Study of Reading, University of Illinois, 1979.

Pearson, P. David, and Dale D. Johnson. *Teaching Reading Comprehension.* New York: Holt, Rinehart & Winston, 1978.

Rankin, Marie. *Children's Interests in Library Books of Fiction.* No. 906. New York: Teachers College Contra Education, 1944.

Wade, Suzanne. *How Interest Affects Learning from Text.* Technical Report No. 506. Cambridge, MA: Bolt, Beranek and Newman, Inc., 1990. ED321237.

2

Where Do Subjects Originate?

"The world is so full of a number of things, I'm sure we should all be as happy as kings," says Robert Louis Stevenson in "Happy Thought" (in *A Child's Garden of Verses*, New York: Philomel, 1990, p. 41). Perhaps this thought is the main ingredient of a subject approach to motivating students to read. There are so many things about which students might take an interest. Surely among all of the world's topics there is something for every student to want to pursue. Topics and subjects already exist—the problem becomes how to help students look at those many "things" and determine their own preferences.

There is ample research that relates comprehension and memory to student interests. Students remember and comprehend topics that are highly interesting to them and relate to their backgrounds or prior knowledge, according to Estes and Vaughn (1973). Often interests are developed, learned, or incorporated into a student's memory when he or she has a strong or positive feeling of satisfaction coming from contact with some person, place, thing, or event. Interest arises when an individual has a feeling of intensity, concern, or curiosity about the person, place, thing, or event. The interest satisfies certain needs. Perhaps that is the reason that interest in a topic is a high motivator, certainly for reading. In fact, interest in topics is one of the reasons that students become readers. A common belief echoed by Ruth Strickland (1957, p.240) is that "a reader is not someone who can read, but one who reads." Janet Hickman (1977, p.375) notes in her article "What Do Fluent Readers Do?" that "fluent readers get to be that way by reading, and by

19

reading a great deal, from something of their own choosing." Given this belief, how do classroom teachers and library media specialists find out what those interests are and capitalize on them?

A number of suggestions are offered in this chapter. The most obvious strategy is to ask the students what they are interested in, and this is the strategy that should be used first. It will yield results. The problem with this strategy, however, is that students may be able to tell their interests based only on their present awareness. How can they express interests in other things in the world about which they are unaware? For the classroom teacher and library media specialist, the trick is identifying present interests while introducing new topics, so that students will continue to expand their possible choices. The second trick is to facilitate the process of turning students' interests into preferences. In fact, classroom teachers and library media specialists can play a major role in promoting and stimulating voluntary reading as suggested and confirmed by A. Irving (1980) and Lesley Mandel Morrow and Carol Simon Weinstein (1986).

There is a difference between interests and preferences. Students might have many interests but not choose to learn more about them. Some interests take precedence over others. Therefore, the difference between a student's interest in a subject and his or her preference for pursuing that interest over another may help an instructor decide how to proceed.

A student might be interested in a certain area but prefer not to read about it. Instead, he or she might prefer to get information about the subject elsewhere. Peers and friends, television, agencies, and so on are information sources too. Forming a preference suggests sampling and deciding that this is a first or second choice. There are many interests that might not be first or second choices. In the process of sampling, students learn that print and nonprint media are good sources for certain kinds of information and for certain kinds of pleasure. As students mature, they develop habits that may center on interests and preferences. For example, an early interest in horses that is actively pursued may help form recreation habits and even vocational directions.

A subject approach to reading motivation centers on finding students' interests and pointing out reading and viewing materials that may satisfy those interests. Perhaps at some point those interests may become preferences. In turn, the preferences may relate to the students' personalities. It is hoped that, through their exploration of interests and forming preferences, young people will develop reading and viewing habits that improve their lives.

FACTORS AFFECTING READING INTERESTS

Research in the area of reading interests, attitudes, and habits reveals several variables that seem to affect students' reading interests. Those correlates include sex, age, intelligence and ability, cultural and racial factors, and socioeconomic factors.

Sex

Whether the reader is male or female appears to be one of the strongest elements in determining reading interests. For example, as early as 1950, George W. Norvell found that during the high school years, the reader's sex was the most powerful determinant of reading preference. Whether the result of stereotyped upbringing or natural biological tendencies, the differences exist. Studies have shown that certain subjects are of more interest to one sex than to the other. For example, Anne G. Scharf (1973) noted that high school males liked biography, sports, world events, war, and crime stories, while females liked drama, autobiography, and poetry. Thomas William Dowan (1971) found boys in grades three through five interested in adventure, tall tales, historical nonfiction, how-to-do-it, sports, and science, while girls were interested in animals, fairy tales, modern fantasy, and children of other lands and in the United States.

Vincent Greaney (1980) has also noted that girls read the most overall, while boys read the most nonfiction. Joan T. Feeley (1982) suggests that interests have not changed for middle graders. And the reader's sex still accounts for differences.

This is not to suggest that the classroom teacher or library media specialist should deliberately offer certain topics to boys as opposed to girls. It does suggest that the instructor should be conscious of those differences and consider introducing the same topics in a multitude of formats and literary forms. For example, most topics are explored in both fiction and nonfiction. Most topics have been addressed in more than one literary form, from nonfiction expository writing to poetry to novels or drama.

Age

As might be expected, age makes a difference in what students find interesting. As students develop, many of their interests shift and grow. Young people change rapidly, both mentally and physically. These changes are reflected in the problems that they encounter. Students move from parents to peers. Relationships change. In effect, students are developing and growing up, and it is to be expected that their interests will change according to the same developmental patterns, from a more self-centered world to one in which they want to know more about others. Pi Lambda Theta's (1974) study of reading interests classified by age reveals some interesting differences for males and females grouped by age. Of interest to those who work with middle-grade students is boys' interest in animals and science, mystery, history, transportation, and sports. Girls the same age select animals, mystery, and people as high on their lists of important interests.

The amount of reading changes with age also, as noted by Greaney (1980). At the end of the primary grades students are reading the most. Then reading seems to taper off, except for those students of high ability.

For the classroom teacher and library media specialist, an understanding of child development is essential for getting clues to the effect of age on interests. One might expect adolescents to be interested in materials in which problems and relationships are explored. Materials about the things that they encounter in their own lives would be high on their lists also. They want to drive, be on their own without parental domination, and succeed in new endeavors.

Intelligence, Ability, and Achievement

Student achievement and the amount of leisure time spent reading are directly related, according to Greaney (1980). Higher intelligence often implies more interests. Intelligence also relates to interests in that students with higher intelligence may have different interests from those of their less intelligent peers. Charlotte S.

Huck (1979) provides a list of characteristics by age and developmental stage. The section on late elementary—ages 10, 11, and 12—is worth review because it reminds us of the changes reflected with age. These, combined with general ability, can be quite powerful in forming reading or general interests.

The ability of a child to comprehend what he or she reads appears significant in the selection of reading topics. Susan Swanton (1984) surveyed gifted and average students' reading interests. Gifted students preferred science fiction and fantasy more than did average students, possibly because of the challenge.

Culture and Race

Racial and cultural backgrounds seem to influence reading interests. Bernice J. Wolfson, Gary Manning, and Maryann Manning (1984) have shown that minority and nonminority children differ to some degree in preferences. According to Sarah Elizabeth Barchas (1971), among many others, minority group children have a higher degree of interest in titles related to their own minority groups.

Classroom teachers and library media specialists should consider what is of special concern to the students with whom they are working. A wide variety of materials representing a multicultural and diverse racial population is likely to be beneficial for students trying to identify with characters in books and other media formats.

Socioeconomic Factors

The socioeconomic levels of students' families influence the interests of students. Isabel Keith Baker (1972) found that reading scores of lower socioeconomic students, those with unskilled or semiskilled fathers, correlated with reading interests, attitudes, and habits. Vincent Greaney (1980) has noted that socioeconomic status makes a difference to the amount students read, with students from higher socioeconomic backgrounds reading more than students from working-class backgrounds.

While the classroom teacher or library media specialist cannot change the economic levels of students' families, they can provide as much incentive as possible for students to read widely. This incentive can take the form of encouragement, modeling, and introduction to materials.

DIAGNOSING STUDENTS' INTERESTS

If the subject approach centers on student interests, how are those interests identified? Is there some magic formula for obtaining this information? After all, the classroom teacher and library media specialist come in contact with hundreds of young adults during their work hours.

Perhaps there is no magic formula, but there is a sort of magic in the interaction that must take place to find out what someone else cares about. The discovery of each student as an individual in his or her own right is a reward in itself. The teaching process is one of finding out, presenting, communicating, and facilitating learning. In order to carry out these tasks, instructors need to know the students with whom they interact.

Finding out someone's interests can be accomplished either informally or formally. Probably the methods are as varied as individuals themselves. While the suggestions offered here for collecting information about students' interests may seem obvious, it is amazing how often they are forgotten because other tasks get in the way.

Informal

Probably one of the most effective ways of learning the interests of students is during conversations. It would be hoped that there is enough time during the course of the school day to converse with students. Conversation implies just that, talking about what is on one's mind. It is during such encounters that the places students frequent, the styles they consider "in," the people they emulate, and the topics that occupy their thoughts most will emerge. This does not occur automatically. Building trusting relationships takes time.

Rapport is often difficult to establish. It becomes a part of the atmosphere of the classroom or library media center. If students feel comfortable in the facility and with the individual, they are likely to share their thoughts. The comfort level can be enhanced by allowing students to help set goals for the setting. In the library media center, the library media specialist may do this in a number of ways. For example, students might be given chances to offer suggestions, plan programs, help establish rules, suggest purchases, and even help evaluate the effectiveness of services.

Much can be learned about students' interests by setting up situations in which they must select options. If the classroom teacher or library media specialist sets up choices during more structured activities, students may select what appeals to them more. Their selections can provide clues about what is of interest to them, even if they sometimes choose as they do because a friend selected that activity. Each choice becomes revealing.

Observation of students can also produce information. What do students do during their free time? What do they select to read? Where do they read? What do they save their money to purchase? What are they working for? Where do they spend most of their time? Is any particular interest taking more time than others? Do the students enjoy any specific physical or intellectual endeavors? How do they express themselves? What television programs or movies do the students watch?

Instructors can watch some of the programs that students mention as favorites. These programs may also give clues about what appeals to the students' humor, the problems that they consider to be important, and what might relate to those concerns. This same strategy is also helpful in considering what students want to buy. Visiting stores or places that cater to students can be revealing. What is there that appeals to students? Where do students "hang out"? Why do they go to certain places?

Information gathered about students may not be written down. In fact, most information gathered in this way is incorporated into thought. One soon has a complex set of ideas about individuals, true or false. Whatever information is collected about the students' interests, it should be used judiciously in the effort to present materials that might be of interest, not to find ways of controlling the students.

Formal

If the students will be engaged in a more formal program, it may be effective to interview them formally. In this case, the classroom teacher or library media specialist may set up a number of formal questions that students would be asked. These questions might be elaborated upon for as much information as possible in order to group students in similar interest groups.

In some instances, volunteers may help in the gathering of information through formal interviews. The disadvantage in this method is that it is by definition a more formal occasion. Students may give answers that they think are expected rather than reveal their true feelings about what interests them. Students' privacy may be at issue, depending on the types of questions asked. However, most students enjoy the individual attention they receive in a formal interview session, and they like the opportunity to give their opinions without worrying about grades.

Many reading clinics and classrooms use information interest inventories. While there are published inventories related to career interests, it is possible for classroom teachers and library media specialists to develop their own questionnaires to elicit general interests. The purpose should be to gather general information quickly about large areas of interest.

Self-prepared interest inventories take some time to develop. The information that might be most helpful has to be identified and the purpose and method of using the information determined before collecting it. Information may be collated manually or in a database. If the information will be used with only one individual, open-ended questions may dominate. If the instructor wishes to group students by interests, a system for finding students with similar interests must be devised. This means that students will need to answer some questions using common terms, which suggests including multiple-choice questions or ranking of choices.

Self-Prepared Interest Inventories with Open-Ended Questions

The following categories might be helpful in identifying interests for an individual student.

- General information such as name, age, address or room number, or teacher
- Favorite subjects in school
- Subjects disliked

- Hobbies or collections
- Pets
- Favorite stories or books
- Books disliked
- Favorite television or radio programs and movies
- Television or radio programs and movies disliked
- Favorite places visited
- Places disliked
- Favorite activities during different times of the day
- People or heroes admired
- People or characters least admired

The interest inventory shown in Figure 4 might be adapted for an individual setting. Answers may be keyed into a database so that the classroom teacher or library media specialist may sort fields by interests. Students may be grouped or activities centered on certain interests identified.

Published Interest Inventories

There are many interest inventories available that are related to career selection. Several of the more popular ones are listed below. There also are reading interest inventories and reading aptitude surveys that may be used to provide clues to the interests and habits of students.

Print—Articles with Suggested Interest Inventories

"A Book Just for You." The Mailbox, Intermediate Edition (October 1990), p. 36.

Forgan, H. W. "Checklist of Recreational Activities." In *The Reading Corner*. Glenview, Illinois: Goodyear, 1977.

Hall, Christine. "The Results of an Information Inventory of the Reading Interests and Backgrounds of Underprepared College Freshmen." *Forum for Reading* 20:2 (Spring-Summer 1989), pp. 15–18.

Heathington, Betty S., and Koskinen, Patricia S. "Interest Inventory for Adult Beginning Readers." *Journal of Reading* 26:3 (December 1982), pp.252–256.

Read the following questions and answer each.

Name: _____

Birthday: _____

Teacher: _____

Read the following list of school subjects. Circle the subject that you would not want to miss. Underline the subject that you wish you did not have to study.

Art	Safety
Dance	Science (biology, geology, physics,
Health	and chemistry)
Home economics	Social studies (geography, world
Industrial arts	history, American history, civics,
Mathematics	and sociology)
Music	Spelling
Physical education	Writing
Reading	

Write a number 1 beside your favorite type of novel, a 2 by your second choice, and a 3 by your third choice. Place an X by the type of novel that you like least of all.

Adventure	Mystery
Animal fiction	Realistic fiction
(dogs, horses, etc.)	Romance
Fantasy	Science fiction
Historical fiction	Sports fiction
Horror	Westerns
Humor	

Rank the following types of reading forms beginning with number 1 for the one that you like the most. The type you like least will be number 11.

Autobiographies	Novels
Biographies	Plays
Fables	Poetry
Folktales	Riddles
Legends	Short stories
Myths	

Figure 4. Reading Interest Inventory

Place an X by the element in a story most important to you. Place an O by the element least important to you.

Plot	Dialogue
Characters	Mood
Setting	Theme

Place an X by the Dewey decimal classification system section that you would most like to browse. Circle the Dewey decimal classification system section that you would least like to browse. Place an O by the Dewey decimal classification system section with which you are least familiar.

000 General	500 Pure science
100 Philosophy	600 Applied science
200 Religion	700 Arts
300 Social science	800 Literature
400 Language	900 Geography and history

Figure 4. Reading Interest Inventory — cont'd.

Jan-Tausch, Evelyn. *Discovery and Measurement of Interests in Reading.* April 1968. ED 026205.

Potter, Thomas C., and Gwenneth Rae. *Informal Reading Diagnosis: A Practical Guide for the Classroom Teacher.* Englewood Cliffs, New Jersey: Prentice-Hall, 1973.

Richet, M. A., L. K. List, and J. W. Lerner. *Reading Problems: Assessment and Teaching Strategies.* Englewood Cliffs, New Jersey: Prentice-Hall, 1989.

Summers, Edward G. "Instruments for Assessing Reading Attitudes: A Review of Research and Bibliography." *Journal of Reading Behavior* 9:2 (Summer 1977), pp. 137–165.

Walker, Susan M., R. G. Noland, and C. M. Greenshields. "The Effect of High and Low Interest Content on Instructional Levels in Informal Reading Inventories." *Reading Improvement* 16 (Winter 1979), pp. 297–300.

Print—Books with Suggested Interest Inventories

Estes Attitude Scales: Measures of Attitudes toward School Subjects. Secondary Form. Austin, Texas: Pro-Ed, 1981.

Fry, Edward B. *Reading Diagnosis: Informal Reading Inventories.* Providence, RI: Jamestown Publishers, 1981.

Interest Checklist. Washington, D.C.: U.S. Department of Labor, 1979.

Interest Inventory for Elementary Grades: George Washington University Series. Washington, D.C.: Center for Psychological Service, 1941.

Inventory of Interests. San Antonio, Texas: Guidance Testing Associates, 1971.

Story Preference Inventory. 1975. ED 236639.

Strong-Campbell Interest Inventory. Stanford, California: Stanford University Press, 1981.

Woodcock-Johnson Psycho-Educational Battery. Allen, Texas: DLM— Teaching Resources, 1978.

Nonprint—Automated Book Programs

BookBrain. Oryx, 4041 N. Central Ave., Phoenix, AZ 85012-3397.

Bookmatch. Educational Development Corporation, P.O. Box 470663, Tulsa, OK 74147.

Byte into Books. Calico, P.O. Box 15916, St. Louis, MO 63114.

Electronic Bookshelf. Electronic Bookshelf, Route 9, Box 64, Frankfort, IN 46041.

DEVELOPING INTEREST GROUPS FOR PEER SHARING AND INTERACTION

Groups are easily established once interests are identified. If the classroom teacher or library media specialist uses primarily informal methods for identifying interests, the grouping procedure may be as simple as asking students who are interested in a certain subject to sign up on a sheet for a group or to sit down together to begin their exploration of a subject.

For those instructors who use more formal methods for finding interests, individual and group records may be kept using manual grids or computer database programs. A sample grid and a database record form are shown in Figure 5.

If grids are used, names of students are listed horizontally and the categories listed vertically. The information for each student from the inventory may then be recorded. Those students matching

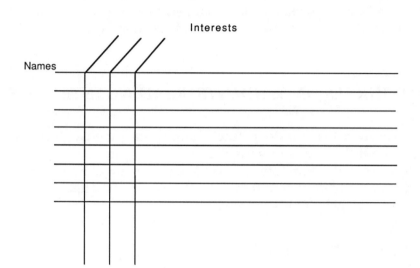

LAST NAME   FIRST NAME

BIRTHDAY   TEACHER

SUBJECT MOST MISSED

SUBJECT LEAST STUDIED

NOVEL CHOICE 1

NOVEL CHOICE 2

NOVEL CHOICE 3

NOVEL CHOICE LEAST

AUTOBIOGRAPHIES   BIOGRAPHIES

FABLES   FOLK TALES   LEGENDS

MYTHS   NOVELS   PLAYS

POETRY   RIDDLES   SHORT STORIES

ELEMENT MOST IMPORTANT

ELEMENT LEAST IMPORTANT

DEWEY BROWSE MOST

DEWEY BROWSE LEAST

DEWEY LEAST FAMILIAR

Figure 5. Sample Grid and Database Record Form

in certain categories is then placed in similar groups to explore their preferred topics further. In like manner, the information may be recorded in established database fields so that searches can be conducted for similar matches.

RESOURCES ON STUDENTS' READING INTERESTS

The more that classroom teachers and library media specialists read about the effects of variables on reading interests, the more they find to help them listen and consider what might be of interest to the students for whom they have responsibility. The following sources may help in this process.

Articles and Dissertations

Anderson, Gary, et al. "Differences in the Free-Reading Books Selected by High, Average, and Low Achievers." *Reading Teacher* 39 (December 1985), pp. 326–330.

Antley, Elizabeth Martin, and Ann L. Fluitt. "Socioeconomic Differences in Reading Interests." In Figurel, J. Allen. *Vistas in Reading: 1966 Proceedings.* Volume 11, Part 1. Newark, Delaware: International Reading Association, 1967, pp. 342–345.

Ashley, L. F. "Children's Reading Interests and Individualized Reading." *Elementary English* 47 (December 1970), pp. 1088–1096.

Baker, Isabel Keith. "A Study of Reading Interests of Fourth Grade Children in Different Socioeconomic Groups." Doctoral Dissertation, Oklahoma State University, 1972. (University Microfilms No. 73-15,048)

Bank, Stanley. "Assessing Reading Interests of Adolescent Students." *Educational Research Quarterly* 10:3 (1986), pp. 8–13.

Barchas, Sarah Elizabeth. "Expressed Reading Interests of Children of Different Ethnic Groups." Doctoral Dissertation, University of Arizona, 1971. (University Microfilms No. 71-29,505)

Bard, Therese B., and John E. Leide. "Elementary School Students' Preferences for Distinguished Children's Books." 1983. ED 239618.

———. "Reading Interests of Children Attending an Elementary School in Hawaii as Indicated by School Library Circulation Records." *CRUS News* 16 (March 1983), pp. 3–4.

Beauchamp, Robert F. "Selection of Books for the Culturally Disadvantaged Ninth Grade Student." Doctoral Dissertation, Wayne State University, 1970. (University Microfilms No. 71-71,235)

Beta Upsilon Chapter, Pi Lambda Theta. "Children's Reading Interests Classified by Age Level." *Reading Teacher* (April 1974), pp. 694–700.

Brenneman, Roger L. "A Comparative Study of the Reading Interests of Amish and English Sixth Graders." ED 024526.

Brown, Carol Lynch. "A Study of Procedures for Determining Fifth Grade Children's Book Choices." Doctoral Dissertation, Ohio State University, 1971. (University Microfilms No. 72-15,178)

Brutton, D. "How To Develop and Maintain Student Interest in Reading." *English Journal* 63 (1974), pp. 74–77.

Campbell, Susan, et al. "Do Children Judge a Book by Its Cover?" 1982. ED 255937.

Carter, Sylvia. "Interests and Reading." In Thomas, James L., and Ruth M. Loring. *Motivating Children and Young Adults To Read.* Phoenix, Arizona: Oryx, 1979.

Childress, Glenda T. "Gender Gap in the Library: Different Choices for Girls and Boys." *Top of the News* 42:1 (Fall 1985), pp. 69–73.

Chiu, Lian-Hwang. "Children's Attitudes Toward Reading and Reading Interests." *Perceptual and Motor Skills* 58:3 (June 1984), pp. 960–962.

Clary, Linda Mixon. "Getting Adolescents To Read." *Journal of Reading* 34:5 (February 1991), pp. 340–345.

Coleman, J. H., and Ann Jungblut. "Children's Likes and Dislikes about What They Read." *Journal of Educational Research* 44 (February 1961), pp. 221–228.

Cooter, Robert B., and J. Estill Alexander. "Interest and Attitude: Affective Connections for Gifted and Talented Readers." *Reading World* 24 (October 1984), pp. 97–102.

Culliton, Thomas E. "Techniques for Developing Reading Interests and Attitudes." In *Reading in the Middle School.* Newark, New Jersey: International Reading Association, 1974, pp. 183–196.

Dowan, Thomas William. "Personal Reading Interests as Expressed by Children in Grades Three, Four, and Five in Selected Florida Public Schools." Doctoral Dissertation, Florida State University, 1971. (University Microfilms No. 72-13,502)

Dysart, Brent. "In Defense of Kids and Their Books." *Journal of Outdoor Education* 19 (1984–1985), pp. 21–22.

Engin, Ann W., Fred H. Wallbrown, and Dorothea H. Brown. "The Dimensions of Reading Attitude for Children in the Intermediate Grades." *Psychology in the Schools* 13:3 (July 1976), pp. 309–316.

Estes, Thomas H., and Joseph H. Vaughn. "Reading Interest and Comprehension: Implications." *Reading Teacher* 27 (November 1973), pp. 149–153.

Fasick, Adele. "How Much Do We Know about What Children Are Reading?" *Emergency Librarian* 12:3 (January-February 1985), pp. 17–20, 22–24.

Feeley, Joan T. "Content Interests and Media Preference of Middle-Graders: Differences in a Decade." *Reading World* 22:1 (October 1982), pp. 11–16.

———. "Interest Patterns and Media Preferences of Boys and Girls in Grades 4 and 5." Doctoral Dissertation, New York University, 1972. (University Microfilms No. 72-20,628)

Frasher, Romona S. "Know Your Reluctant Reader's Interest." *Reading World* 18 (October 1978), pp. 67–71.

Geeslin, Dorine H., and Richard C. Wilson. "Effect of Reading Age on Reading Interests." *Elementary English* 49 (May 1972), pp. 750–756.

Goostree, Renee Close. "A Study of the Reading Interests and Attitudes of Fourth, Fifth, and Sixth Grade Gifted Children in the State of Missouri." Master's Thesis, Southwest Missouri State University, 1981. ED 209842.

Greaney, Vincent. "Factors Related to Amount and Type of Leisure Time Reading." *Reading Research Quarterly* 15:3 (1980), pp. 337–357.

Heather, Pauline. *Young People's Reading: A Study of the Leisure Time Reading of 13–15 Year Olds.* Paper presented at the Annual Meeting of the United Kingdom Reading Association, Newcastle on Tyne, England, July 19–23, 1982. ED 225130.

Heathington, Betty S. "What To Do about Reading Motivation in the Middle School." *Journal of Reading* 22:8 (1979), pp. 709–713.

Heathington, Betty S., and Patricia S. Koskinen. "Interest Inventory for Adult Beginning Readers." *Journal of Reading* 26:2 (December 1982), pp. 252–256.

Hickman, Janet. "What Do Fluent Readers Do?" *Theory into Practice* 16:5 (December 1977), pp. 372–375.

Holmes, Betty C., and Richard Ammon I. "Teaching Content with Trade Books: A Strategy." *Childhood Education* 61:5 (May-June 1985), pp. 366–370.

Hummel, Jeffrey W., and Peter J. L. Fisher. "Reading Attitudes and Reading Interests of Urban Intermediate Grade Students." *Psychology in the Schools* 22:4 (October 1985), pp. 470–472.

Hunt, Lyman C., Jr. "The Effect of Self-Selection, Interest, and Motivation upon Independent, Instructional, and Frustrational Levels." *Reading Teacher* 24:2 (1970), pp. 146–151, 158.

Isaacs, Kathleen T. "'Go Ask Alice': What Middle School Students Choose To Read." *New Advocates* 5:2 (Spring 1992), pp. 129–143.

———. "Independent Reading: Middle School Choices (Library Connections)." *ALAN Review* 17:2 (Winter 1990), pp. 35–36, 42.

Johns, J. "Reading Preferences of Urban Students in Grades Four through Six." *Journal of Educational Research* 68 (1975), pp. 306–309.

Johns, Jerry, and Davis, Susan J. "Reading Interests of Middle School Students." *Ohio Reading Teacher* 24:3 (Spring 1990), pp. 47–50.

Jones, Margarite G. "The Reading Attitudes and Interests of Fifth Graders." Master's Thesis, Kean College of New Jersey, 1983. ED 228626.

Karrenbrock, Marilyn H. "Children's Preferences in Book-Related Characteristics." *Public Libraries* 23:4 (Winter 1984), pp. 138–140.

Keller, Zero. "What My Students Taught Me about Children's Books." *Bookseller* 3942 (July 11, 1981), pp. 118–119, 121.

King, Ethel. "Critical Appraisal of Research on Children's Reading Interests, Preferences and Habits." *Canadian Education and Research Digest* 7 (December 1967), pp. 312–326.

Kiser, George Edward. "A Study of Selected Indicators of Children's Interest-in-Reading." Doctoral Dissertation, University of Kentucky, 1968. (University Microfilms No. 69-17,528)

Klug, Beverly J. "Utilizing Literature To Motivate Remedial Readers." 1989. ED 305609.

Lamme, Linda Leonard. "Are Reading Habits and Abilities Related?" *Reading Teacher* 30:1 (1976), pp. 21–27.

Langer, Robert S. "Reading Interests and School Achievement." *Reading Improvement* 7 (Spring 1970), pp. 18–19.

Langerman, Deborah. "Books and Boys: Gender Preferences and Book Selection." *School Library Journal* 36:3 (March 1990), pp. 132–136.

Lau, Sing, and Sau M. Cheung. "Reading Interests of Chinese Adolescents: Effects of Personal and Social Factors." *International Journal of Psychology* 23:6 (1988), pp. 695–705.

Lauritzen, Carol. "Children's Reading Interests Classified by Age Level." *Reading Teacher* 27 (April 1974), pp. 694–700.

Lawson, Cornelia V. "Children's Reasons and Motivations for the Selection of Favorite Books." Doctoral Dissertation, University of Arkansas, 1972. (University Microfilms No. 72-10,208)

Liebler, Roberta. "Reading Interests of Black and Puerto Rican, Inner City, High School Students." *Graduate Research in Education and Related Disciplines* 6:2 (Spring 1973), pp. 23–43.

Mellon, Constance A. "Leisure Reading Choices of Rural Teens." *School Library Media Quarterly* 18:4 (Summer 1990), pp. 223–228.

Mendoza, Alicia. "Reading to Children: Their Preferences." *Reading Teacher* 38:6 (February 1985), pp. 522–527.

Mertz, Maia P. "Understanding the Adolescent Reader." *Theory into Practice* 14:3 (June 1975), pp. 179–185.

Moffit, Mary Anne S., and Wartella, Ellen. "Youth and Reading: A Survey of Leisure Reading Pursuits of Female and Male Adolescents." *Reading Research and Instruction* 31:2 (Winter 1992), pp. 1–17.

Moray, G. "What Does Research Say about the Reading Interests of Children in the Intermediate Grades?" *Reading Teacher* 31 (1978), pp. 763–768.

Morrow, Lesley Mandel, and Carol Simon Weinstein. "Encouraging Voluntary Reading: The Impact of a Literature Program on Children's Use of Library Corners." *Reading Research Quarterly* 21:3 (Summer 1986), pp. 330–346.

Oliver, Lin. "The Reading Interests of Children in Primary Grades." *Elementary School Journal* 77:5 (May 1977), pp. 400–406.

Palmer, Princess A., and Barbara C. Palmer. "Reading Interests of Middle School Black and White Students." *Reading Improvement* 20:2 (Summer 1983), pp. 151–155.

Robinson, Helen. "What Research Says to the Reading Teacher." *Reading Teacher* 8 (February 1955), pp. 173–176.

Sauls, C. W. "The Relationship of Selected Factors to the Recreational Reading of Sixth Grade Students." Doctoral Dissertation, Louisiana State University and Agricultural and Mechanical College, 1971. (University Microfilms No. 71-29,390)

Scharf, Anne G. "Who Likes What in High School?" *Journal of Reading* 16 (May 1973), pp. 604–607.

Schulte, Emerita S. "The Independent Reading Interests of Children in Grades Four, Five, and Six." Doctoral Dissertation, Ohio State University, 1967. (University Microfilms No. 68-3063)

Simpson, Ray H., and Anthony Soares. "Best and Least-Liked Short Stories in Junior High School." *English Journal* 54 (February 1965), pp. 108–111.

Sizemore, Robert Alexander. "The Reading Interests and Preferences of Deviates in Mental Ability and Educational Attainment in the Seventh and Eighth Grades." Doctoral Dissertation, Northwestern University, 1962. (University Microfilms No. 63-1369)

Smith, Lawrence L., and C. Rosanne Joyner. "Comparing Recreational Reading Levels with Reading Levels from an Informal Reading Inventory." *Reading Horizons* 30:4 (Summer 1990), pp. 293–299.

Smith, Lynn C., et al. *Locating the Recreational Level of Elementary Grades Students.* Paper presented at the Annual Meeting of Southeastern Regional Conference of the International Reading Association, November 4–6, 1982. ED 225106.

Soares, Anthony T., and Ray H. Simpson. "Interest in Recreational Reading of Junior High School Students." *Journal of Reading* 11 (October 1967), pp. 14–21.

Spangler, Katherine L. "Reading Interests vs. Reading Preferences: Using the Research." *Reading Teacher* 36:9 (May 1983), pp. 876–878.

Stanchfield, J. M., and S. R. Fraim. "A Follow-Up Study on the Reading Interests of Boys." *Journal of Reading* 22:8 (1979), pp. 748–752.

Steiert, Katherine. "The Designing of an Inventory To Investigate Recreational Reading Interests of Pupils in Grades Five and Six." Doctoral Dissertation, Kent State University, 1966. (University Microfilms No. 67-9432)

Strickland, Ruth G. "Children, Reading and Creativity." *Elementary English* 34 (1957), pp. 234–241.

Summers, Edward G., and Ann Lukasevich. "Reading Preferences of Intermediate-Grade Children in Relation to Sex, Community, and Maturation (Grade Level): A Canadian Perspective." *Reading Research Quarterly* 18:3 (Spring 1983), pp. 347–360.

Swanton, Susan. "Minds Alive: What and Why Gifted Students Read for Pleasure." *School Library Journal* 30 (March 1984), pp. 99–102.

Tibbetts, Sylvia Lee. "Intelligence and Children's Reading Preferences." *California Journal of Educational Research* 26:2 (March 1975), pp. 89–91.

———. "Sex Differences in Children's Reading Preferences." *Reading Teacher* 28 (December 1974), pp. 279–281.

Usova, G. M. "Techniques for Motivating Interest in Reading for the Disadvantaged High School Student." *Reading Improvement* 15 (1978), pp. 36–38.

Wolfson, Bernice J., Gary Manning, and Maryann Manning. "Revisiting What Children Say Their Reading Interests Are." *Reading World* 24:2 (December 1984), pp. 4–10.

Books

Alexander, J. Estill. *Attitudes and Reading.* Newark, Delaware: International Reading Association, 1976.

Cleary, Florence Damon. *Blueprints for Better Reading: School Programs for Promoting Skill and Interest in Reading.* New York: H. W. Wilson, 1972.

Forgan, Harry W. *Read All about It! Using Interests and Hobbies To Motivate Young Readers.* Santa Monica, California: Goodyear, 1979.

Huck, Charlotte S. *Children's Literature in the Elementary School.* New York: Holt, 1979.

Irving, A. *Promoting Voluntary Reading for Children and Young People.* Paris: UNESCO, 1980.

Kujoth, J. S. *Reading Interests of Children and Young Adults*. Metuchen, New Jersey: Scarecrow, 1970.

Norvell, George W. *The Reading Interests of Young People*. Boston: D. C. Heath, 1950.

————. *What Boys and Girls Like To Read*. Morristown, New Jersey: Silver Burdette, 1958.

Pilgrim, Geneva Hanna, and Mariana K. McAllister. *Books, Young People, and Reading Guidance*. New York: Harper, 1968.

Varlejs, Jana. *Young Adult Literature in the Seventies: A Selection of Readings*. Metuchen, New Jersey: Scarecrow, 1978.

SOURCES FOR LOCATING MATERIALS ON SUBJECTS

There are a number of selection sources that may be valuable for locating materials on a given topic. These sources either cite recommended books or suggest ways of locating titles that might be evaluated. Some of the sources are general and arranged by Dewey decimal classification system; others include helpful subject indexes.

Sources of Sources

Building Library Media Collections; Bibliography: Selection Sources. Baltimore: Maryland State Department of Education, 1988.

General Reference Books for Adults: Authoritative Evaluations of Encyclopedias, Atlases, and Dictionaries. New York: Bowker, 1988.

Kohn, Rita. *Once Upon a Time for Young People and Their Books: An Annotated Resource Guide*. Metuchen, New Jersey: Scarecrow, 1986.

Whitaker, Cathy Seitz. *A Guide to Directories, Indexes, Bibliographies and Other Sources*. Jefferson, North Carolina: McFarland, 1990.

General Sources Related to Subjects

Blackburn, G. Meredith, III. *Index to Poetry for Children and Young People: 1982–1987*. New York: H. W. Wilson, 1989.

Blostein, Fay. *Invitations, Celebrations: A Handbook of Ideas and Techniques for Promoting Reading in Junior and Senior High Schools*. Toronto: Ontario Library Association, 1980.

Brewton, John E., and Sara W. Brewton. *Index to Children's Poetry*. New York: H. W. Wilson, 1942.

————. *Index to Children's Poetry: First Supplement*. New York: H. W. Wilson, 1954.

————. *Index to Children's Poetry: Second Supplement*. New York: H. W. Wilson, 1965.

Brewton, John E., Sara W. Brewton, and G. Meredith Blackburn III. *Index to Poetry for Children and Young People: 1964–1969*. New York: H. W. Wilson, 1972.

Brewton, John E., G. Meredith Blackburn III, and Lorraine A. Blackburn. *Index to Poetry for Children and Young People, 1970–1975*. New York: H. W. Wilson, 1978.

Brewton, John E., G. Meredith Blackburn III, and Lorraine A. Blackburn. *Index to Poetry for Children and Young People: 1976–1981*. New York: H. W. Wilson, 1983.

Burns, Grant. *The Sports Pages*. Metuchen, New Jersey: Scarecrow, 1989.

Children's Catalog. New York: H. W. Wilson, 1909–.

Cummins, Julie, and Blair Cummins. *Choices: A Core Collection for Reluctant Readers*. Evanston, Illinois: John Gordon Burke, 1990.

Davis, Barbara Kerr. *Read All Your Life: A Subject Guide to Fiction*. Jefferson, North Carolina: McFarland, 1989.

Dewey, Patrick R. *Interactive Fiction and Adventure Games for Microcomputers: An Annotated Directory*. Westport, Connecticut: Meckler, 1988.

Educational Film and Video Locator. New York: Bowker, 1990.

Edwards, Harriet. *Children Living Apart from Their Mothers*. Hicksville, New York: Mayflower, 1989.

First Stop: The Master Index to Subject Encyclopedias. Phoenix, Arizona: Oryx, 1989.

Gaffney, Maureen. *Using Media To Make Kids Feel Good*. Phoenix, Arizona: Oryx, 1988.

Gillespie, John T. *More Juniorplots: A Guide for Teachers and Librarians*. New York: Bowker, 1977.

Gillespie, John T., and Diana L. Lembo. *Introducing Books: A Guide for Middle Grades*. New York: Bowker, 1970.

————. *Juniorplots: A Book Talk Manual for Teachers and Librarians.* New York: Bowker, 1967.

Gillespie, John T., and Corinne J. Naden. *Best Books for Children: Preschool through Grade 6.* New York: Bowker, 1990.

————. *Juniorplots 3: A Book Talk Guide for Use with Readers Ages 12–16.* New York: Bowker, 1987.

————. *Seniorplots: A Book Talk Guide for Use with Readers Ages 15–18.* New York: Bowker, 1989.

Gomberg, Karen Cornell. *Books Appeal: Get Teenagers into the School Library.* Jefferson, North Carolina: McFarland, 1987.

Helbig, Alethea K., and Agnes Regan Keeping Perkins. *Dictionary of American Children's Fiction, 1859–1959: Books of Recognized Merit.* New York: Greenwood, 1985.

————. *Dictionary of American Children's Fiction, 1960–1984: Recent Books of Recognized Merit.* New York: Greenwood, 1986.

Hendrickson, Linnea. *Children's Literature: A Guide to Criticism.* Boston: G. K. Hall, 1987.

Johnson, Carolyn M. *Discovering Nature with Young People: An Annotated Bibliography and Selection Guide.* Westport, Connecticut: Greenwood, 1987.

Junior High School Catalog. New York: H. W. Wilson, 1965–.

Kennedy, DayAnn M., Stella S. Spangler, and Mary Ann Vanderwerf. *Science and Technology in Fact and Fiction: A Guide to Children's Books.* New York: Bowker, 1990.

————. *Science and Technology in Fact and Fiction: A Guide to Young Adult Books.* New York: Bowker, 1990.

Kobrin, Beverly. *Eye Openers! How To Choose and Use Children's Books about Real People, Places, and Things.* New York: Penguin, 1988.

McBride, William G. *High Interest Easy Reading: A Booklist for Junior and Senior High School Students.* Urbana, Illinois: National Council of Teachers of English, 1990.

Nakamura, Joyce. *High-Interest Books for Teens.* Detroit: Gale Research, 1988.

National Association of Independent Schools. *Books for Secondary School Libraries.* New York: Bowker, 1981.

Nelson, Nancy Melin. *CD-ROMs in Print.* Westport, Connecticut: Meckler, 1988.

Peterson, Carol Sue, and Ann D. Fenton. *Index to Children's Songs.* New York: H. W. Wilson, 1979.

Pettus, Eloise S. *Master Index to Summaries of Children's Books.* Metuchen, New Jersey: Scarecrow, 1985.

Rochelle, Mercedes. *Historical Art Index, A.D. 400–1650: People, Places, and Events Depicted.* Jefferson, North Carolina: McFarland, 1989.

Senior High School Catalog. New York: H. W. Wilson, 1967–.

Short Story Index: 1984–1988. New York: H. W. Wilson, 1989.

Software for Schools. New York: Bowker, 1989.

Spirt, Diana L. *Introducing Bookplots 3: A Book Talk Guide for Use with Readers Ages 8–12.* New York: Bowker, 1988.

————. *Introducing More Books: A Guide for the Middle Grades.* New York: Bowker, 1978.

Subject Guide to Children's Books in Print. New York: Bowker, 1991.

Whitehead, Robert J. *A Guide to Selecting Books for Children.* Metuchen, New Jersey: Scarecrow, 1984.

The Young Adult Reader's Adviser. New York: Bowker, 1991.

3

People

REAL PEOPLE

People, as a subject, often interest students because the students sense the common actions and feelings of human behavior. When students read about people—their likes and dislikes, successes and failures, and friends and enemies—bonds are created with others. These bonds traverse time, allowing students a sense of life before their own existence. What actions and people helped form the environment in which they live? The possibilities for studying and reading about people who have achieved in all fields are almost overwhelming given the kinds of resources currently available. Whether students select biographies and autobiographies, newspaper and periodical articles, or fictionalized accounts of people's lives, they will find multiple choices for captivating their imaginations.

Thus, a subject approach focusing on people involves many classifications of people by job types, interests, regions, accomplishments, nationalities, sex, and so on. Whether students read about politicians and leaders, artists, scientists, sports figures, social scientists, educators, literary figures, or humanitarians, they are likely to find something in common with certain figures. People of all races and sexes have had similar ideas and feelings that may be shared. In some cases, it will be the differences that students find intriguing. Pursuing a subject approach using people as the subject establishes a place for students to see their own possibilities by looking at others.

A focus on people does not imply use of biography alone. In fact, biography is only one possible literary form or genre. Students will find examples of short stories, poetry, plays, novels, folk stories, and even jokes that highlight people. Selecting a real or fictional person becomes a way of exploring all kinds of literary forms in different ways. These literary forms help the student look at the topic or subject from varied points of view.

Many resources are available to students and faculty for identifying fascinating people. The resources range from the biography collection, usually easily browsed, to biographical reference sources or indexes that suggest names of individuals and specific sources about them. Using a variety of biographical references makes identifying both the living and the dead a challenge.

Resources Related to Real People

The following biographical reference sources may include names of individuals interesting to students. While some are strictly alphabetically arranged, others include special sections arranged chronologically, regionally, or professionally. Although reference sources are useful for specific reference questions, nothing prohibits students' use of these sources for browsing. In fact, when students are unaware of possibilities, browsing through such materials can help them to understand the parameters of a given topic. It can form a basis for organizing thought. Students see the span of topics and build their own categories and classifications for later choices.

Abbott, David. *The Biographical Dictionary of Scientists: Astronomers.* New York: Peter Bedrick, 1984.

————. *The Biographical Dictionary of Scientists: Biologists.* New York: Peter Bedrick, 1984.

————. *The Biographical Dictionary of Scientists: Chemists.* New York: Peter Bedrick, 1984.

————. *The Biographical Dictionary of Scientists: Engineers and Inventors.* New York: Peter Bedrick, 1984.

————. *The Biographical Dictionary of Scientists: Mathematicians.* New York: Peter Bedrick, 1984.

————. *The Biographical Dictionary of Scientists: Physicists.* New York: Peter Bedrick, 1984.

Adams, Russell L. *Great Negroes, Past and Present.* Chicago: Afro-Am Publishing, 1976.

Almanac of Famous People. Detroit: Gale Research, 1989.

American Men and Women of Science: A Biographical Directory of Today's Leaders in Physical, Biological and Related Sciences. New York: Bowker, 1989.

Asimov, Isaac. *Asimov's Biographical Encyclopedia of Science and Technology: The Lives and Achievements of 1510 Great Scientists from Ancient Times to the Present, Chronologically Arranged.* Garden City, New York: Doubleday, 1982.

Baigell, Matthew. *Dictionary of American Art.* New York: Harper, 1979.

Baker's Biographical Dictionary of Musicians. New York: Schirmer/Macmillan, 1984.

Bartke, Wolfgang. *A Biographical Dictionary and Analysis of China's Party Leadership 1922–1988.* New York: Bowker, 1990.

———. *Who's Who in the Republic of China.* New York: Bowker, 1991.

Beard, Charles A., and William Beard. *Charles Beard's the Presidents in American History.* New York: Scribner's, 1985.

Biographical Dictionary of American Educators. Westport, Connecticut: Greenwood, 1978.

Biographical Dictionary of Modern Peace Leaders. Westport, Connecticut: Greenwood, 1985.

Biography Index. New York: H. W. Wilson, 1946–.

Blaug, Mark. *Great Economists Since Keynes: An Introduction to the Lives and Works of One Hundred Modern Economists.* New York: Barnes & Noble, 1985.

Breen, Karen. *Index to Collective Biographies for Young Readers.* New York: Bowker, 1988.

Bruccoli, Matthew J., and Richard Layman. *Dictionary of Literary Biography.* Detroit: Gale Research, 1987.

Butler, Alban. *Butler's Lives of the Saints.* New York: Harper, 1985.

Butterworth, Neil. *A Dictionary of American Composers.* New York: Garland, 1984.

Campbell, Dorothy. *Index to Black American Writers in Collective Biographies.* Littleton, Colorado: Libraries Unlimited, 1983.

Celebrity Register. Detroit: Gale Research, 1990.

Chicorel, Marietta. *Chicorel Index to Biographies.* New York: Chicorel Library Publishing, 1974.

Cloyd, Iris. *Who's Who among Black Americans.* Detroit: Gale Research, 1990.

Cohen-Stratyner, Barbara N. *Biographical Dictionary of Dance.* New York: Schirmer/Macmillan, 1982.

Colby, Vineta. *World Authors 1980–1985.* New York: H. W. Wilson, 1990.

Commire, Anne. *Something about the Author.* Detroit: Gale Research, 1971–.

———. *Yesterday's Authors of Books for Children.* Detroit: Gale Research, 1977–.

Concise Dictionary of American Literary Biography. Detroit: Gale Research, 1987–.

Concise Dictionary of Scientific Biography. New York: Scribner's, 1981.

Contemporary Artists. New York: St. Martin's, 1983.

Contemporary Dramatists. New York: St. Martin's, 1982.

Contemporary Poets. New York: St. Martin's, 1985.

Current Biography. New York: H. W. Wilson, 1940–.

Daintith, John. *A Biographical Encyclopedia of Scientists.* New York: Facts on File, 1981.

DeFord, Miriam Allen, and Joan S. Jackson. *Who Was When? A Dictionary of Contemporaries.* New York: H. W. Wilson, 1976.

DeGregorio, William A. *A Complete Book of U.S. Presidents.* New York: W. W. Norton, 1984.

Delaney, John. *Dictionary of Saints.* Garden City, New York: Doubleday, 1980.

Delpar, Helen. *The Discoverers: An Encyclopedia of Explorers and Exploration.* New York: McGraw-Hill, 1979.

DeMontreville, Doris, and Elizabeth D. Crawford. *Fourth Book of Junior Authors and Illustrators.* New York: H. W. Wilson, 1978.

DeMontreville, Doris, and Donna Hill. *Third Book of Junior Authors.* New York: H. W. Wilson, 1972.

Dictionary of American Biography. New York: Scribner's, 1990.

Dictionary of American Medical Biography. Westport, Connecticut: Greenwood, 1984.

Ebony Pictorial History of Black America. Chicago: Johnson, 1971–1973.

Eggenberger, David I. *The McGraw-Hill Encyclopedia of World Biography.* New York: McGraw-Hill, 1973.

Ewen, David. *American Songwriters.* New York: H. W. Wilson, 1986.

———. *Composers since 1900.* New York: H. W. Wilson, 1969.

———. *Composers since 1900: First Supplement.* New York: H. W. Wilson, 1981.

———. *Great Composers 1300–1900.* New York: H. W. Wilson, 1966.

———. *Musicians since 1900: Performers in Concert and Opera.* New York: H. W. Wilson, 1978.

Falk, Byron A., and Valerie Falk. *Personal Name Index to "The New York Times Index" 1975–1981 Supplement.* New York: Roxbury Data Interface, 1986.

Fink, Gary M. *Biographical Dictionary of American Labor.* Westport, Connecticut: Greenwood, 1984.

Fleming, Margaret, and Jo McGinnis. *Portraits: Biography and Autobiography in the Secondary School.* Urbana, Illinois: National Council of Teachers of English, 1985.

Friedman, Leon, and Fred I. Israel. *The Justices of the United States Supreme Court, 1789–1978: Their Lives and Major Opinions.* New York: Chelsea House, 1980.

Fucini, Joseph J., and Suzy Fucini. *Entrepreneurs: The Men and Women behind Famous Brand Names and How They Made It.* Boston: G. K. Hall, 1985.

Fuller, Muriel. *More Junior Authors.* New York: H. W. Wilson, 1963.

Haskins, James. *Leaders of the Middle East.* Hillside, New Jersey: Enslow, 1985.

Holtze, Sally Holmes. *Fifth Book of Junior Authors and Illustrators.* New York: H. W. Wilson, 1983.

———. *Sixth Book of Junior Authors and Illustrators.* New York: H. W. Wilson, 1989.

Hubbard, Linda S. *Notable Americans.* Detroit: Gale Research, 1988.

Index to All Books: Who's Who Publications. Chicago: Marquis, 1980.

Ingram, John N. *Biographical Dictionary of American Business Leaders.* Westport, Connecticut: Greenwood, 1983.

International Who's Who. Detroit: Gale Research, 1989.

Kane, Joseph Nathan. *Facts about the Presidents: From George Washington to George Bush: Two Hundred Fascinating Years of Presidential History.* New York: H. W. Wilson, 1989.

Kunitz, Stanley J. *American Authors 1600–1900.* New York: H. W. Wilson, 1977.

———. *Twentieth Century Authors: First Supplement.* New York: H. W. Wilson, 1955.

Kunitz, Stanley J., and Vineta Colby. *European Authors 1000–1900.* New York: H. W. Wilson, 1967.

Kunitz, Stanley J., and Howard Haycraft. *British Authors before 1800.* New York: H. W. Wilson, 1952 (4th printing, 1965).

———. *British Authors of the Nineteenth Century.* New York: H. W. Wilson, 1936 (7th printing, 1973).

———. *The Junior Book of Authors.* 2nd ed., rev. New York: H. W. Wilson, 1951 (6th printing, 1970).

———. *Twentieth Century Authors.* New York: H. W. Wilson, 1942 (7th printing, 1973).

Laclotte, Michel, and Alistair Smith. *Larousse Dictionary of Painters.* New York: Larousse, 1981.

Logan, Rayford, and Michael R. Winston. *Dictionary of American Black Biography.* New York: W. W. Norton, 1982.

Macmillan Biographical Encyclopedia of Photographic Artists and Innovators. New York: Macmillan, 1983.

Marks, Claude. *World Artists 1950–1980.* New York: H. W. Wilson, 1984.

———. *World Artists 1980–1990.* New York: H. W. Wilson, 1990.

May, Hal, and James G. Lesniak. *Contemporary Authors New Revision Series.* Detroit: Gale Research,1981–.

Nakamura, Joyce. *Children's Authors and Illustrators: An Index to Biographical Dictionaries.* Detroit: Gale Research, 1976–.

———. *Something about the Author Autobiography Series.* Detroit: Gale Research, 1971–.

———. *Writers for Young Adults.* Detroit: Gale Research, 1988.

New Grove Dictionary of Music and Musicians. New York: Grove's Dictionaries of Music, 1980.

Newsmakers. Detroit: Gale Research, 1990.

Nicholsen, Margaret E. *People in Books, First Supplement: A Selective Guide to Biographical Literature Arranged by Vocations and Other Fields of Reader Interest.* New York: H. W. Wilson, 1977.

Pennington, Piers. *The Great Explorers: Stories of Men Who Discovered and Mapped the Unknown Areas of the World.* New York: Facts on File, 1979.

Polner, Murray. *American Jewish Biographies.* New York: Facts on File, 1982.

Rubenstein, Charlotte Streiffer. *American Women Artists from Early Indian Times to the Present.* Boston: G. K. Hall, 1982.

Slatkin, Wendy. *Women Artists in History: From Antiquity to the 20th Century.* Englewood Cliffs, New Jersey: Prentice-Hall, 1985.

Southwick, Leslie H. *Presidential Also-Rans and Running Mates, 1788–1980*. Jefferson, North Carolina: McFarland, 1984.

Stroud, Richard H. *National Leaders of American Conservation*. Washington, D.C.: Smithsonian Institution Press, 1985.

Tapsell, R. F. *Monarchs, Rulers, Dynasties, and Kingdoms of the World*. New York: Facts on File, 1983.

Trotsky, Susan M. *Contemporary Authors*. Detroit: Gale Research, 1986–.

Turner, Roland, and Steven L. Goulden. *Great Engineers and Pioneers in Technology, Volume I: From Antiquity through the Industrial Revolution*. New York: St. Martin's, 1981.

Unterburger, Amy L. *Who's Who among Hispanic Americans*. Detroit: Gale Research, 1990.

Vronskaya, Jeanne. *A Biographical Dictionary of the Soviet Union 1917–1988*. New York: Bowker, 1989.

Wakelyn, Jon L. *Biographical Dictionary of the Confederacy*. Westport, Connecticut: Greenwood, 1977.

Wakeman, John. *World Authors 1950–1970*. New York: H. W. Wilson, 1975.

———. *World Authors 1970–1975*. New York: H. W. Wilson, 1980.

———. *World Authors 1975–1980*. New York: H. W. Wilson, 1985.

———. *World Film Directors*. 2 vols. New York: H. W. Wilson, 1987, 1988.

Webster's American Biographies. Springfield, Massachusetts: Merriam-Webster, 1979.

Webster's American Military Biographies. Springfield, Massachusetts: Merriam-Webster, 1978.

Webster's New Biographical Dictionary. Springfield, Massachusetts: Merriam-Webster, 1983.

Weis, Frank W. *Lifelines: Famous Contemporaries from 600 B.C. to 1975*. New York: Facts on File, 1982.

Whitman, Alden. *American Reformers*. New York: H. W. Wilson, 1985.

———. *Nobel Prize Winners*. New York: H. W. Wilson, 1987.

Who's Who in America. Chicago: Marquis, 1899–.

Who's Who in American Art. New York: Bowker, 1990.

Who's Who in American Politics. New York: Bowker, 1989.

Who's Who in Black America. Northbrook, Illinois: Who's Who among Black Americans/Educational Communications, 1985.

Who's Who in European Politics. New York: Bowker, 1990.

Who's Who in South African Politics. New York: Bowker, 1990.

Who's Who in the Soviet Union Today: Political and Military Leaders. New York: Bowker, 1990.

Zadrozny, Mark. *Contemporary Authors Autobiography Series.* Detroit: Gale Research, 1984–.

Zarnowski, Myra. *Learning about Biographies: A Reading-and-Writing Approach for Children.* Urbana, Illinois: National Council of Teachers of English, 1990.

Sample Activity Related to Real People: Mahatma Gandhi

Mohandas Karamchand Gandhi is a good figure to introduce to students, especially if you also want to tie in the subject of peace. His byname became Mahatma, or Great-Souled. The students may begin with consideration of his two names, one given at birth and the second later. Capturing the horrific drama with a glimpse of Gandhi's assassination, the library media specialist might consider using an excerpt from a movie about Gandhi. Following the viewing of the excerpt, the library media specialist should pose the questions, "How did this man come to that end?" "For what was he known?" Students may discuss what captivated or intrigued them in the film, such as the clothing, the people, or the event.

The library media specialist should explain that Gandhi was a real person, well known for his peace efforts. Because he was a real person, those efforts were documented in daily newspapers around the world. The library media specialist may share some examples of newspaper articles about Gandhi from the book, *Chronicle of the 20th Century* (Mount Kisco, New York: Chronicle, 1987). This source provides a year-by-year picture of world events as posted in the daily news. For example, there are articles about Gandhi in March 1907 (p. 98) regarding him as a leader in South Africa, in March 1922 (p. 289) regarding his imprisonment for civil disobedience, and so forth, until his assassination in January 1948 (p. 635). The library media specialist should check the index to mark the major places where the articles mentioning Gandhi are shown, so that students may follow up and look at them on their own.

The library media specialist may help students use a database to locate articles about a person so that they can see the firsthand reporting as a primary source. The best source may be the *New York Times Index*. The index in print form includes citations about Gandhi under a number of years, 1948 being a good place to start. When students have found the appropriate listings, they should read the actual articles. The library media specialist can show students how they can check the headline for clues about an article's purpose or main idea, and how they can read or skim the first and second paragraphs for answers to questions such as who, what, where, when, how, and why. By reading a series of articles, students should develop their own perceptions about the person as reported during that individual's lifetime. Depending on the person selected, students may scour other resources, such as books and videotapes, to see how authors have interpreted the person and the events surrounding his or her life.

Following this activity, the library media specialist may display the materials for locating newspaper articles. The students may select a figure from sports, history, civil rights, or another area, and read a series of articles about the person. The library media specialist may want to use this as a way of introducing all kinds of biographical sources and materials. Examples of biographies, audiovisual materials, and reference materials can be included in the display.

The major point of the exercise is the motivation of students to investigate a real person in whom they have some interest. Browsing these sources is a legitimate activity!

Student Resources Related to Mahatma Gandhi

Print

(IL Signifies Interest Level; RL Signifies Fry Readability Level)

Autobiography and Quotations

Gandhi, Mahatma. *An Autobiography, or, The Story of My Experiments with Truth*. New York: Penguin, 1982. IL: 8–9+.

———. *The Essential Gandhi: His Life, Work, and Ideas—An Anthology.* Noroton, Connecticut: Vintage, 1962. IL: 8–9+.

———. *Gandhi in India: In His Own Words.* Hanover, New Hampshire: University Press of New England, 1987. IL: 8–9+.

————. *Mahatma Gandhi*. Mankato, Minnesota: Creative Education, 1985. IL: 2–9+.

————. *Words of Gandhi*. New York: Newmarket, 1982. IL: 5–9+. RL: 8.

Biographical Sketches

"Gandhi." In *People: A History of Our Time*. New York: Gallery, 1986.

"Gandhi." In Donovan, Frank. *Famous Twentieth Century Leaders*. New York: Dodd, 1964.

"Gandhi." In Fox, Mary. *Pacifists: Adventures in Courage*. New York: Reilly & Lee, 1971.

"Gandhi." In Garfinkel, Bernard. *They Changed the World: The Lives of Forty-Four Great Men and Women*. New York: Platt, 1973.

"Gandhi." In Haskins, James. *Resistance: Profiles in Nonviolence*. Garden City, New York: Doubleday, 1970.

"Gandhi." In Kelen, Emery. *Fifty Voices of the Twentieth Century*. New York: Lothrop, 1970, pp. 52–55.

"Gandhi." In McNeer, May, and Lynd Ward. *Armed with Courage*. Nashville, Tennessee: Abingdon, 1957, pp. 83–98.

Biography

Bains, Rae. *Gandhi: Peaceful Warrior*. Mahwah, New Jersey: Troll Associates, 1990. IL: 4–7.

Bush, Catherine. *Gandhi*. Edgemont, Pennsylvania: Chelsea House, 1985. IL: 4–7.

Cheney, Glenn Alan. *Mohandas Gandhi*. New York: Watts, 1983. IL: 4–7.

Coolidge, Olivia. *Gandhi*. Boston: Houghton Mifflin, 1971. IL: 5–8.

Copley, A. R. H. *Gandhi: Against the Tide*. Oxford: Basil Blackwell, 1987. IL: 8–9+.

Faber, Doris, and Harold Faber. *Mahatma Gandhi*. New York: Messner, 1986. IL: 5–7.

Fischer, Louis. *Gandhi: His Life and Message for the World*. New York: New American Library, 1954. IL: 7–9+. RL: 8.

————. *The Life of Gandhi*. New York: Collier, 1950. IL: 5–8.

Freitas, F. *Bapu*. Pomona, California: Auromere, 1979. IL: 3–8.

Gold, Gerald. *Gandhi: A Pictorial Biography*. New York: Newmarket, 1983. IL: 8–9+.

Goldston, Robert C. *The Death of Gandhi, January 30, 1948: India's Spiritual Leader Helps His Nation with Independence.* New York: Watts, 1973. IL: 4–7.

Grenier, Richard. *The Gandhi Nobody Knows.* New York: T. Nelson, 1983. IL: 8–9+.

Hunter, Nigel. *Gandhi.* New York: Bookwright, 1986. IL: 4–7.

Joshi, Uma. *Stories from Bapu's Life.* Pomona, California: Auromere, 1979. IL: 4–8.

Kumar, Chandra, and Mohinder Puri. *Mahatma Gandhi: His Life and Influence.* New York: Watts, 1982. IL: 8–9+.

Kytle, Calvin. *Gandhi: Soldier of Nonviolence.* Cabin John, Maryland: Seven Locks, 1982. IL: 8–9+.

Mehta, Ved. *Mahatma Gandhi and His Apostles.* New York: Penguin, 1976. IL: 8–9+.

Nanda, Bal Ram. *Gandhi and His Critics.* New York: Oxford University Press, 1985. IL: 8–9+.

Nicholson, Michael. *Mahatma Gandhi: The Man Who Freed India and Led the World in Non-Violent Change.* Milwaukee, Wisconsin: Gareth Stevens, 1988. IL: 5–8.

Rawding, F. W. *Gandhi and the Struggle for India's Independence.* Minneapolis: Lerner, 1980. IL: 4–7.

Redpath, Ann. *Mahatma Gandhi.* Mankato, Minnesota: Creative Education, 1985. IL: 4–7+.

Shankar, R. *Story of Gandhi.* Pomona, California: Auromere, 1979. IL: 4–8. RL: 7.

Shirer, William L. *Gandhi: A Memoir.* New York: Washington Square, 1979. IL: 8–9+.

Spink, Kathryn. *Gandhi.* New York: Hamish Hamilton, 1981. IL: 5–8.

Exposition

Besides encyclopedia articles found under the terms GANDHI, MAHATMA; GANDHI, MOHANDAS KARAMCHAND; or INDIA, students may find books such as those listed below helpful.

Attenborough, Richard. *In Search of Gandhi.* London: Bodley Head, 1982.

Borman, William. *Gandhi and Nonviolence.* Albany: State University of New York Press, 1986.

Periodical Articles

There are many articles available about Gandhi. Students may want to read samples such as these:

Brown, Judith. "M. K. Gandhi." *History Today* 30 (May 1980), pp. 16–22.
"The Mahatma's Legacy." *Newsweek* 100 (December 13, 1982), p. 67.

Plays

Briley, John. *Gandhi, a Screenplay.* London: Duckworth, 1982.

Nonprint

Gandhi. Washington, D.C.: National Public Radio. OP-78-09-28. (60-min. sound recording)
Gandhi. New York: RCA/Columbia Pictures, 1982. (188-min. videocassette)
Gandhi. Evanston, Illinois: Journal Films, 1984, 1987. (27-min. videocassette)
Mahatma Gandhi: Silent Revolution. Chicago: Pilgrim Films/International Film Bureau, 1968. (38-min. videocassette)
Mahatma Gandhi: Soul Force. Deerfield, Illinois: Learning Corporation of America, 1978. (24-min. videocassette)
Nine Hours to Rama. Los Angeles: Twentieth Century Fox, 1963. (125-min. 16mm film)
The Words of Gandhi. New York: Caedmon, 1984. CDL5 1740. (sound recording)

Organizations as Sources of Information

Embassy of India
Library of Information Service of India
2107 Massachusetts Avenue, NW
Washington, DC 20008
(202) 265-5050

Gandhi Memorial Center
4748 Western Avenue
Bethesda, MD 20816

Gandhi Peace Foundation
221 Deen Dayal Upadhyaya Marg
New Delhi, India 110 002
11 272396

Method: Using Newspaper Microfiche/Microforms and Newspaper Indexes

Using the newspaper as a motivational technique, students may unfold information about the world around them locally, nationally, and internationally. On the one hand, the information is timely; on the other hand, information from the past can be skimmed or read in a leisurely manner if the arrangement is understood. The choices of what kinds of information to read are equally wide, from sports to comics or from national crises to personal help finding a job. And it is a relatively inexpensive medium.

Using a newspaper method focuses on current information needs as well as background information with a research orientation. The method highlights a print format for providing the impetus for reading. The articles as well as organization and information categories may form the manner of introducing students to information and the value of reading. Students incorporate flexible reading skills by practicing on current issues or skimming and scanning columns of sources.

The newspaper covers many subjects, such as local, state, national, and international news; weather; advertisements; science reports; sports events; theater and movie reviews; book reviews; editorials and letters to editors; obituaries; games; human interest; business; real estate; career opportunities; television and radio; legal notices; job opportunities; home decorating; gardening; art; and maps and charts. Because of this diversity, students may learn the differences between reading very critically and more superficial scanning. Reading about personalities in the newspaper can emphasize those differences.

In most cases, introduction to the use of the newspaper begins with the highlighting of the needs that a newspaper fulfills. Formal introductions are more useful in instructional settings, while casual discussion and use may be more meaningful to students. By skimming and browsing through newspapers on their own, students may identify the organizational patterns and types of material they contain. In either case, students should practice using the format.

Because computers and telecommunications have changed the news medium, students may find that elements of the print medium show up in new electronic forms. Understanding both forms may help them see how their information needs can be fulfilled.

Resources Related to the Newspaper Microfiche/ Microforms and Newspaper Indexes Method

Print

Newspaper Directories and Indexes: Book Editions

The book edition indexes listed below vary in the length of time between updates.

The Cover Story Index: 1960–1989. Fort Atkinson, Wisconsin: Highsmith, 1989.

The IMS Ayer Directory of Publications. Washington, Pennsylvania: IMS, annual.

Milner, Anita Cheek. *Newspaper Indexes: A Location and Subject Guide for Researchers.* Volumes 1–3. Metuchen, New Jersey: Scarecrow, 1977–1982.

Names in the News Index. New Canaan, Connecticut: Newsbank, 1985–present.

New York Times Index. New York: New York Times, annual.

Newsbank Index. New Canaan, Connecticut: Newsbank, 1982–present. (Note other titles for specific subjects, such as Housing and Urban Renewal, or Welfare and Poverty.)

Newspapers in Microform. Washington, D.C.: Library of Congress, 1973–present.

Newspapers in Microform: Foreign Countries 1948–1983. Washington, D.C.: Library of Congress, 1984.

The Official Washington Post Index. Fair Lawn, New Jersey: Research Publications, 1988.

Schwarzlose, Richard Allen. *Newspapers: A Reference Guide.* Westport, Connecticut: Greenwood, 1987.

The Serials Directory: An International Reference Book. Birmingham, Alabama: EBSCO, 1990.

The Times Index (London). London: Newspaper Archive Developments, 1978–present.

Wall, Celia Jo. *Newspaper Libraries: A Bibliography, 1933–1985.* Washington, D.C.: Special Libraries Association, 1986.

There are a number of catalogs offering newspapers in microform. For example, University Microfilms International (300 North Zeeb Road, Ann Arbor, MI 48106) includes more than 7,000 titles in its catalog. Students with access to newspaper indexes may locate articles and use the resources of libraries with microfiche collections. UMI also provides database access to other newspapers.

Books for Students

Carey, Helen H., and Judith E. Greenberg. *How To Read a Newspaper.* New York: Watts, 1983. IL: 5–8.

Books and Articles for Classroom Teachers and Library Media Specialists

Abbott, Janice. *Meet the Press: Reading Skills for Upper-Intermediate and More Advanced Students.* New York: Cambridge University Press, 1981.

About Journalism. Deerfield, MA: Channing L. Bete, 1978.

Aiex, Nola Kortner. *Using Newspapers as Effective Teaching Tools.* ERIC Digest No. 10. Bloomington, Indiana: ERIC Clearinghouse on Reading and Communication Skills, 1988. ED 300847.

Anderson, Frances J. *Classroom Newspaper Activities: A Resource for Teachers, Grades K–8.* Springfield, Massachusetts: Charles C. Thomas, 1985.

Anderson, Thelma. *Assessing the Impact of Newspaper in Education Programs: Changes in Student Attitudes, Newspaper Reading, and Political Awareness.* Newspaper Readership Project Research Report. New York: Newspaper Advertising Bureau, 1982. ED 229752.

Beals, Paul E. "The Newspaper in the Classroom: Some Notes on Recent Research." *Reading World* 23:4 (May 1984), pp. 381–382.

Becher, Nancy A. *Let's Make the Newspaper Connection.* Paper presented at the Annual Meeting of the New York State Reading Association, Kiamesha Lake, New York, November 2–5, 1982. ED 232137.

Becker, Sharon, and Stuart Kendall. *Using the Weekly Newspaper in Education.* Milwaukee, Wisconsin: Milwaukee Journal/Milwaukee Sentinel, 1982. ED 224033.

Benedict, Mary, et al. "High School Students and the Newspaper: Educating Media Consumers." *Journalism Quarterly* 53:2 (1976), pp. 280–286.

Bibliography: NIE Publications—More Than 100 Teacher Guides and Curriculum Materials To Aid the Classroom Use of Newspapers. Washington, D.C.: American Newspaper Publishers Association Foundation, 1986. ED 308541.

Callahan, Tim, and Randall Felton. "The Newspaper in the Social Studies Classroom: An Issue Oriented Curriculum." 1980. ED 22187.

Cheyney, Arnold B. *Press: A Handbook Showing the Use of Newspapers in the Elementary Classroom.* Stevensville, Michigan: Educational Service, 1978.

———. *Teaching Reading Skills through the Newspaper.* Newark, Delaware: International Reading Association, 1984.

———. *The Writing Corner.* Glenview, Illinois: Goodyear, 1979.

Children and Newspapers: Changing Patterns of Readership and Their Effects: Report on the Study of America's Children and the Mass Media. New York: Newspaper Advertising Bureau, 1980.

Chusmir, Janet. "The Origin of Newspaper in Newspaper in Education Week." *Journal of Reading* 32:5 (February 1989), pp. 453–454.

Cole, Helen W. *Newspaper in Education.* Waco, Texas: Waco Tribune-Herald, 1978.

Coole, Sandra. *Newswriting.* Raleigh, North Carolina: News Observer/Raleigh Times, 1984.

Creating a Newspaper. Mobile, Alabama: Berkeley Small, 1982.

Criscuolo, Nicholas P. "Newspapers Can Sharpen Children's Reading and Writing Skills." *PTA Today* 12:6 (April 1987), p. 21.

Cummings, Alysa. *Problem Solving*. Philadelphia Inquirer Newspaper in Education Supplement. Philadelphia: Philadelphia Inquirer, 1989.

Daily Newspapers in American Classrooms: A National Study of Their Impacts on Student Attitudes, Readership and Political Awareness: Report on the Study of America's Children and the Mass Media. New York: Newspaper Advertising Bureau, 1980.

Decker, Howard F. *Newspaper Workshop: Understanding Your Newspaper*. New York: Globe, 1972.

Degl'Innocenti, Riccardo, and Maria Ferraris. "Database as a Tool for Promoting Research Activities in the Classroom: An Example in Teaching Humanities." *Computers and Education* 12:1 (1988), pp. 904–910.

DeRoche, Edward. *The Newspaper*. Santa Barbara, California: ABC-CLIO, 1991.

Diamond, Sandra, and Linda Riekes. *Newspapers and Law-Related Education: Grades 5–9*. Washington, D.C.: American Newspaper Publishers Association Foundation, 1981. ED 254436.

———. *Newspapers and Law-Related Education: Grades 10–12*. Washington, D.C.: American Newspaper Publishers Association Foundation, 1981. ED 254437.

Douglas, John Henry. *Parent Power!* San Diego, California: Enterprise, 1977.

Educators: Try NIE. Washington, D.C.: American Newspaper Publishers Association Foundation, 1986. ED 309428.

Filvaroff, Joan. *Newspaper Activities: Upper Level*. Austin, Texas: Austin American-Statesman Educational Services, 1983.

Gentry, Carolyn S. *Photojournalism*. Jacksonville: Florida Times-Union, 1976.

Greatsinger, Calvin. *Your Daily Paper*. Syracuse, New York: New Readers, 1977.

Greenup, Tess. *Newspaper Activities for Young Consumers*. Albuquerque, New Mexico: Albuquerque Journal/Tribune, 1983. ED 246002.

Griffin, Charlene M. "The Effect of the Use of Selected Newspaper Articles in the Teaching of Certain Reading/Thinking Skills." Thesis, Rutgers State University of New Jersey, 1979. ED 169479.

Hamrick, Lesanne. *Newspaper in Education Activity Book.* Temple, Texas: Temple Daily Telegram, 1981. ED 250703.

Hawks, Gail. "Dollars and Sense: The Newspaper as an Economic Resource (Use the News)." *Journal of Reading* 32:2 (November 1988), pp. 166–168.

Hazard, John, and Ezra Stieglitz. *NIE Teacher Activity Book.* Providence, Rhode Island: Providence Journal, 1978.

Heitzmann, William Ray. *What Research Says to the Teacher: The Newspaper in the Classroom.* Washington, D.C.: National Education Association, 1986.

Herrmann, Polly. *Newspapers Are for Kids, Too! A Newspaper in Education Handbook for Parents and Eddy Torial Brings Big News for Small People (Fun Activities with the Newspaper for Kids).* Binghamton, New York: Press/Sun-Bulletin, 1981. ED 278041.

Kossack, Sharon. "Use the News: Newspapers Provide the Main Gain." *Journal of Reading* 30:1 (October 1986), pp. 74–75.

Lamb, Jane. *The Complete Newspaper Resource Book.* Portland, Maine: J. Weston Walch, 1985.

Lenhart, Michael. *Newspaper Capers: Activities To Acquaint Students with Newspapers.* Santa Barbara, California: Learning Works, 1986.

Lisnik, Charron, et al. *Maine Newspaper-in-Education: An Activities Book for Educators.* Bangor, Maine: Bangor Daily News, 1979. ED 205998.

Livingston, Carolyn. "All the News That's Fit for the Music Classroom." *Music Educators Journal* 75:9 (May 1989), pp. 37–39.

Lowell, Stephen S. *The Newspaper Comes to the Classroom.* Portland, Maine: J. Weston Walch, 1973.

Mass Media in the Family Setting: Social Patterns in Media Availability and Use by Parents—Report on a Study of America's Children and the Mass Media. New York: Newspaper Advertising Bureau, 1980.

Mathews, Nancy N. "Sports News You Can Use." *Update on Law Related Education* 7:2 (Spring 1983), pp. 11–15.

Merina, Anita. "Extra! Extra! Teachers Discover New Resource: Newspapers." *NEA Today* 8 (November 1989), p. 25.

Moments in Time: 50 Years of Associated Press News Photos. New York: Associated Press, 1984.

Monda, Lisa E., et al. "Use the News: Newspaper and LD Students." *Journal of Reading* 31:7 (April 1988), pp. 678–679.

Morse, Julie C. *Using the Newspaper in Upper Elementary and Middle Grades.* Washington, D.C.: American Newspaper Publishers Association Foundation, 1986.

News Currents: N.I.E. Teacher's Guide. Madison, Wisconsin: Knowledge Unlimited, 1977.

The Newspaper as an Effective Teaching Tool: A Brief Introduction to the Newspaper in Education Concept. Washington, D.C.: American Newspaper Publishers Association Foundation, 1981. ED 236690.

Newton, Ray. *Newspaper in Education: New Readers for Newspapers.* Paper presented at the Annual Meeting of the Western Social Science Association, Fort Worth, Texas, April 24–27, 1985. ED 260373.

Newton, Richard F., and Peter F. Sprague. *The Newspaper in the American History Classroom.* Washington, D.C.: American Newspaper Publishers Association Foundation, 1974.

Olson, Marilyn. *Using the Newspaper To Teach Language Arts for Middle Grades and Up.* Palo Alto, California: Dale Seymour, 1981.

Palmer, Barbara C., et al. *An Investigation of the Effects of Newspaper-Based Instruction on Reading Vocabulary, Reading Comprehension, and Writing Performance of At-Risk Middle and Secondary School Students: Final Report.* Knight Foundation, 1989. ED 315732.

Partlow, Hugh. *Learning from Newspapers.* Toronto: Canadian Daily Newspaper Publishers Association, 1976.

Pasley, Sally Grimes, and Dee Koppel Williams. *Using the Newspaper.* New York: Cambridge University Press, 1987.

Passell, Peter. *How To Read the Financial Pages.* New York: Warner, 1986.

Rhoades, Lynn, and George Rhoades. "Using the Newspaper To Teach Cognitive and Affective Skills." *Clearinghouse* 59:4 (December 1985), pp. 162–164.

Richardson, Lynn J. *Cover to Cover: A Language Arts Newspaper Guide.* Johnson City, Tennessee: Johnson City Press-Chronicle, 1980.

Robinson, John P., and Leo W. Jeffries. *The Changing Role of Newspapers in the Age of Television.* Philadelphia: Association for Education in Journalism, 1979.

Sargent, Eileen E. *The Newspaper as a Teaching Tool.* Norwalk, Connecticut: Reading Laboratory, 1975.

Shapley, Barbara. "Newspaper Research: A Recent Study Reveals Relevant Data." *Social Studies Teacher* 9:2 (November 1987–January 1988), pp. 11–12.

Short, J. Rodney, and Bev Dickerson. *The Newspaper: An Alternative Textbook.* Belmont, California: David S. Lakes, 1980.

Sorgman, Margo, and Marilou Sorenson. "Utilization of the Newspaper in the Micro-Society Classroom." *Georgia Social Science Journal* 14:1 (Winter 1983), pp. 18–22.

Stabler, Charles Norman. *How To Read the Financial News.* New York: Barnes & Noble, 1965.

Target Date. Tucson, Arizona: Tucson Newspapers, 1983.

Teacher's Guide: Newspaper in the Classroom Project. Nashville: The Tennessean, 1972.

Thorndyke, Perry W. *Knowledge Acquisition from Newspaper Stories.* Santa Monica, California: RAND Corporation, 1979.

Understanding the News Media. Oxford, Ohio: Instructional TV Association, 1976.

Using the New York Times Index. Pittsburgh, Pennsylvania: Pittsburgh Regional Library Center, 1979. (slide set)

Vigilante, Nicholas, and Sharon Kossack. "Newspapers Enhance Mathematics (Use the Newspaper)." *Journal of Reading* 32:1 (October 1988), pp. 70–71.

Wajnryb, Ruth. "Communicative Use of the Newspaper Texts in Classroom Reading: The Read-Ask-and-Tell Approach." *Reading in a Foreign Language* 4:2 (Spring 1988), pp. 107–118.

Walker, Alice. "Creating a Newspaper Index: Microcomputers to the Rescue." *Wilson Library Bulletin* 61 (October 1986), p. 26.

Wells, James, et al. "Newspapers Facilitate Content Area Learning: Social Studies." *Journal of Reading* 31:3 (December 1987), pp. 270–272.

Yankelovich, Skelly and White, Inc. *Changing Needs of Changing Readers: A Qualitative Study of the New Social Contract between Newspaper Editors and Readers.* Easton, Pennsylvania: American Society of Newspaper Editors, 1979.

Yeaton, Connie S., and Karen Trusty Braeckel. *A Salute to Our Constitution and the Bill of Rights: 200 Years of American Freedom. Using the Newspaper To Discover How the Constitution and Bill of Rights Work.* Indianapolis: Indianapolis Newspapers, 1986. ED 278601.

Your Daily Newspaper. Baton Rouge, Louisiana: State Times and Morning Advocate, 1980.

Nonprint

Databases

The following databases are examples of electronic sources available related to news or newspapers. Check the source for specific information.

> *Dialog Information Services*
> 3460 Hillview Avenue
> Palo Alto, CA 94304
> (800) 334-2564
>
> *Information Access*
> 362 Lakeside Drive
> Foster City, CA 94404
> (800) 227-84311
>
> *University Microfilms International*
> 300 North Zeeb Road
> Ann Arbor, MI 48106
> (800) 521-0600
>
> *H. W. Wilson*
> 950 University Avenue
> Bronx, NY 10452
> (800) 367-6770

Academic Index. Available from Information Access.

American Men and Women of Science Online. Available from Dialog or Orbit Search Service.

AP News. Available from Dialog.

Chicago Tribune. Available from Dialog.

Chronolog Newsletter. Available from Dialog.
Current Digest of the Soviet Press. Available from Dialog.
Facts on File. Available from Dialog.
Legaltrac. Available from Information Access.
Middle East: Abstracts and Index. Available from Dialog.
National Newspaper Index. Available from Information Access and Dialog.
New York Times Index. Available from University Microfilms.
Newsearch. Available from Dialog.
Newspaper Abstracts. Available from Dialog.
Online Chronicle. Available from Dialog.
PAIS International. Available from Dialog.
UPI News. Available from Dialog.
USA Today Decision Line. Available from Dialog.
Washington Post Electronic Edition. Available from Dialog.
Wilsondisc. Available from H. W. Wilson.
Wilsonline. Available from H. W. Wilson.
World Affairs Report. Available from Dialog.

Films

Getting the Newspaper. Chicago: Encyclopedia Britannica Educational Corporation, 1967. (15-min 16mm film)
How To Read Newspapers. Deerfield, Illinois: Coronet, 1970. (13-min. 16mm film)
Lisa Makes the Headlines. Deerfield, Illinois: Learning Corporation of America, 1982. (26-min. 16mm film)
Newspaper Story. Chicago: Encyclopedia Britannica Educational Corporation, 1973. (27-min. 16mm film)
What Is It? Bloomington: Indiana University, 1977. (15-min. 16mm film)

FICTIONAL PEOPLE

American literary heritage is full of folk and mythical characters. Simple browsing in the library within the Dewey decimal system's 398 and 290 sections attests to this, as shelf after shelf spills over with books on legendary figures, fairy folk, and gods and goddesses. These figures have personalities and become real to students as they suspend time and become involved in the reading experience. Students relate to many of these figures' actions. There are heroes/heroines and villains with whom to cope. This is a wonderful place to begin, because there are plenty of materials from which students may choose. An American society with its contributions from many cultures and races adds to the rich reading possibilities because there are also enough materials for multicultural experiences.

Folk or Mythic Figures

Who are folk or mythical characters about whom students may read? Given the incredible number of folktales and myths told in books and films in library media centers across the United States, the problem of selecting a story can be difficult. Assuming that students listen to stories daily, they will slowly become familiar with many of the "classics." There will be many stories with which students will have to become familiar on their own, either through browsing or through use of reference sources.

Sometimes folk and mythical characters are considered flat. They often follow stereotypes that can be identified easily. Their personal characteristics do not change during the course of a story. Characters' actions match their stereotyped personalities. Wicked characters do wicked tricks to their innocent victims. Good characters spread their goodness. Students can count on the characters to perform as they expected.

Resources Related to Folk or Mythic People

The books and reference sources listed below include names and descriptions of many folk and mythical characters. The classroom teacher and library media specialist may investigate these sources to identify interesting characters to pursue.

Avery, Catherine B. *The New Century Handbook of Greek Mythology and Legend.* New York: Meredith, 1962.

Barber, Richard W. *A Companion to World Mythology.* New York: Delacorte, 1980.

Baumann, Hans. *The Stolen Fire: Legends of Heroes and Rebels from Around the World.* New York: Pantheon, 1974.

Bell, Robert E. *Dictionary of Classical Mythology; Symbols, Attributes, and Associations*. Santa Barbara, California: ABC-CLIO, 1982.

Boswell, Fred, and Jeanetta Boswell. *What Men or Gods Are These? A Genealogical Approach to Classical Mythology*. Metuchen, New Jersey: Scarecrow, 1980.

Branston, Brian. *Gods and Heroes from Viking Mythology*. New York: Schocken, 1982.

Briggs, Katharine M. *An Encyclopedia of Fairies: Hobgoblins, Brownies, Bogies, and Other Supernatural Creatures*. New York: Pantheon, 1978.

Bulfinch, Thomas. *Bulfinch's Mythology; The Age of the Fable; The Age of Chivalry; Legends of Charlemagne*. New York: Crowell, 1970.

Burland, Cottie Arthur. *Gods and Heroes of War*. New York: Putnam, 1974.

———. *North American Indian Mythology*. New York: Paul Hamlyn, 1965.

Carlyon, Richard. *A Guide to the Gods*. New York: Morrow, 1981.

Carruth, Gorton, and Eugene Ehrlich. *Young Reader's Companion*. New York: Bowker, 1992.

Cavendish, Richard, and Trevor Ling. *Mythology: An Illustrated Encyclopedia*. London: Rizzoli, 1980.

Christie, Anthony. *Chinese Mythology*. London: Hamlyn, 1968.

Cohen, Daniel. *The Encyclopedia of Monsters*. New York: Dodd, 1982.

Cook, Elizabeth. *The Ordinary and the Fabulous: An Introduction to Myths, Legends and Fairy Tales for Teachers and Storytellers*. New York: Cambridge University Press, 1976.

Cotterell, Arthur. *A Dictionary of World Mythology*. New York: Putnam, 1980.

Courlander, Harold. *Tales of the Yoruba Gods and Heroes*. New York: Crown, 1972.

D'Aulaire, Ingri, and Edgar Parin D'Aulaire. *Norse Gods and Giants*. Garden City, New York: Doubleday, 1967.

Davidson, Hilda Roderick Ellis. *Gods and Myths of Northern Europe*. New York: Penguin, 1964.

Dorson, Richard. *America in Legend; Folklore from the Colonial Period to the Present*. New York: Pantheon, 1973.

Downing, Christine. *The Goddess: Mythological Images of the Feminine*. New York: Crossroad, 1981.

Dowson, John. *A Classical Dictionary of Hindu Mythology and Religion*. Mystic, Connecticut: Lawrence Verry, 1973.

Eliade, Mircea. *Gods, Goddesses and Myths of Creation: A Thematic Source Book of the History of Religions.* New York: Harper, 1974.

Feder, Lillian. *Crowell's Handbook of Classical Literature.* New York: Crowell, 1964.

Gifford, Douglas. *Warriors, Gods and Spirits from Central and South American Mythology.* New York: Schocken, 1983.

Gimbutas, Marija. *The Goddesses and Gods of Old Europe 6500–3500 B.C.: Cult Images.* Los Angeles: University of California Press, 1982.

Grant, Michael, and John Hazel. *Gods and Mortals in Classical Mythology.* New York: Dorset, 1979.

Grueber, Helen A. *The Myths of Greece and Rome.* London: London House, 1965.

Hamilton, Edith. *Mythology.* New York: New American Library, 1940.

Harris, Geraldine. *Gods and Pharaohs from Egyptian Mythology.* New York: Schocken, 1983.

Hendricks, Rhoda A. *Mythologies of the World: A Concise Encyclopedia.* New York: McGraw-Hill, 1981.

Hindu Myths: A Sourcebook. New York: Penguin, 1975.

Ions, Veronica. *Indian Mythology.* New York: Hamlyn, 1967.

Ireland, Norma. *Index to Fairy Tales, 1949–1972; Supplements 1973 and 1979; including Folklore, Legends and Myths in Collections.* Westwood, Massachusetts: Faxon; Metuchen, New Jersey: Scarecrow.

Kaster, Joseph. *Putnam's Concise Mythological Dictionary.* New York: Putnam, 1963.

Kohn, Rita. *Mythology for Young People: A Reference Guide.* New York: Garland, 1985.

Leach, Maria. *Funk and Wagnall's Standard Dictionary of Folklore, Mythology, and Legend.* New York: Harper, 1984.

Man, Myth and Magic: The Illustrated Encyclopedia of Mythology, Religion, and the Unknown. Freeport, New York: Marshall Cavendish, 1985.

McGowen, Tom. *Encyclopedia of Legendary Creatures.* Chicago: Rand McNally, 1981.

McHargue, Georgess. *The Impossible People: A History Natural and Unnatural of Beings Terrible and Wonderful.* New York: Holt, Rinehart & Winston, 1972.

Mercantante, Anthony. *Who's Who in Egyptian Mythology.* New York: Clarkson B. Potter, 1978.

Monaghan, Patricia. *The Book of Goddesses and Heroines.* New York: Dutton, 1981.

Munch, Peter A. *Norse Mythology: Legends of the Gods and Heroes.* Detroit: Singing Tree, 1968.

Naravane, V. S. *A Dictionary of Indian Mythology.* New York: Advent, 1984.

Norton, Eloise Speed. *Folk Literature of the British Isles; Readings for Librarians, Teachers, and Those Who Work with Children and Young Adults.* Metuchen, New Jersey: Scarecrow, 1978.

Palmer, Robin. *Centaurs, Sirens and Other Classical Creatures: A Dictionary—Tales and Verse from Greek and Roman Mythology.* New York: Walck, 1969.

Parrinder, Geoffrey. *African Mythology.* London: Hamlyn, 1967.

Picard, Barbara Leonie. *Celtic Tales: Legends of Tall Warriors and Old Enchantments.* New York: Criterion, 1965.

Rovin, Jeff. *The Encyclopedia of Superheroes.* New York: Facts on File, 1985.

Saunders, Tao Tao Liu. *Dragons, Gods and Spirits from Chinese Mythology.* New York: Schocken, 1983.

Schmidt, Joel. *Larousse Greek and Roman Mythology.* New York: McGraw-Hill, 1980.

Schwab, Gustav. *Gods and Heroes: Myths and Epics of Ancient Greece.* New York: Random House, 1977.

Senor, Michael, and Geoffrey Parringer. *The Illustrated Who's Who of Mythology.* New York: Macmillan, 1985.

Shapiro, Max S., and Rhoda A. Hendricks. *Mythologies of the World: A Concise Encyclopedia.* Garden City, New York: Doubleday, 1979.

Sierra, Judy. *Cinderella.* Oryx Multicultural Folktale Series. Phoenix, Arizona: Oryx, 1992.

Stone, Merlin. *Ancient Mirrors of Womanhood: A Treasury of Goddesses and Heroine Lore from Around the World.* Boston: Beacon, 1984.

Tremain, Ruthven. *The Animal's Who's Who.* New York: Scribner's, 1982.

Tyler, Hamilton A. *Pueblo Gods and Myths.* Norman: University of Oklahoma Press, 1964.

Usher, Kerry. *Heroes, Gods and Emperors from Roman Mythology.* New York: Schocken, 1984.

Walker, Barbara G. *The Woman's Encyclopedia of Myths and Secrets.* New York: Harper, 1983.

Ward, James M., with Robert J. Kuntz. *Deities and Demigods: Cyclopedia.* Geneva, Wisconsin: TSR Games, 1980.

Zimmerman, J. E. *Dictionary of Classical Mythology.* New York: Harper, 1964.

Sample Activity Related to Folk or Mythic People: John Henry

Using a variety of stories about folk or mythological characters, the library media specialist or classroom teacher may read about a different legendary figure or character each day. After students have had one or two weeks to consider some of the figures, the library media specialist should explain that there are many such figures. Instructors should share the sources of stories so that students learn about where they can find more.

The library media specialist may suggest that students select a figure, read about a particular event in the life of that figure, and then make props and prepare a short play for a story theater performance.

In this case, John Henry is the example. First, students would locate as many versions of the story of John Henry as possible. While they read all about the figure, they select one event or part of the legend to develop into a story theater presentation. The library media specialist and classroom teacher help the students with their first adventure so that the experience can be replicated with other fictionalized folk heroes.

In this exercise, the students should understand that the experience does not require learning very specific lines. Instead, they read and reread the story so that they can almost retell it without a book. The objective is not to memorize lines, but to play the story with natural dialogue such as they feel that the characters might use.

After the students have read the selected version of the story as many times as possible, they may reduce the story to main events. If possible, students should reduce the sequence of events to between five and ten points. Using these points, the students may see how well they remember the story to retell it to each other. A group of three to five students should tell the story to each other, going from point to point and elaborating as they go.

The students may decide that there are some lines or phrases that they all want to repeat throughout the story. When the students are confident telling the story in their own words, they can consider what simple props they might use to act out the story, and then construct or gather them. The play should not be too elaborate. Some scenery might be painted, but students may use their imaginations.

At this point, students may write out a simple outline following the main events in the story. They may decide on parts for each individual and write down some of the dialogue and actions.

Scripts may be shared and the students may practice with all characters. In the case of John Henry, students might decide to have John Henry, an engineer in the engine, and onlookers. The students may make a cardboard or paper engine and get a hammer, bandannas, and the kind of hat used in the mines. The scene might be dark except for a light shining on John Henry and the steam engine. Students may practice the timing of their lines using dialogue that sounds realistic and appropriate. They should set up the lights and props. Finally, the students perform. They then may critique their play and perform again.

Resources Related to John Henry

Articles and Stories

Botkin, Benjamin A. *Treasury of American Folklore*. New York: Crown, 1944.

"John Henry." In *The Life Treasury of American Folklore*. New York: Time, 1961, p. 168.

"John Henry." In *World Book Encyclopedia*.

Folk Literature

"The Birth of John Henry." In Emerich, Marion V., and George Korson. *Child's Book of Folklore*. New York: Dial, 1947, p. 198.

Felton, H. W. *John Henry and His Hammer*. New York: Alfred A. Knopf, 1950.

"John Henry." In Blair, Walter. *Tall Tale America: A Legendary History of Our Humorous Heroes*. New York: Coward-McCann, 1944, pp. 203–219.

"John Henry." In Carmer, Carl. *The Hurricane's Children*. New York: McKay, 1965, pp. 122–128.

"John Henry." In Malcolmson, Anne. *Yankee Doodle's Cousins*. Boston: Houghton Mifflin, 1941, pp. 101–107.

"John Henry and the Machine in West Virginia." In Rugoff, Milton Allan. *A Harvest of World Folk Tales*. New York: Viking, 1968, pp. 85–91.

"John Henry and the Steam Drill." In Miller, Olive B. *Heroes, Outlaws, and Funny Fellows*. Garden City, New York: Doubleday, 1939.

Keats, Ezra Jack. *John Henry: An American Legend*. New York: Alfred A. Knopf, 1965.

Killens, John Oliver. *A Man Ain't Nothin' but a Man: The Adventures of John Henry*. Boston: Little, Brown, 1975.

Naden, Corinne J. *John Henry, Steel Driving Man*. Mahwah, New Jersey: Troll Associates, 1980.

Nonfiction

Sanford, Steve. *A Natural Man: The True Story of John Henry*. Boston: D. R. Godine, 1986.

Plays

"John Henry." In Kamerman, Sylvia E. *Holiday Plays Around the Year*. Boston: Plays, 1983, pp. 239–246.

"John Henry." In Kamerman, Sylvia E. *Plays of Black Americans: Episodes from the Black Experience in America, Dramatized for Young People*. Boston: Plays, 1987.

Poetry

"John Henry." In Adshead, Gladys L., and Anis Duff. *Inheritance of Poetry*. Boston: Houghton Mifflin, 1948, p. 172.

"John Henry." In Bontemps, Arna. *Golden Slippers: An Anthology of Negro Poetry for Young Readers*. New York: Harper, 1941, pp. 34–37.

"John Henry." In Cole, William. *Rough Men, Tough Men*. New York: Viking, 1969, p. 225.

"John Henry." In Untermeyer, Louis. *Magic Circle: Stories and People in Poetry*. New York: Harcourt, 1952, pp. 277–279.

Songs

A number of versions of the song about John Henry exist. The following sources may help in locating the words and music.

Arnett, Hazel. *I Hear America Singing!* New York: Praeger, 1975.

Bluegrass Complete. New York: Dover, 1978.

Carmer, Carl. *America Sings: Stories and Songs of Our Country's Growing.* New York: Alfred A. Knopf, 1942.

Cohen, Norm. *Long Steel Rail: The Railroad in American Folksongs.* Urbana: University of Illinois Press, 1981.

Cyporyn, Dennis. *The Bluegrass Songbook.* New York: Macmillan, 1972.

Ewen, David. *Songs of America: A Cavalcade of Popular Songs.* New York: Harper, 1947.

Forucci, Samuel L. *A Folk Song History of America.* Englewood Cliffs, New Jersey: Prentice-Hall, 1984.

Fowke, Edith, and Joe Glazer. *Songs of Work and Protest.* New York: Dover, 1975.

Glass, Paul. *Songs and Stories of Afro-Americans.* New York: Grosset & Dunlap, 1971.

Golden Encyclopedia of Folk Music. Winona, Minnesota: Hal Leonard, 1985.

Hansen, Charles. *400 Super Song Fest: Folk Songs of Today.* New York: Folk World, 1973.

Hurst, Jack. *Nashville's Grand Ole Opry.* New York: Abrahms, 1975.

Lomax, John A., and Alan Lomax. *Best Loved American Folk Songs (Folk Songs U.S.A.).* New York: Grosset & Dunlap, 1947.

The Norman Rockwell Family Songbook. New York: Abrahms, 1984.

1002 Jumbo for Me and You: The Children's Song Book. Miami Beach, Florida: Shattenger International, 1983.

Seeger, Pete. *American Favorite Ballads: Tunes and Songs.* New York: Oak, 1961.

Seeger, Pete, and Bob Reiser. *Carry It On! A History in Song and Picture of Working Men and Women of America.* New York: Simon & Schuster, 1985.

Silverman, Jerry. *Folk Song Encyclopedia.* New York: Chappell, 1975.

Professional Books

Chappell, Louis W. *John Henry: A Folklore Study.* Jena, Germany: Walter Biederman, 1933.

Johnson, Guy B. *John Henry: Tracking Down a Negro Legend.* Chapel Hill: University of North Carolina Press, 1929.
Williams, Brett. *John Henry: A Bio-Bibliography.* Westport, Connecticut: Greenwood, 1983.

Sound Recordings

The ballad of John Henry has been recorded by many singers—Rich Dehr, Tennessee Ernie Ford, Josh White, Pete Seeger, and others. The story has also inspired other forms of music, as shown below.

Copland, Aaron. *Appalachian Spring; Cortege Macabra: From "Grohg"; Letter from Home; John Henry.* New York: EMI; manufactured for Angel Records by Capitol, 1988.
———. *Lincoln Portrait and Other Works.* Beachwood, Ohio: Telarc, 1987. (sound recording)

Films and Videos

John Henry. New York: BFA, 1972. (11-min. 16mm film)
Legend of John Henry. Pasadena, California: Barr Films, 1974. (2 sound filmstrips)
Stories and Poems from Long Ago: John Henry. Springfield, Virginia: Children's Television International, 1990. (Distributed by GPN.) (15-min. videocassette)

Method: Story Theater

Story theater is simple drama without formal scripts. In this situation, the individuals learn a story by reading and reading and reading it! They identify all of the key points or events and develop a short outline to follow in retelling it. When students learn the story, they retell it in their own words. In other words, they become the storytellers. Students may memorize repetitive passages. For example, Jack's giant might still say "Fe, Fi, Fo, Fum."

Students then consider the story, outline it, develop a very simple script, and prepare props to tell the story. After practice, the students act out the story in their own version.

Story theater allows students to work within small groups to learn, perform, and retell. Groups may organize to fit the size of a story, and they will differ according to the story told. The advantage of story theater is that it helps students to develop a sense of plot while increasing their own repertoire of knowledge. While students may lose the beauty of more formal written language from text, they incorporate stories into their own language. Story theater allows students to develop their own reality of what they have read. The props are almost symbols for certain important parts of a story.

Students who have practice in this simple form of drama will find it easier to watch plays, read dramatic works, and participate in dramatic activities. They are comfortable "acting."

Resources Related to the Story Theater Method

Bolton, G. "Changes in Thinking about Drama in Education." *Theory into Practice* 24 (1985), pp. 151–157.

———. *Drama as Education*. London: Longman, 1984.

Christian, Catherine D. "Instructional Practices: Tales from the Magic Forest." *Communication Education* 28:3 (July 1979), pp. 233–237.

Davidson, Josephine. *Teaching and Dramatizing Greek Myths*. Englewood, Colorado: Teacher Ideas, 1989.

Horne, Catharine. *Word Weaving: A Storytelling Workbook*. San Francisco: San Francisco Education Fund, 1980. ED 225161.

Kaplan, Don. "Tracking the Bandersnatch and Other Slithy Foes." *Teacher* 94:7 (1977), pp. 41–44.

Morgan, Norah, and Julean Morgan. "Enriching Language through Drama." *Language Arts* 65:1 (January 1988), pp. 34–40.

San Jose, Christine. "Story Drama in the Content Areas." *Language Arts* 65:1 (January 1988), pp. 26–33.

Book Characters

Why is there an interest in book characters? Perhaps it is because authors imbue them with presence that allows readers to believe that characters are real. Reading about characters who appear in more than one book or story can be very motivating to some students. Students want to know what happened next. What happened after the book ended? Did the character really live happily ever after? Adolescents know that there is a next day, another situation to solve, and new experiences. Just as they continue to become more aware and to have new experiences, they may feel that a character deserves to be read about again. They may have such strong identification with a character that they want some advice based on what that character does in the next book.

Resources Related to Fictional Book Characters

The reference sources listed below provide background about characters in works of fiction. Some of these sources suggest similarities among characters.

Amos, William. *Originals: An A–Z of Fiction's Real-Life Characters.* Boston: Little, Brown, 1986.

Benet, William Rose. *The Reader's Encyclopedia.* New York: Crowell, 1965.

Browne, Ray B. *Contemporary Heroes and Heroines.* Detroit: Gale Research, 1990.

Carpenter, Humphrey, and Mari Pritchard. *The Oxford Companion to Children's Literature.* New York: Oxford University Press, 1984.

Carruth, Gorton, and Eugene Ehrlich. *Young Reader's Companion.* New York: Bowker, 1992.

Fetros, John G. *Dictionary of Factual and Fictional Riders and Their Horses.* Hicksville, New York: Exposition, 1979.

Fisher, Margery. *Who's Who in Children's Books: A Treasury of the Familiar Characters of Childhood.* New York: Holt, 1975.

Freeman, William. *Dictionary of Fictional Characters.* Boston: Writer, 1974.

Harris, Laurie Lanzen. *Characters in 20th-Century Literature: A Guide to Major Characters in World Fiction.* Detroit: Gale Research, 1990.

Kohn, George C. *Dictionary of Culprits and Criminals.* Metuchen, New Jersey: Scarecrow, 1986.

Magill, Frank N. *Cyclopedia of Literary Characters.* Englewood Cliffs, New Jersey: Salem, 1963.

Nowlan, Robert Anthony, and Gwendolyn Wright Nowlan. *The Name Is Familiar: Who Played in the Movies.* New York: Neal-Schuman, 1990.

Taggart, Jean E. *Pet Names.* Metuchen, New Jersey: Scarecrow, 1962.

Sample Activity Related to Fictional Book Characters: Anastasia Krupnik

For this example activity, the teacher or library media specialist supplies students with multiple copies of Lois Lowry's Anastasia books, so that Anastasia may be introduced to the students. The library media specialist may select the appropriate book title for study depending on the age of the readers.

In this example, a group of eight seventh-grade students would be involved. In *Anastasia on Her Own*, she is 13 and in seventh grade, so for such a group selections might be taken from this book. For example, students may read the section where Sam comes down with the chicken pox beginning on page 45. The group would then share sections before talking in general about being left in charge. They may speculate about the situations that might occur.

The students may then have an opportunity to select and read at least one of the Anastasia books. When the students meet again with their background reading done, they have an opportunity to role play some situations that might be similar to those that happen to Anastasia. This role play would be based on the Anastasia character. The library media specialist may read all of the books and identify a number of situations.

Sample Situations

1. Anastasia gets a job in a fast-food place. Friends come in and make a mess. She has to tell them to clean it up. One of the messy friends is a boy whom she would love to know better.
2. Anastasia is responsible for a neighbor's pet and the pet gets lost.
3. Anastasia learns how to use the computer and takes on typing assignments for others, completing their papers. She gets two papers mixed up in the machine and tries to get the papers back.

Following a period of one week to allow time for reading a selected title, the students meet again with the library media specialist. At the beginning of the meeting, the library media specialist talks about the titles that they read and what they thought about

the escapades of Anastasia. Students identify what kind of character they think Anastasia is. Students comment and retell some of
their favorite episodes from the books. The library media specialist
may ask one or two of the more outgoing students to act out some
of the things that Anastasia does. The library media specialist may
tell the students to pretend that they have lost jewelry down the
kitchen sink or that they are giving advice to their mothers about
the clothes they wear. The students act out these situations.

Following these initial warm-up role-playing situations, the
library media specialist may explain that the group will role-play
situations similar to those that occur in the books. The participants
will act out the situations and the audience will listen and observe
politely. When volunteer participants are ready, the library media
specialist may provide a sample situation.

Students may act out the situation and their ending. When this
is completed and bows are taken, the audience and participants
may discuss the reasons for their actions. What was the character
feeling? What was the character trying to do? Why did the character
try that solution? Some students may have come up with different
endings. At this point they may volunteer to act out their versions.
Again bows may be taken and discussions follow. Finally, the
students may evaluate the performances and the solutions, and
then decide why they think the character might act in the way that
she did.

Resources Related to Anastasia Krupnik

Print

Lowry, Lois. *Anastasia, Again!* Boston: Houghton Mifflin, 1981.
IL: 4–7. RL: 5.

———. *Anastasia, Ask Your Analyst.* Boston: Houghton Mifflin, 1984. IL: 4–7. RL: 3.

———. *Anastasia at Your Service.* Boston: Houghton Mifflin, 1982.
IL: 4–7. RL: 5.

———. *Anastasia Has the Answers.* Boston: Houghton Mifflin, 1986.
IL: 4–7. RL: 6.

———. *Anastasia Krupnik.* Boston: Houghton Mifflin, 1979. IL: 4–7.
RL: 4.

————. *Anastasia on Her Own.* Boston: Houghton Mifflin, 1985. IL: 4–7. RL: 6.

————. *Anastasia's Chosen Career.* Boston: Houghton Mifflin, 1987. IL: 4–7. RL: 6.

————. *All about Sam.* Boston: Houghton Mifflin, 1988. IL: 4–7. RL: 4.

Nonprint

Anastasia Krupnik. Hightstown, New Jersey: American School Publishers, 1986. (3 sound filmstrips)

Method: Role Playing

Role playing is a powerful method for involving students in situations. During role play, an individual suspends his or her own persona and takes on another in a given situation. In other words, it is a structured way of pretending. Role play allows students to relate to others in situations set up outside the immediate realm of reality. Using role play can help clarify information about self and others. If the situations are meaningful to the individual, the act of becoming involved in a "pretend" situation can help that person to apply what he or she learns to other situations. Role play may help students understand social problems, improve interpersonal relations, recognize experiences they have in common with others, and express feelings in another situation. If the situations are synthesized carefully, fewer risks are presented to the individuals acting or taking on the roles.

In order to organize for role playing, more than one person is usually needed. Effective role-play situations often work best with small groups numbering four to nine individuals, although larger groups work too. In larger groups, not all participants have opportunities to participate in the discussion.

Role playing allows insight into character behavior, traits, and motivations. The procedures for role playing can be summarized into a few steps:

1. Select a situation that may be dramatized by students. When using it with literature study or to motivate reading, the book situations chosen should be understandable to the students involved.

2. Help students feel comfortable by having warm-up exercises. Students may all participate in some simple actions, such as pretending they are taking an elevator crammed with people, one of whom has a delicious-smelling pizza.
3. Explain the selected situation. Outline the situation by describing the setting, the initial actions, and the problem.
4. Explain the roles that participants or actors will play. When volunteers accept roles, outline how long they have, what they are to do, and where they are to do it.
5. Explain the role that the audience will play while watching the actors as well as following the acting. It helps to stress good manners, such as listening, observing, not making rude remarks, and clapping when the volunteers are finished.
6. Have the volunteers role-play the selected situation.
7. Discuss the actions portrayed in the role play and the logic of the play. Students should have an opportunity to talk about what happened and why they think it was a logical solution, and so on.
8. Role-play the situation again if audience members would have handled the situation differently. If there are disagreements, let others volunteer to give their reenactments.
9. Evaluate the role play, the audience participation, and the discussion.

Resources Related to the Role-Playing Method

Articles

Cacha, Frances P. "Holidays in Anticipation of Spring." *Social Studies* 67:1 (1976), pp. 35–36.

Cappetta, Ann, and Joan Scranton. "An Historical Act!" *School Arts* 85:9 (May 1986), pp. 20–22.

Davison, Joyce G. "Real Tears: Using Role Plays and Simulation." *Curriculum Review* 23:2 (April 1984), pp. 91–94.

Duncombe, Sydney, and Michael H. Heikkinen. "Role-Playing for Different Viewpoints." *College Teaching* 36:1 (Winter 1988), pp. 3–5.

Dyson, Pauline Ucci. "Dramatizing History with a Victorian Tea." *Teaching History: A Journal of Methods* 11:2 (Fall 1986), pp. 71–76.

Froehle, Thomas C., et al. "Enhancing the Effects of Modeling through Role-Play Practice." *Counselor Education and Supervision* 22:3 (March 1983), pp. 197–206.

Greathouse, Lillian R., and Joseph S. Karmos. "A New Look at Two Established Teaching Methods: Case Studies and Role Playing." *Journal of Studies in Technical Careers* 9:4 (Fall 1987), pp. 361–367.

Hickey, M. Gail. "Mock Trials for Children." *Social Education* 54:1 (January 1990), pp. 43–44.

Horwitz, Elaine K. "Getting Them All into the Act: Using Audience Participation To Increase the Effectiveness of Role-Play Activities." *Foreign Language Annals* 18:3 (May 1985), pp. 205–208.

Hurst, Joe B., and Daniel L. Merritt. "Pre-Structured and Semi-Structured Role-Playing." *Social Studies* 67:1 (1976), pp. 14–18.

Karjala, Eugene, and Raymond E. White. "American History through Music and Role Play." *History Teacher* 17:1 (November 1983), pp. 33–59.

Keller, Clair W. "Role Playing and Simulation in History Classes." *History Teacher* 8:4 (1975), pp. 573–581.

Laird, Dugan, and Ruth Sizemore House. "How To Turn Bystanders into Role Players." *Training* 21:4 (April 1984), pp. 41–43.

Major, Robert L. "Role Playing in the Classroom." *Momentum* 11:3 (October 1980), pp. 14–15.

Moore, Betty Jean. "Problem Stories for Role Playing." *Language Arts* 52 (November-December 1975), pp. 1113–1115.

Mullins, Emmett R. "An Activity on Equality or . . . . The Sneetches Revisited." *Georgia Social Science Journal* 13:3 (Fall 1982), pp. 32–34.

O'Neill, Cecily. "Dialogue and Drama: The Transformation of Events, Ideas, and Teachers." *Language Arts* 66:2 (February 1989), pp. 147–159.

Saunders, Danny. "'Reluctant Participants' in Role Play Simulations: Stage Fright or Bewilderment?" *Simulation/Games for Learning* 15:1 (March 1985), pp. 3–15.

Schunckle, George M. "Action Approaches to Learning." *Social Studies* 69:5 (1978), pp. 212–217.

Slaney, Noel. "Conversations Libres: Beyond the Conversation Card." *British Journal of Language Training* 24:2 (Fall 1986), pp. 98–103.

Surplus, Susan Hake. "Overcoming Role-Play Resistance." *Training* 20:12 (December 1983), pp. 93–94, 97.

Tabor, Jewel L. "Classroom Ideas: The Trial of Susan B. Anthony." *Social Education* 50:4 (April-May 1986), pp. 311–313.

Wolen, Inez. "Social Studies/Arts: A Little Drama at the Art Museum." *Teacher* 97:3 (November-December 1979), pp. 108, 110–111.

Books

Biddle, Bruce Jesse. *Role Theory: Expectations, Identities, and Behaviors.* New York: Academic Press, 1979.

Case, Doug, and Ken Wilson. *Off-Stage! Sketches from the English Teaching Theatre.* New York: Heinemann Educational Books, 1979.

Cottrell, June. *Teaching with Creative Dramatics.* Skokie, Illinois: National Textbook, 1975.

Dianna, Michael A. *Vitalizing Your Social Studies Class with Role-Playing.* 1983. ED 237372.

Dormant, Diane. *Rolemaps.* Englewood Cliffs, New Jersey: Educational Technology Publications, 1980.

Fletcher, Jerry L. *Human Growth Games: Explorations and Research Prospects.* Beverly Hills, California: Sage, 1978.

Furness, Pauline. *Role Play in the Elementary School: A Handbook for Teachers.* Denver: Hart, 1976.

Hall, Christine K. *Writing before Reading: A Role-Playing Model.* Paper presented at the Annual Meeting of the International Reading Association, Philadelphia, Pennsylvania, April 13–17, 1986. ED 272852.

Hawley, Robert C. *Value Exploration through Role-Playing.* Amherst, Massachusetts: Educational Research Associates, 1974.

Holmes, John Eric. *Fantasy Role Playing Games.* New York: Hippocrene, 1981.

Jennings, Sue. *Remedial Drama: A Handbook for Teachers and Therapists.* New York: Theatre Arts Books, 1974.

Johnson, Keith, and Keith Morrow. *Communication in the Classroom: Applications and Methods for a Communicative Approach.* New York: Longman, 1981.

Jones, Ken. *Interactive Learning Events: A Guide for Facilitators.* New York: Nichols, 1988.

Kerr, J. Y. K., et al. *Games, Simulations and Role-Playing.* London: English-Teaching Information Centre, 1977. ED 148176.

Livingston, Carol. *Role Play in Language Learning.* New York: Longman, 1983.

Livingston, Ian. *Dicing with Dragons: An Introduction to Role-Playing Games.* New York: New American Library, 1982.

Milroy, Ellice. *Role-Play: A Practical Guide.* Riverside, New Jersey: Pergamon, 1982.

Parisi, Lynn. *Creative Role-Playing Exercises in Science and Technology.* Boulder, Colorado: Social Science Education Consortium, 1986. ED 269329.

Role Playing: A Practical Manual for Group Facilitators. La Jolla, California: University Associates, 1980.

Sarason, Irwin G., and Barbara R. Sarason. *Constructive Classroom Behavior: A Teacher's Guide to Modeling and Role-Playing Techniques.* New York: Behavioral Publications, 1974.

Shaftel, Fannie R., and George Shaftel. *Role Playing in the Curriculum.* Englewood Cliffs, New Jersey: Prentice-Hall, 1982.

Thompson, John Francis. *Using Role Playing in the Classroom.* Bloomington, Indiana: Phi Delta Kappa Educational Foundation, 1978.

Van Ments, Morry. *The Effective Use of Role-Play: A Handbook for Teachers and Trainers.* New York: Nichols, 1989.

Wohlking, Wallace, and Patricia J. Gill. *Role Playing.* Englewood Cliffs, New Jersey: Educational Technology Publications, 1980.

Yawkey, Thomas Daniels. *Role Playing as an Imaginative Experience for Language Growth.* University Park: Pennsylvania State University, 1978. ED 161524.

4

Places

Although it is exciting to travel to unusual areas, sometimes it can be just as fun to read about them. Adults who read travel books and daydream about where they would like to visit can attest to the joy of reading about various places. It may be the seeking out of someplace different or the investigation of a familiar place formerly unknown that motivates, or it may be the pleasure of placing oneself in another setting. Whatever the motives involved, students often enjoy reading or hearing about other places. This may take many forms and relates to the development of prior knowledge deemed so important in reading comprehension. For example, students may enjoy finding out about both real and fictional places. In each case, students may consider reading about buildings and special sites, towns, cities, regions, states, and countries. Reading offers an opportunity to investigate and see another place.

RESOURCES RELATED TO GEOGRAPHICAL STUDIES

Geography and travel materials could occupy several volumes. These general sources may be helpful to the classroom teacher or library media specialist getting started.

Goddard, Stephen. *A Guide to Information Sources in the Geographical Sciences.* New York: Barnes & Noble, 1983.

Harris, Chauncy D. *A Geographical Bibliography for American Librar-ies.* Washington, D.C.: Association of American Geographers, 1985.

Hays, Greg, and Joan Wright. *Going Places: The Guide to Travel Guides.* New York: Bowker, 1988.

Hoopes, David. *Global Guide to International Education.* New York: Facts on File, 1984.

Kister, Kenneth K. *Kister's Atlas Buying Guide: General English-Lan-guage World Atlases Available in North America.* Phoenix, Arizona: Oryx, 1984.

Lewis, Lawrence T. "Geographical Software for IBM Personal Computers: Programs and Vendors." *Journal of Geography* 84:5 (September-October 1985), pp. 224–225.

Makower, Joel, and Laura Bergheim. *The Map Catalog.* New York: Random House, 1987.

Reference Sheet on Geography. Boulder, Colorado: ERIC Clearing-house for Social Studies/Social Science Education, 1982.

U.S. Geological Survey. *Maps for America: Cartographic Products, USGA and Others.* Washington, D.C.: Government Printing Office, 1981.

Because information about places changes so quickly, asking to be placed on the mailing lists of publishers and producers of materials about countries is very worthwhile. Consistently examining catalogs of such companies allows one to remain current. There are many such companies, including Rand McNally, Lerner Publications, Nystrom Education Media, Children's Press, and so forth. Check the bibliographies listed to see which companies have materials about places. Locate current addresses in *Books in Print* and write to those for whom there is an interest.

REAL PLACES

Buildings, Towns, Cities, and States

Reading about real buildings, sites, towns, cities, regions, or states can provide quite an impetus if introduced with skill on the part of the teacher or library media specialist. Every place has its own history, feeling, and look. For individuals with some imagination, reading about different places can be quite fascinating. There are so many beautifully illustrated books available that it is exciting even for the least visual learner. Poring over *National Geographic Magazine* can be more than a separate journey, it can be inspirational to know that one is not limited to the space one currently occupies.

Resources Related to Finding Information about Buildings, Towns, Cities, and States

The following sources are general in nature and may be used in connection with atlases and encyclopedias; general atlases and maps are not listed here. In addition, some local and state school library associations prepare bibliographies about their own particular regions or areas. These can be helpful in identifying resources.

Burns, William A. *Enjoying the Arts: Museums.* New York: Rosen, 1977.

Cantor, George. *Historic Black Landmarks: A Traveler's Guide.* Detroit: Gale Research, 1991.

Carpenter, Allan. *Facts about Cities.* New York: H. W. Wilson, 1990.

Chase, Valerie, et al. *Educator's Guide to the National Aquarium in Baltimore.* Baltimore: National Aquarium in Baltimore, 1984. ED 265066.

Eastman, John. *Who Lived Where: A Biographical Guide to Homes and Museums.* New York: Facts on File, 1983.

Exploring America's Scenic Highways. Washington, D.C.: National Geographic Society, 1985.

Frome, Michael. *National Park Guide.* Chicago: Rand McNally, 1991.

Kane, Joseph Nathan, Steven Anzovin, and Janet Podell. *Facts about States.* New York: H. W. Wilson, 1989.

Long, Kim. *Encyclopedia of Field Trips and Educational Destinations.* Santa Barbara, California: ABC-CLIO, 1991.

Miller-Lachmann, Lyn. *Our Family, Our Friends, Our World: An Annotated Guide to Significant Multicultural Books for Children and Teenagers.* New York: Bowker, 1992.

Norris, John, and Joann Norris. *Amusement Parks: An American Guidebook.* Jefferson, North Carolina: McFarland, 1986.

"Physical Geography Slide Sets of America's National Parks." *Journal of Geography* 83:3 (May-June 1984), pp. 131–132.

Reading for Young People Series. Chicago: American Library Association, 1979–present. (titles include regions of the United States)

Sclar, Charlotte L. *The Smithsonian: A Guide to Its National Public Facilities in Washington D.C.* Jefferson, North Carolina: McFarland, 1985.

Strait, Jerry L., and Sandra S. Strait. *Vietnam War Memorials: An Illustrated Reference to Veterans Tributes Throughout the United States*. Jefferson, North Carolina: McFarland, 1988.

Thum, Marcella. *Exploring Black America: A History and Guide*. New York: Atheneum, 1975.

Thum, Marcella, and Gladys Thum. *Exploring Military America*. New York: Atheneum, 1982.

Van Meer, Mary, and Michael Anthony Pasquarelli. *Free Attractions, USA*. Sante Fe, New Mexico: John Muir, 1984.

Zucker, Barbara Fleisher. *Children's Museums, Zoos, and Discovery Rooms*. Westport, Connecticut: Greenwood, 1987.

Sample Activity Related to Place: Field Trips

The teacher or library media specialist can pull together materials about the local community and have students peruse the materials and then help plan a field trip. The example given here involves students visiting Washington, D.C.

The students first look at different travel guides about the city. In pairs, they examine information about the many places that could be visited. A map may be displayed so that students can get their bearings. Each pair in the class selects a place that they consider worthwhile, and then begins research on this particular place within the city. After this reading, the classroom teacher asks each pair to make a report to the class about the site they have chosen. Pairs report on what they learned about the selected area.

The classroom teacher then places a large schedule on the board with blocks of time for each day. He or she explains that time will limit the places that can be visited, so decisions need to be made. A list of the reports made by pairs is made, and the pairs then lobby for visiting their selected sites. A vote is taken, and the sites gaining the most votes are selected. In this case, there were several sites preordained by the classroom teacher. However, the top places are selected. Using the maps, sites close to each other are planned to be visited within the same day.

The classroom teacher asks groups of three students each to sign up for one of the selected sites to do more research work. Each triad is given the assignment to prepare a worksheet for their site. Questions are prepared to be used at each site by the entire group. The questions are typed up, and sources for further reading are given as bibliographical references. Students prepare worksheets for the entire group making the visit; these are arranged in notebooks according to the scheduled day and time of the field trip.

Resources Related to Local City, Town, or State

As an example, the following materials about the District of Columbia have been selected. Two of the most useful sources for materials for students include Allan Carpenter's *Facts about Cities* (New York: H. W. Wilson, 1990) and Joseph Nathan Kane, Steven Anzovin, and Janet Podell's *Facts about the States* (New York: H. W. Wilson, 1989). These resources include sources for obtaining information and bibliographies.

Fiction

(IL Signifies Interest Level; RL Signifies Fry Readability Level)

Burnham, Sophy. *Dogwalker*. New York: Warner, 1979. IL: 5–7. RL: 6.
Lindberg, Anne. *People in Pineapple Place*. New York: Harcourt, 1982. IL: 4–6. RL: 6.

Nonfiction

Bluestone, Carol, and Susan Irwin. *Washington D.C. Guidebook for Kids*. Washington, D.C.: Noodle, 1987.
Brown, Richard. *A Kid's Guide to Washington*. New York: Harcourt, 1989. IL: 4–7.
Carpenter, Allan. *The New Enchantment of America: District of Columbia*. Chicago: Children's Press, 1979. IL: 4–8. RL: 6.
Cox, Brian. *500 Things To Do in Washington for Free and 100 Things To Do for Less Than a Buck*. Newark, New Jersey: New Century, 1983.

Going Places with Children. Rockville, Maryland: Green Acres School, 1989.

Krementz, Jill. *A Visit to Washington.* New York: Scholastic, 1987. IL: 6–8.

Loewen, N. *Washington D.C.* Vero Beach, Florida: Rourke, 1990 IL: 5–8. RL: 6.

Lumley, K. W. *District of Columbia: In Words and Pictures.* Chicago: Children's Press, 1981. IL: 3–6. RL: 4.

Reef, Catherine. *Washington, D.C.* Minneapolis: Dillon, 1989.

Stein, R. Conrad. *The Story of the Burning of Washington.* Chicago: Children's Press, 1985. IL: 3–6.

Nonprint

America's National Shrines. (Includes the Washington Monument and Mount Vernon.) Chicago: Nystrom, 1974. (10 sound filmstrips)

The Capitol. Irwindale, California: Barr Films, 1975. (sound filmstrip)

History of Washington DC. Chicago: Society for Visual Education, 1982. (sound filmstrip)

Our Nation's Capital. Westminster, Maryland: Random House, 1979. (2 sound filmstrips)

Washington, City Out of the Wilderness. Chicago: Films Incorporated, 1975. (2 sound filmstrips)

Washington DC. Washington, D.C.: National Geographic Society, 1983. (20-min. videocassette)

Washington, DC by Augustin. Lincoln, Nebraska: GPN, 1975. (videocassette)

Washington DC: L'Enfant's Dream, Our Heritage. Hollywood, California: Handel Film, 1984. (videocassette)

Method: Field Trip

A field trip is a method in which a teacher or library media specialist arranges to undertake a trip or excursion for educational purposes. When the instructor makes the arrangements, it is usually through the school, although such trips are not necessarily only school related. Such arranged trips allow students to travel to specific places where the materials of instruction may be observed and studied directly in their functional setting. In other words, students go to the site and learn, immersing themselves in the atmosphere of the setting they are interested in.

Selecting a place should involve scrutiny of the interests or goals and objectives of the study. Travel can be very expensive, so if there is not enough interest or the goals are unclear, much can be lost.

Advance planning makes most field trips successful. Even with a great deal of planning, however, there will probably be little glitches in most trips. What are some of the areas that should be considered in making the trip?

Depending on the distance and length of time for the trip, the classroom teacher and library media specialist should consider making all arrangements. Before making any arrangements, they must consider the legalities and permissions that might be required.

Those planning the trip should obtain and read carefully any information about the place being visited: location, distance from school, and times of operation. There is nothing worse than going to a museum to find it closed.

Transportation will be among the first considerations. What will the transport be? How will it be paid for? If the trip is to last overnight, food and sleeping arrangements must be made. Students must be told what kinds of clothing and other items would be appropriate to bring along.

Planning the trip itself thoroughly becomes a must. What will students do during the transport to the site? What kinds of investigations will be suggested? These should be in keeping with the interests and learning objectives the trip is designed to address. What kinds of questions need to be formulated and answered after the trip? If there will be a tour, discussion of manners and general behavior is a likely topic, along with what students might expect to see. A specific schedule is probably a good idea if the trip is a day or longer. Buddy systems usually help if there are large numbers of students.

Finally comes the trip itself. If the plans have been carefully worked out, there is a likelihood of success. The classroom teacher and library media specialist should be ready for discussion and should have plenty of follow-up materials available for further reading.

Resources Related to the Field Trip Method

Print

Archer, A. C. "What Does Industry Want Teachers To Know?" *Physics Education* 19:5 (September 1984), pp. 216–218.

Baer, Vicki E. "Getting To Know the Neighbors: An Information Exchange Between Two Middle Schools." *Computing Teacher* 15:8 (May 1988), pp. 20–23.

Baker, Beverly, and Jean Sellar. "Science Come Alive in the Natural History Museum." *Curriculum Review* 22:5 (December 1983), pp. 71–74.

Beinhorn, George. "How To Take a Walk with Kids: And Still Enjoy the Scenery." *Instructor* 94:8 (April 1985), pp. 46–48, 51.

Bischoff, Henry. "A Walking Tour of an Ethnic Neighborhood: Communities as Outdoor Classrooms for Teaching Immigration History." *Social Studies* 78:5 (September-October 1987), pp. 202–205.

Carroll, Rives. "Exploring the History of a Neighborhood: A Community Project." *Social Studies* 76:4 (July-August 1985), pp. 150–154.

Chandler, Theodore A. "These Policy Tips Make the Most of Field Trips." *American School Board Journal* 172:6 (June 1985), pp. 30, 41.

Chetelat, Frank J. "Art, Animals and Learning." *School Arts* 85:2 (October 1985), pp. 22–23.

DeRosa, Bill. "Field Trips: An Effective Supplement to Humane Education." *Children and Animals* 10:2 (April 1986), p. 12.

Dicott, Mark S. "A Field Trip to Gettysburg: A Model Experience." *History Teacher* 20:4 (August 1987), pp. 487–496.

Dilworth, R. Anne. *The Capitol Experience in Washington, D.C.* Arlington, Virginia: Arlington County Public Schools, 1983.

Ediger, Marlow. *A Visit to a Pig "Hatchery" on the Farm.* 1985. ED 262931.

"The Field Trip: Frill or Reality?" *Instructor* 94:9 (May 1985), pp. 14–15.

Finson, Kevin D., and Larry G. Enochs. "Student Attitudes Toward Science-Technology-Society Resulting from Visitation to a Science Technology Museum." *Journal of Research in Science Teaching* 24:7 (October 1987), pp. 593–609.

Fischer, Richard B. "Successful Field Trips." *Nature Study* 37:3–4 (March 1984), pp. 24–27.

"Frugal Field Trips." *Instructor* 93:2 (September 1983), pp. 58–62.

Garbutt, Barb. "What? A Field Trip on the Playground?" *Inside Out: Michigan Outdoor Education Association Newsletter* 5:2 (Spring 1983), p. 7.

Greenslade, Cleo B. "A Walk Back." *Social Studies* 79:2 (March-April 1988), pp. 47–50.

Hamilton, Thomas R. "How-To-Do-It: A Transect Study of a Barrier Beach." *American Biology Teacher* 50:2 (February 1988), pp. 107–109.

Harrison, Jo Ann. "The Effects of Educational Programs in Art Museums on the Artistic Perceptions of Elementary School Children." *Journal of Research and Development in Education* 21:3 (Spring 1988), pp. 44–52.

James, Lila Jean. "A Museum Field Trip, a Controlled Environment." *Outdoor-Communicator* 18:2 (Fall 1986–Winter 1987), pp. 31–32.

Jenness, Mark. "Schoolyard Hikes." *Science and Children* 24:6 (March 1987), pp. 23–25.

Katulka, Lawrence. "The Boston Massacre." *Social Science Record* 22:2 (Fall 1985), pp. 44–45.

Keown, Duane. "Let's Justify the Field Trip." *American Biology Teacher* 46:1 (January 1984), pp. 43–48.

Long, Kim. *Encyclopedia of Field Trips and Educational Destinations.* Santa Barbara, California: ABC-CLIO, 1991.

Magahay, Wendy, et al. "Get Those Kids Out of Here! Using No-Cost or Low-Cost Field Trips." *TESL Talk* 14:4 (Fall 1983), pp. 54–58.

McClure, John W. "The Great American Geological Field Trip." *Science Activities* 25:1 (February-March 1988), pp. 8–16.

McCoy, Martha A. "What To Do before the Downbeat." *Music Educators Journal* 69:8 (April 1983), pp. 34–35.

McKenzie, Garry D., et al. "The Importance of Field Trips." *Journal of College Science Teaching* 16:1 (September-October 1986), pp. 17–20.

McLure, John W. "Free Tips for Geology Trips." *Science Teacher* 52:7 (October 1985), pp. 40–43.

McMahon, Sue, and Mary Stubbs. "Scavenging for the Past." *Southern Social Studies Quarterly* 14:1 (Fall 1988), pp. 57–62.

Muse, Corey, et al. "Teachers Utilization of Field Trips: Prospects and Problems." *ClearingHouse* 56:3 (November 1982), pp. 122–126.

Pfoutz, Bonnie. *If These Walls Could Talk: The Story of Arlington House before the Civil War.* Arlington, Virginia: Arlington County Public Schools, 1983.

Piekarz, Ann Lorette. "Go to the Experience, or Let It Come to You . . . But Let It Happen!" *Illinois Schools Journal* 61:1–4 (1982), pp. 49–54.

Redleaf, Rhoda. *Field Trips: An Adventure in Learning.* Saint Paul, Minnesota: Toys 'n' Things Press, 1980. ED 224560.

Rosenheck, Donna. "Field Trips Abroad." *Social Education* 52:5 (September 1988), pp. 344–346.

Russell, Helen Ross. "Ten Minute Field Trips: Using the School Grounds To Teach." *Nature Study* 37:3–4 (March 1984), p. 8.

Sanderson, P. L. "The Pollution Detectives: Part II. Lead and Zinc Mining." *School Science Record* 69:249 (June 1988), pp. 721–728.

Schwartz, Mary Jo. "An 8000-Mile, 38-Day Field Trip for High School Students." *Journal of Geological Education* 36:3 (May 1988), pp. 177–181.

Sesow, F. William, and Tom McGowan. "Take the Field Trip First." *Social Studies* 75:2 (March-April 1984), pp. 68–70.

Steiner, Linda. "Field Trips Provide Learning Experience for Students, Staff." *Journalism Educator* 42:1 (Spring 1987), pp. 39–41.

Tyson, Eleanor S. "What? No Field Trips." *Illinois Schools Journal* 64:1–4 (1984), pp. 49–55.

Van De Walle, Carol. "Water Works." *Science and Children* 25:7 (April 1988), pp. 15–17.

Weible, Thomas. "Using Community Resources To Enhance the Rural School Curriculum." *Small School Forum* 5:2 (Winter 1983–1984), pp. 13–14.

West, Leo R. "Training in Pennsylvania." *Social Studies Journal* 12 (Spring 1983), pp. 4–8.

Wood, Jacalyn K. "Take a Field Trip Close to Home." *Science and Children* 24:2 (October 1986), pp. 26–27.

Zeller, Terry. "Let's Teach Art with Originals." *Art Education* 36:1 (January 1983), pp. 43–46.

Zielinski, Edward J. *So You Want To Take a Field Trip.* 1987. ED 299079.

Nonprint

Field Trips. Maine Public Broadcasting Network, 1983. (Distributed by GPN.) (18 15-min. videocassettes. Titles: *The Potato Farm; Between High Tide and Low; Power from Water; Yacht Building; Television: It's Done with Mirrors; The Little Time Machine; Harvesting Our Forest; Making Paper; The Play's the Thing; Growing Salmon; Update: Defense; The Weaver; The Maine Bear; Aquaculture; Early Man in Maine; The Bangor River; "Jax"*; and *Maple Syrup Making.*)

Country and Continent

Students may find the study of countries deadly boring if it is presented as a study of facts. However, there are many pictorial works and histories available that can make the exploration of countries quite exciting.

Resources Related to Country and Continent

Albright, Charlotte F. "Teaching the Middle East: Topics and Resources." *Indiana Social Studies Quarterly* 35:2 (Fall 1982), pp. 77–87.

Bibliography of Children's Books from Asia 1980: An Annotated Bibliography of Illustrated Books for Children in Asia. Tokyo: Asian Cultural Centre for UNESCO, 1980.

Boek en Jeugd. (Annual List from Bureau Boek en Juegd, Taco Scheltemastraat 5, Postbus 93054, Den Haag, Netherlands.)

Boker for Barn Og Ungdom. (Annual List from Statens Bibliotektilsyn, Munkesdamsveien 62, N-1301 Oslo, Norway.)

Bookbird. International Board on Books for Young People.

Booklist. Chicago: American Library Association. (Often includes sections related to regions or groups.)

Borne Boger. (Annual List from Bibliotekscentralen, Telegrafve 5, 2750 Ballerup, Denmark.)

Butlar, Lois, and Lubomyr R. Wynar. *Building Ethnic Collections: An Annotated Guide for School Library Media Centers and Public Libraries.* Littleton, Colorado: Libraries Unlimited, 1977.

Chandras, Kananur V. *Arab, Armenian, Syrian, Lebanese, East Indian, Pakistani and Bangladeshi Americans: A Study Guide and Source Book.* Saratoga, California: R&E, 1977.

China Resources: A Guide for the Classroom. Stanford, California: SPICE, Stanford University, 1986.

Herscovich, Pearl, and Philomena Hauck. "Geography and History Skills: An Annotated Bibliography of Recent Canadian Teaching Resources." *History and Social Science Teacher* 22:2 (1986), pp. 29–34.

Jassim, Charlene. *India: A Myriad of Cultures. Three Learning Modules for Middle School Students.* 1989. ED 322042.

La Revue des Livres pour Enfants. (Quarterly from La Joie par les Livres, 8, Rue Saint-Bon, F-75004, Paris, France.)

Makino, Yasuko. *Japan through Children's Literature: An Annotated Bibliography.* Westport, Connecticut: Greenwood, 1985.

Metcalf, Fay, and Catherine Edwards. *Materials for Teaching about Europe: An Annotated Bibliography for Educators.* Washington, D.C.: Atlantic Council of the United States, 1986.

Miller, E. Willard, and Anthony R. De Souza. "Resources on the Geography of Canada." *Journal of Geography* 83:5 (September-October 1984), pp. 256–260.

National Resource List for Teaching about Latin America. Stanford, California: SPICE, Stanford University, 1983.

Posner, Arlene, and Arne de Kejier. *China: A Resource and Curriculum Guide.* Washington, D.C.: Center for Teaching about China, 1976.

Povsic, Francis F. *Eastern Europe in Children's Literature: An Annotated Bibliography of English-Language Books.* Westport, Connecticut: Greenwood, 1986.

Schedario. (Bimonthly from Centro Didaticco Nazionale, Sezione di Letteratura, Giovanile, Via Michelangelo Buonarotti 10, 50122, Firenze, Italy.)

Schon, Isabel. *A Bicultural Heritage: Themes for the Exploration of Mexico and Mexican-American Culture in Books for Children and Adolescents.* Metuchen, New Jersey: Scarecrow, 1978.

Sen, Sondra. *The Asian Indians in America: A Curriculum Resource Handbook for Teachers.* New York: Association of Asian Indians in America.

Serina, Loreta, and Fe Aldave Yap. *Children's Literature in the Philippines: An Annotated Bibliography of Philipino and English Works, 1901–1979.* Manila, Philippines: National Books Store, 1980.

Simony, Maggy. *Traveler's Reading Guide: Ready-Made Reading Lists for the Armchair Traveler*. New York: Facts on File, 1987.

Teaching about China: Cultural Expressions. Washington, D.C.: Center for Teaching about China, 1983.

Teaching about China: People and Daily Life. Washington, D.C.: Center for Teaching about China, 1982.

"Vietnam: A Teacher's Guide" (Special issue). *Focus on Asian Studies* 1 (Fall 1983).

Vi Laser Pa Fritid. (Annual from Bibliotekstjanst, AB, Box 200, Tornavagen 9, S-22100 Lund, Sweden.)

World Bibliography Series. Santa Barbara, California: ABC-CLIO. (More than 90 volumes on specific countries.)

Sample Activity Related to Country: Japan

In this research project method, a group of four to six students gathers around a cart on which has been placed multiple materials about the country of Japan. Outlines of information from an encyclopedia may also be written on a large chart and placed on or near the cart so that students can consider the kinds of topics they might investigate.

As the students look through the materials, they discuss what interests them. They may select a chairperson who will help keep them on target. Another chart can give a list such as the one that follows, giving students suggested steps for carrying out the project:

1. Previewing materials about the topic
2. Brainstorming with other group members
3. Selecting a specific topic
4. Asking questions about what you want to learn
5. Deciding where you might look for the necessary answers to the questions
6. Gathering information about the questions (card catalog, reference books, films, etc.)
7. Reporting to the group
8. Organizing the information (outlining)
9. Gathering more information and arranging it in the organization pattern set

10. Summarizing the information
11. Putting the information into a product

Students may begin following the steps outlined in the chart. As they work, the classroom teacher or library media specialist may want to monitor their progress to make sure they are on a successful path. Depending on the product, the students may need time to share what they have learned with others. They may put on a program, write something, or make something. The emphasis is on the process of individualized searching and studying and then communicating what has been learned.

Student Resources Related to Japan

Students can find many resources about Japan. A useful bibliography includes Yasuko Makino's *Japan Through Children's Literature* (Westport, Connecticut: Greenwood, 1985). There are so many materials available that the following list represents only a sampling.

Fiction

Coerr, Eleanor. *Sadako and the Thousand Paper Cranes.* New York: Putnam, 1977. IL: 3–6.

Goodman, Robert B., and Robert A. Spicer. *Momotaro: Peach Boy.* Honolulu: Island Heritage, 1972. IL: 3–6.

Miyazawa, Kenji. *Winds from Afar.* Palo Alto, California: Kodansha, 1972. IL: 4–6.

Paterson, Katherine. *The Master Puppeteer.* New York: Harper, 1975. IL: 7–9.

———. *Of Nightingales That Weep.* New York: Crowell, 1974. IL: 5–7.

Say, Allen. *The Inn-Keeper's Apprentice.* New York: Harper, 1979. IL: 6–8.

Watkins, Yoko Kawashima. *So Far from the Bamboo Grove.* New York: Lothrop, Lee & Shepard, 1986.

Winthrop, Elizabeth. *Journey to the Bright Kingdom.* New York: Holiday House, 1979. IL: 3–6.

Nonfiction

Blumberg, Rhoda. *Commodore Perry in the Land of the Shogun.* New York: Lothrop, Lee & Shepard, 1985. IL: 5–8.

Bruce, Jeannette. *Judo: The Gentle Beginning.* New York: Crowell, 1975. IL: 4–7.

Elkin, Judith. *A Family in Japan.* Minneapolis: Lerner, 1987. IL: 3–6.

Epstein, Samuel, and Beryl Epstein. *A Year of Japanese Festivals.* Champaign, Illinois: Garrard, 1974. IL: 4–7.

Greene, Carol. *Japan.* Chicago: Children's Press, 1983. IL: 5–8.

Japan. New York: Time/Life, 1985. IL: 6–9+.

Japan at War. New York: Time/Life, 1980. IL: 6–9+.

Japan: Early History. Milwaukee, Wisconsin: Raintree, 1991. IL: 4–8. RL: 4.

Japan: Geography and Economy. Milwaukee, Wisconsin: Raintree, 1991. IL: 4–8. RL: 4.

Japan: Modern History. Milwaukee, Wisconsin: Raintree, 1991. IL: 4–8. RL: 4.

Japan: People and Culture. Milwaukee, Wisconsin: Raintree, 1991. IL: 4–8. RL: 4.

Japan-in-Pictures. Minneapolis: Lerner, 1989. IL: 3–6.

Lewis, Richard. *There Are Two Lives.* New York: Simon & Schuster, 1970. IL: 3–6.

Marrin, Albert. *Victory in the Pacific.* New York: Atheneum, 1983. IL: 6–8.

Maruki, Toshi. *Hiroshima No Pika.* New York: Lothrop, Lee & Shepard, 1982. IL: 4–7.

Parker, Steve. *Japan.* Morristown, New Jersey: Silver Burdette, 1988. IL: 4–6.

Roberson, John R. *Japan: From Shogun to Sony, 1543–1984.* New York: Atheneum, 1985. IL: 6–9.

Steffoff, Rebecca. *Japan.* New York: Chelsea House, 1988. IL: 5–8. RL: 6.

Tada, Tatsuji. *Japanese Recipes.* Rutland, Vermont: Tuttle, 1967. IL: 5–9.

Tames, Richard. *Japan, the Land and Its People.* Morristown, New Jersey: Silver Burdette, 1987. IL: 5–8.

———. *Passport to Japan.* New York: Watts, 1988. IL: 6–8.

Zich, Arthur. *The Rising Sun.* New York: Time/Life, 1977. IL: 7–9+.

Nonprint

Japan. Washington, D.C.: National Geographic Society, 1987. (25-min. videocassette)

The Japanese. Lincoln: University of Nebraska-Lincoln Television/The Nebraska ETV Network, 1988. (Distributed by GPN.) (videodisc)

The Japanese, Part 1: Full Moon Lunch. New York: Japan Society, 1978. (58-min. 16mm film)

The Japanese, Part 2: The Blind Swordsman. New York: Japan Society, 1978. (57-min. 16mm film)

The Japanese, Part 3: Farm Song. New York: Japan Society, 1978. (57-min. 16mm film)

Living Treasures of Japan. Washington, D.C.: National Geographic Society, 1987. (59-min. videocassette)

Marie: Ama Diver. Glendale, California: Cyprus, 1979. (sound filmstrip)

Our World Neighbors: Japan. New York: Imperial Educational Services, 1987. (4 sound filmstrips)

Seeing Japan. New York: Random House, 1987. (6 sound filmstrips)

Method: Individual Study

During individual study, the student makes a preliminary survey of subject areas and decides on an area that he or she might like to pursue. This type of study involves some form of agreement. Students usually talk with their teachers and agree to study certain topics. Adults make the commitment to themselves.

As the process of locating information begins, usually a set of particular steps occurs. These steps are outlined in a number of sources; following is a summary of steps that seem to be generally accepted in individual study:

1. Choose a general topic.
2. Review the information generally available about the topic and the ground that might need to be covered.
3. Narrow or expand the topic depending on the time and area of interest.
4. Develop a thesis.
5. Ask questions related to the thesis.

6. Plan for the search (sources and subjects to look for).
7. Find the materials and use those sources to find more sources.
8. Analyze what has been found.
9. Organize the information analyzed (rough outline or web).
10. Evaluate the organization.
11. Draft an outline.
12. Consider the information and take notes on paper.
13. Keep records and organize notes around the outline.
14. Revise the outline.
15. Draft a paper or prepare a product.
16. Compile a bibliography.
17. Revise the paper or product, looking for gaps or problems.
18. Evaluate the final product.

Resources Related to the Individual Study Method

There are many articles available on the research process, as well as guides for writing papers. Besides those materials that may be found in local library media centers, the following sources offer insight into the research process.

Eisenberg, Michael B., and Robert E. Berkowitz. *Information Problem-Solving: The Big Six Skills Approach to Library and Information Skills Instruction.* Norwood, New Jersey: Ablex, 1990.

Kuhlthau, Carol Collier. *Teaching the Library Research Process.* West Nyack, New York: Center for Applied Research in Education, 1985.

Stripling, Barbara K., and Judy M. Pitts. *Brainstorms and Blueprints: Teaching Library Research as a Thinking Process.* Littleton, Colorado: Libraries Unlimited, 1988.

FICTIONAL PLACES

In many fantastical works, in fantasy, science fiction, descriptive poetry, and other forms, readers may find a variety of imaginary places. These settings have one thing in common: they exist only in the imaginations of the authors and of readers willing to suspend belief to accept the authors' views. These places may be worlds, countries, cities, or universes that are populated with beings.

The books selected as examples here include those that take place in the world created by L. Frank Baum. However, there are many other worlds that might be explored. The simulation or role-playing method is chosen because it lends itself to pretending and interacting.

Resources Related to Fictional Places

Dowrick, Stephanie. *Land of Zeus: The Greek Myths Retold by Geographic Place of Origin*. Garden City, New York: Doubleday, 1976.

Fonstad, Karen Wynn. *The Atlas of Middle Earth*. Boston: Houghton Mifflin, 1981.

————. *The Atlas of Pern*. New York: Del Rey, 1984.

————. *The Atlas of the Land*. New York: Ballantine, 1985.

Frimmer, Steven. *Neverland; Fabled Places and Fabulous Voyages of History and Legend*. New York: Viking, 1976.

May, Julian. *A Pliocene Companion*. Boston: Houghton Mifflin, 1984.

Velasco, Raymond L. *Star Wars: A Guide to the Star Wars Universe*. New York: Ballantine, 1984.

Sample Activity Related to Fictional Places: Oz

In this activity, the students use a number of resources to make up their own simulation about Oz. This requires reading and viewing before planning of the simulation can begin. Copies of the materials and the map in *An Atlas of Fantasy* should be used. Of definite use is the reference source *Who's Who in Oz*.

Several simulations may be played at a time. Basically, one person is the Wizard and plans the plot or story for a particular game. Players (besides the Wizard) in the simulation game may number one or more; five is probably a maximum for involvement. The Wizard begins the session and maps out a plan for the players. The plot is written out at the beginning, but not shown to the players.

Each player assumes a character based on his or her own readings. For example, a player might choose to be Dorothy or Tip from *The Marvelous Land of Oz*. The students are provided with the map of Oz as found in the fantasy atlas. They may learn all that they can about their characters by reading the books and referring to *Who's Who in Oz*. A spinner may be used to determine move choices and activities. For example, a 1 might mean "move player down the road to the next stop." The Wizard for the game being played makes up the meanings for the spinner numbers.

Each player has special characteristics that he or she must identify before starting to play. For example, the Scarecrow wanted brains. The Wizard maps out the plot of the story, the reason the players must get to a certain spot, and the problems they will encounter. These problems are written on small cards by the Wizard. The person playing the Wizard must be something of a story-teller, because he or she will describe the events that happen at certain spots. If the Wizard is extremely adventurous and creative, he or she may make up his or her own map version for the particular play.

When the Wizard is ready, the students begin the play, with the first person spinning. Play continues until the students have finished the plot laid out by the Wizard.

Resources Related to Oz

Association

> *International Wizard of Oz Club*
> 220 North 11th Street
> Escanaba, MI 49829

Books

Baum, L. Frank. *Dorothy and the Wizard in Oz*. Chicago, IL: Rand McNally, 1971. IL: 4–7.

———. *Dorothy and the Wizard in Oz*. New York: Dover, 1984. IL: 4–7.

———. *The Emerald City of Oz*. New York: Ballantine, 1985. IL: 4–7.

———. *Glinda of Oz*. Chicago: Contemporary Books, 1977. IL: 4–7.

———. *The Land of Oz*. New York: Airmont, 1968. IL: 4–7.

———. *The Land of Oz*. New York: Ballantine, 1983. IL: 4–7.

———. *The Little Wizard Stories of Oz*. New York: Schocken, 1985. IL: 4–7.

———. *The Lost Princess of Oz*. New York: Ballantine, 1980. IL: 4–7.

———. *The Magic of Oz*. Chicago: Reilly & Lee, 1977. IL: 4–7.

———. *The Marvelous Land of Oz*. New York: Morrow, 1985. IL: 4–7.

———. *Ozma of Oz*. Chicago: Rand McNally, 1971. IL: 4–7.

———. *Ozma of Oz*. New York: Ballantine, 1984. IL: 4–7.

———. *Ozma of Oz*. New York: Dover, 1985. IL: 4–7.

———. *Ozma of Oz*. Chicago: Reilly & Britton, 1989. IL: 4–7.

———. *The Patchwork Girl of Oz*. New York: Ballantine, 1985. IL: 4–7.

———. *Rinkitink in Oz*. Chicago: Contemporary Books, 1916. IL: 4–7.

———. *The Road to Oz*. Chicago: Contemporary Books, 1977. IL: 4–7.

———. *The Scarecrow of Oz*. New York: Ballantine, 1985. IL: 4–7.

———. *Tik-Tok of Oz*. New York: Ballantine, 1980. IL: 4–7.

———. *The Tin Woodman of Oz*. New York: Ballantine, 1981. IL: 4–7.

———. *The Wonderful Wizard of Oz*. New York: Dover, 1960. IL: 3–7. RL: 6.

———. *The Wonderful Wizard of Oz*. New York: Morrow, 1987. IL: 3–7. RL: 6.

Cosgrove, Rachel. *The Hidden Valley of Oz*. Chicago: Reilly & Lee, 1951. IL: 4–7.

McGraw, Eloise J., and Lauren M. Wagner. *Merry-Go-Round in Oz*. Chicago: Reilly & Lee, 1963. IL: 4–7.

Neill, John R. *Lucky Bucky in Oz*. Chicago: Reilly & Lee, 1949. IL: 4–7.

———. *The Scalawagons of Oz*. Chicago: Reilly & Lee, 1941. IL: 4–7.

———. *The Wonder City of Oz*. Chicago: Reilly & Lee, 1940. IL: 4–7.

Snow, Jack. *The Magical Mimics in Oz*. Chicago: Reilly & Lee, 1946. IL: 4–7.

———. *The Shaggy Man of Oz*. Chicago: Reilly & Lee, 1949. IL: 4–7.

———. *Who's Who in Oz*. New York: Peter Bedrick, 1988. IL: 4–7.

Post, J. B. *An Atlas of Fantasy*. New York: Ballantine, 1979. IL: 4–7.

Thompson, Ruth Plumly. *Captain Salt of Oz*. Chicago: Reilly & Lee, 1936. IL: 4–7.

———. *The Cowardly Lion of Oz*. New York: Ballantine, 1985. IL: 4–7.

———. *The Giant Horse of Oz*. New York: Ballantine, 1985. IL: 4–7.

———. *The Gnome King of Oz*. New York: Ballantine, 1985. IL: 4–7.

———. *Grampa in Oz*. New York: Ballantine, 1985. IL: 4–7.

———. *Handy Mandy in Oz*. Chicago: Reilly & Lee, 1937. IL: 4–7.

———. *The Hungry Tiger of Oz*. New York: Ballantine, 1985. IL: 4–7.

————. *Jack Pumpkinhead of Oz*. New York: Ballantine, 1985. IL: 4–7.
————. *Kabumpo in Oz*. Chicago: Reilly & Lee, 1922. IL: 4–7.
————. *The Lost King of Oz*. New York: Ballantine, 1985. IL: 4–7.
————. *Ojo in Oz*. Chicago: Reilly & Lee, 1933. IL: 4–7.
————. *Ozoplanning with the Wizard of Oz*. Chicago: Reilly & Lee, 1939. IL: 4–7.
————. *Pirates in Oz*. New York: Ballantine, 1986. IL: 4–7.
————. *The Purple Prince of Oz*. New York: Ballantine, 1986. IL: 4–7.
————. *The Royal Book of Oz*. New York: Ballantine, 1985. IL: 4–7.
————. *The Silver Princess in Oz*. Chicago: Reilly & Lee, 1938. IL: 4–7.
————. *Speedy in Oz*. Chicago: Reilly & Lee, 1934. IL: 4–7.
————. *The Wishing Horse of Oz*. Chicago: Reilly & Lee, 1935. IL: 4–7.
————. *The Yellow Knight of Oz*. New York: Ballantine, 1986. IL: 4–7.

Professional Books

The Annotated Wizard of Oz: The Wonderful Wizard of Oz. New York: C. N. Potter, 1973.
Baum, Frank Joslyn. *To Please a Child: A Biography of L. Frank Baum, Royal Historian of Oz*. Chicago: Reilly & Lee, 1961.
Gardiner, Martin, and Russell B. Nye. *The Wizard of Oz and Who He Was*. East Lansing: Michigan State University Press, 1957.
Moore, Raylyn. *Wonderful Wizard, Marvelous Land*. Bowling Green, Ohio: Bowling Green University Press, 1974.

Plays

"Wizard of Oz." In Burack, Abraham Saul, and Alice Crossley. *Popular Plays for Classroom Reading*. Boston: Plays, 1974.
"Wizard of Oz." In Kamerman, Sylvia. *Fifty Plays for Junior Actors*. Boston: Plays, 1966.
"Wizard of Oz." In Mahlmann, Lewis, and David Cadwalader Jones. *Puppet Plays for Young Readers*. Boston: Plays, 1974.
"Wizard of Oz." In Sanders, Sandra. *Creating Plays with Children*. New York: Scholastic, 1970.

Nonprint

Return to Oz. Dayton, Ohio: Twyman Films, 1970. (16mm film)
Wizard of Oz. Mahwah, New Jersey: Troll Associates, 1987. (59-min. videocassette)

The Wizard of Oz. Pasadena, California: Audio Book Contractors. (sound recording)

The Wizard of Oz. Chicago: Encyclopedia Britannica Educational Corporation. (sound filmstrip)

The Wizard of Oz. Culver City, California: MGM/UA Home Video, 1939. (101-min. videocassette)

The Wizard of Oz. Teaching Resources Film, 1975. (sound filmstrip)

The Wizard of Oz and the Land of Oz. Newport Beach, California: Books on Tape, 1989. (90-min. sound recording)

Wizard of Oz: The Original Sound Track Album. S-3996ST. Culver City, California: MGM Records, 1939. (sound recording)

Method: Simulation

A simulation is a method for a student or participant to replicate a situation in order to participate in the system. The student sets goals, makes decisions, and analyzes information. In the model, the participant has some of the rules delineated and the situation is usually simplified or clarified. The situation may be a real-world replication or a situation that takes on the characteristics of a real world. For example, there are simulations that model life processes, governments, and even events that have occurred in history. Simulations are motivating for those who like detail and development of characters. They may be interested in a particular situation and enjoy the fantasy and make-believe possible in playing the simulation. Simulations are often described as games because they involve a form of play.

There are a number of advantages in using simulations. Often, students are naturally motivated in the play. They can experiment in the simulation rather than in real life. Usually games require critical thinking about the particular situation. Students must draw on a wide range of their own experiences. This means that although the situation may be simplified in a simulation, the level of abstraction likely has not been lowered. Students must interact with others to complete the simulation.

Certainly there are disadvantages to using simulations as well. Flexible grouping of individuals is required, and students may become overly involved in the imaginary world. In some cases, simulations have been criticized because they are considered play.

Also, commercial simulation games can be expensive, so choices must be made with care.

Resources Related to the Simulation Method

Associations

> *Players Association*
> TSR Ltd.
> The Mill, Rathmore Road
> Cambridge, England
>
> *Role-Playing Game Association (RPGA) Network*
> P.O. Box 515
> Lake Geneva, WI 53147

Articles

Addison, Linda. "Simulation Gaming and Leadership Training for Gifted Girls." *Gifted Child Quarterly* 23:2 (Summer 1979), pp. 288–296.

Bartling, Debra, and Barry P. Johnson. "Future Games." *Man/Society/Technology* 38:5 (February 1979), pp. 26–27.

Bell, David C. "Simulation Games: Three Research Paradigms." *Simulation & Games* 6 (September 1975), pp. 271–287.

Bennett, Paul W. "Abolition Under Attack: A Role Playing Simulation in American History." *History and Social Science Teacher* 21:2 (Winter 1985–1986), pp. 103–108.

Brand, Charles A. "Learning from Simulation Games: Effects of Grouping." *Simulation & Games* 11 (June 1980), pp. 163–176.

Cline, Starr. "Simulation: A Teaching Strategy for the Gifted and Talented." *Gifted Child Quarterly* 23:2 (Summer 1979), pp. 269–287.

Cruikshank, Donald R. "The Uses of Simulations in Teacher Preparation: Past, Present, and Future." *Simulation & Games* 19:2 (June 1988), pp. 133–156.

Easterly, Jean. "Simulation Game Design: A Philosophic Dilemma." *Simulation & Games* 9 (March 1978), pp. 23–28.

Hegarty, W. Harvey. "Changes in Students' Attitudes as a Result of Participating in a Simulated Game." *Journal of Educational Psychology* 65 (February 1975), pp. 136–140.

Orbach, Eliezer. "Simulation Games and Motivation for Learning: A Theoretical Framework." *Simulation & Games* 10 (March 1979), pp. 3–40.

Pierfy, David A. "The Historical Development of Simulation Gaming." *MSCSS Journal* 4 (Fall 1981), pp. 23–26.

Place, Daniel R. "Social Studies Materials: A Stimulating Experience." *Social Studies Review* 16:1 (1976), pp. 78–80.

Reid, Norman. "Simulation Techniques in Secondary Education: Affective Outcomes." *Simulation & Games* 11 (March 1980), pp. 107–121.

Schreifels, Beverly. "Breathe Life into a Dead Subject." *Learning* 11:8 (March 1983), pp. 84–85.

Sisk, Dorothy. "Simulation: Learning by Doing Revisited." *Gifted Child Quarterly* 19:2 (1975), pp. 175–180.

Smith, Gerald R. "Simulation: A Bridge between Theory and Practice." *Performance and Instruction* 20 (April 1981), pp. 18–20.

Van Sickle, Ronald L. "Decision-Making in Simulation Games." *Theory and Research in Social Education* 5 (December 1977), pp. 84–95.

Watson, Hugh J. "An Empirical Investigation of the Use of Simulation." *Simulation & Games* 9 (December 1978), pp. 477–482.

Books

Balent, Matthew. *Palladium Books Presents a Compendium of Weapons, Armour and Castles.* Detroit: Palladium, 1989.

Birt, David, and Jon Nichol. *Games and Simulations in History Education Today.* New York: Longman, 1975.

Boocock, Sarane S., and E. O. Schild. *Simulation Games in Learning.* Beverly Hills, California: Sage, 1968.

Galloway, Bruce. *Fantasy Wargaming.* Briarcliff Manor, New York: Stein & Day, 1981.

Gibbs, G. Ian. *Dictionary of Gaming, Modeling and Simulations.* Beverly Hills, California: Sage, 1978.

Glazier, Ray. *How To Design Educational Games.* Cambridge, Massachusetts: Games Central, 1976.

Guetzkow, Harold. *Simulation in Social Science.* Englewood Cliffs, New Jersey: Prentice-Hall, 1962.

Gugax, Gary. *Master of the Game.* New York: Perigee, 1989.

————. *Role-Playing Mastery.* New York: Perigee, 1987.

Heitzmann, William Ray. *What Research Says to the Teacher: Educational Games and Simulations.* Washington, D.C.: National Education Association, 1974.

Holmes, John Eric. *Fantasy Role Playing Games.* New York: Hippocrene, 1981.

Horn, Robert, and Ann Cleaves. *The Guide to Simulations/Games for Education and Training.* Beverly Hills, California: Sage, 1980.

Jones, Ken. *Simulations: A Handbook for Teachers.* London: Kegan Paul, 1980.

Kachaturoff, Grace. *Simulations in the Consumer Economics Classroom: Consumer Education Training Module.* Ypsilanti: Eastern Michigan University, 1978. ED 167436.

Livingston, Ian. *Dicing with Dragons: An Introduction to Role-Playing Games.* New York: New American Library, 1982.

Nesbit, William A. *Simulation Games for the Social Studies Classroom.* New York: Foreign Policy Association, 1971.

Niles, Douglas. *Dungeoneer's Survival Guide: The Sourcebook for AD&D Game Adventures in the Unknown Depths of the Underdark.* Lake Geneva, Wisconsin: TSR, 1986.

Schuette, Kim. *The Book of Adventure Games.* Van Nuys, California: Arrays, 1981.

Stadsklev, Ron. *Handbook of Simulation Gaming in Social Education, Part 2: Directory of Noncomputer Materials.* University: University of Alabama, 1979.

Townsend, Carl. *Conquering Adventure Games.* Forest Grove, Oregon: Dilithium, 1981.

Wilson, Cathy R., and Mark C. Schug. *A Guide to Games and Simulations for Teaching Economics.* New York: Joint Council on Economic Education, 1979.

Conventions

DragonCon
Ed Kramer
Box 148
Clarkston, GA 30021

Game Fair
TSR, Ltd.
The Mill, Rathmore Road
Cambridge, England

Games Day, Games Workshop
Chewton Street, Hilltop
Eastwood
Nottingham NG16 3HY, England

GenCon Convention
TSR, Inc.
P.O. Box 756
Lake Geneva, WI 53147

Origins; Games Manufacturers; Game Designers Worldship
P.O. Box 1646
Bloomington, IL 61702-1646

Periodicals

Challenge
Games Design Workshop
P.O. Box 1646
Bloomington, IL 61702-1646

Dragon Magazine
TSR, Inc.
P.O. Box 111
Lake Geneva, WI 53147

Dungeon Magazine
TSR, Inc.
P.O. Box 111
Lake Geneva, WI 53147

Polyhedron Magazine
TSR, Inc.
P.O. Box 111
Lake Geneva, WI 53147

Simulation-Gaming News
Box 3039, University Station
Moscow, ID 83843

Simulation & Gaming:
An International Journal of Theory, Design, & Research
2455 Teller Road
Newbury Park, CA 91320

White Dwarf
Games Workshop
Chewton Street, Hilltop
Eastwood
Nottingham NG16 3HY, England

U.S. address:
9110-F Red Branch Road
Columbia, MD 21045

White Wolf
White Wolf Publishing
1298 Winter Place
Anniston, AL 36201

Publishers

Chaosium Games
950A 56th Street
Oakland, CA 94608

FASA
P.O. Box 6930
Chicago, IL 60680

Game Design Workshop
P.O. Box 1646
Bloomington, IL 61702

Games Workshop
Chewton Street, Hilltop
Eastwood
Nottingham NG16 3HY, England

U.S. address:
3431 Benson Avenue
Baltimore, MD 21227

Ice
P.O. Box 1605
Charlottesville, VA 22902

Mayfair Games
P.O. Box 48539
Niles, IL 60648

Palladium Game
5927 Lonyo
Detroit, MI 48210

R. Talsorian Games
Box 2288
Aptos, CA 95001-2288

Steve Jackson Games
Box 18957
Austin, TX 78760

TSR, Inc.
P.O. Box 756
Lake Geneva, WI 53147

West End Games
RD 3, Box 2345
Honesdale, PA 18431

5

Things

The subject approach focuses heavily on nouns, or things that are named, touched, and seen. In other words, "things" play an important part in forming interests. These things may be real or imaginary. Whatever item strikes one's interest becomes a potential subject approach topic.

An interest in things using the subject approach as motivation may stem from the need to investigate the concrete world surrounding us. Human beings seem interested in using tools to solve problems. Curiosity in exploring the environment is evident from birth. Many individuals move from curiosity to collecting "things." Young people collect all manner of items: baseball cards, dolls, patches, jewelry, charms, stamps, coins, and so forth. Collections occupy time and energy as items pile up and get categorized or classified. Such collecting behavior becomes part of hobby behavior.

Classroom teachers and library media specialists may capitalize on such interest in things to motivate reading in areas where there is an interest. Topical exploration of "things" can be organized and classified. For example, it might be classified into animate and inanimate things in a fictional world or the real world.

ANIMATE THINGS

Resources Related to Animate Things

There are so many reference materials related to animals that it would be difficult to present an inclusive list of sources here.

However, the following resources, including some general nature encyclopedias and indexes as well as handbooks and teaching articles, may provide ideas for further activities. There are many field guides specific to plant and animal identification (birds, insects, trees) that have not been included. These individual titles would be equally invaluable. Many lists and resources may be found in periodicals such as *American Biology Teacher: Journal of the National Association of Biology Teachers; Appraisal: Science Books for Children; Science and Children; Science Books and Films; The Science Teacher;* and *Science.* Resources are located in more specialized journals and magazines.

Alexander, Gretchen M., and Lisa K. Alexander. *Science and Reading: Partners in Learning.* Paper presented at the National Science Teachers Association Convention, Cincinnati, Ohio, 1985.

Alexander, Neil. *The Encyclopedia of Animal Biology.* New York: Facts on File, 1987.

Berry, R. J., and A. Hallam. *The Encyclopedia of Animal Evolution.* New York: Facts on File, 1987.

Bramwell, Martyn. *Warwick Illustrated Encyclopedia of Nature.* New York: Watts, 1989.

Brown, Vinson. *Building Your Own Nature Museum: For Study and Pleasure.* New York: Arco, 1984.

———. *Investigating Nature Through Outdoor Projects: 36 Strategies for Turning the Natural Environment into Your Own Laboratory.* Harrisburg, Pennsylvania: Stackpole, 1983.

Chinery, Michael. *Dictionary of Animals.* New York: Arco, 1984.

———. *Illustrated World of Nature.* New York: Watts, 1988.

Comstock, Anna B. *Handbook of Nature-Study.* Ithaca, New York: Cornell University Press, 1986.

Cornell, Joseph B. *Sharing Nature with Children.* Nevada City, California: Dawn, 1979.

Davis, Elisabeth B. *Guide to Information Sources in the Botanical Sciences.* Littleton, Colorado: Libraries Unlimited, 1987.

Durrell, Gerald. *Amateur Naturalist.* New York: Alfred A. Knopf, 1982.

Farrand, John. *The Audubon Society of Animal Life.* New York: Crown, 1982.

Hanauer, Ethel. *Biology Experiments for Children.* New York: Dover, 1968.

Heyward, Vernon H. *Popular Encyclopedia of Plants.* New York: Cambridge University Press, 1982.

Hillman, Lawrence. *Nature Puzzlers.* Englewood, Colorado: Teacher Ideas, 1989.

Jarman, Catherine. *Atlas of Animal Migration.* New York: Crowell, 1974.

Kennedy, DayAnn M., Stella S. Spangler, and Mary Ann Vanderwerf. *Science and Technology in Fact and Fiction: A Guide to Children's Books.* New York: Bowker, 1990.

————. *Science and Technology: A Guide to Young Adult Books.* New York: Bowker, 1990.

Klein, Stanley. *The Encyclopedia of North American Wildlife.* New York: Facts on File, 1983.

Lerner, Carol. *Plant Families.* New York: Morrow, 1989.

Lowery, Lawrence, and Carol Verbeeck. *Explorations in Life Science.* Belmont, California: David S. Lake, 1987.

Macmillan Illustrated Animal Encyclopedia. New York: Macmillan, 1984.

Martin, E. A. *A Dictionary of Life Science.* New York: Pica, 1984.

McFarland, David. *The Oxford Companion to Animal Behavior.* New York: Oxford University Press, 1981.

Mitchell, John. *The Curious Naturalist.* Englewood Cliffs, New Jersey: Prentice-Hall, 1980.

Moore, Peter D. *The Encyclopedia of Animal Ecology.* New York: Facts on File, 1987.

Nayman, Jacqueline. *Atlas of Wildlife.* New York: Crowell, 1972.

Sisson, Edith A. *Nature with Children of All Ages: Activities and Adventures for Exploring, Learning, and Enjoying the World around Us.* Englewood Cliffs, New Jersey: Prentice-Hall, 1982.

Slater, Peter J. B. *Encyclopedia of Animal Behavior.* New York: Facts on File, 1987.

Smith, Howard. *A Naturalist's Guide to the Year.* New York: Dutton, 1985.

Toothill, Elizabeth. *The Facts on File Dictionary of Biology.* New York: Facts on File, 1981.

————. *The Facts on File Dictionary of Botany.* New York: Facts on File, 1984.

Tremain, Ruthven. *The Animal's Who's Who.* New York: Scribner's, 1982.

Wood, Gerald. *The Guinness Book of Animal Facts and Feats*. New York: Sterling, 1982.

Real Things

Animate objects by definition are alive—in motion and energized. Children exhibit interest in animals from an early age, and usually this interest continues. Some express interest in pets; some are curious about animals in the wild. Some students may enjoy reading about or viewing media forms showing accurate nonfiction views of all classifications of animals. Others may want to read fictional stories about people and animals interacting or animals on their own.

Horses

What motivates students, often girls, to read about animals? Perhaps motivation involves the different patterns often found in the fictional horse book. For example, in some stories, the horse is the main character, acting out a series of behaviors assumed by the author. In other books, the main character is a human being who interacts with the horse. Often in such situations, the human character wins an award or overcomes some seemingly insurmountable problem.

Students who are interested in horses will find ample nonfiction sources available, ranging from material on raising and caring for horses to horse racing.

Resources Related to Studying Horses

Grimshaw, Anne. *The Horse: A Bibliography of British Books 1851–1976*. Phoenix, Arizona: Oryx, 1982.

Jones, William E. *A Descriptive Bibliography of One Thousand One Horse Books*. Fort Collins, Colorado: Printed Horse, 1972.

Wear, Terri A. *Horse Stories: An Annotated Bibliography of Books for All Ages*. Metuchen, New Jersey: Scarecrow, 1987.

Sample Activity Related to Horses

Most classrooms and library media centers have bulletin boards, and many students have such boards in their own rooms at home. This activity offers a chance for students to create their own bulletin boards centered on reading about horses.

During a session in the classroom or library media center, the major ideas and concepts for completing a bulletin board are presented to students. It will help if a bulletin board is on display that includes all of the elements discussed. The art ideas and concepts found in the checklist presented in Figure 6 can be introduced by the art teacher, with each section pointed out and demonstrated. Design suggestions can be provided so that students may draw their own preliminary plans using the planning chart for decision making on the bulletin board.

In designing their boards, the students may follow these steps:

1. Decide on the area to be covered and used.
2. Use a pencil, paper, and ruler to draw the space. Graph paper can be helpful.
3. Decide on the message and how it will be represented.
4. Decide on the sizes of materials, objects, and letters. Manipulate the materials on the paper until the design appeals to the senses.
5. Decide on the colors and visuals.

When the plans are completed, the students may collect the materials upon which they have based their plans and put up the display. Using the planning sheet as an evaluation guide, the students may judge the success of the plan.

To make this more of a competition, the activity can be varied through the use of small bulletin boards. Groups of two to five students may plan their own small bulletin boards and prepare them. The small bulletin boards may be arranged around the room, and each student can use the planning sheet to evaluate the bulletin boards. Based on the evaluations, the students may rank their choices for most effective bulletin board. The number-one choice of each student should be totaled and shared.

In completing your bulletin board, consider each question on this checklist. These are the criteria by which your bulletin board will be evaluated.

Concept and Design
- ❐ Is the idea or message that you want to convey clear and evident to the observer?

Layout
- ❐ Is the background carefully fastened to the board and in an appropriate color?
- ❐ Is the written message coordinated with the visual images? Are the messages positioned on the board so the eyes will focus on them quickly? (Do the words form a Z pattern? Are they in a circle? Are the words in groupings all over the board?)
- ❐ Are shapes used effectively to create mood (angular or rounded)?
- ❐ Is there even spacing to help read and understand the message?
- ❐ Do the materials form texture in the design?
- ❐ Is there balance (symmetrical, asymmetrical)?
- ❐ Is there a clear point of interest?
- ❐ Does it all fit together?

Illustrations
- ❐ Are illustrations used effectively? Describe the kinds of art, for instance, freehand, clip art, computer art, silhouettes, cutouts, three-dimensional art, painted works, origami, plaster of paris objects.

Lettering
- ❐ Is the appropriate lettering used? Describe the lettering (paper, plastic, wood; raised letters).
- ❐ Do the letters provide the message or theme and focus the idea?
- ❐ Are the sizes and styles of letters appropriate? Describe the types of lettering used, such as calligraphy, clip art, rub-on, computer type, cutout letters, marker hand-drawn and crayon hand-drawn, mechanical letters, painted, stencils.

Color
- ❐ Do the selected colors draw attention to the message, unify the bulletin board, and show relationships of words and illustrations?
- ❐ Does the background color contrast with the lettering? Is it suitable to the topic?

Figure 6. Bulletin Board Checklist

Student Resources Related to Horses

Folklore

(IL Signifies Interest Level; RL Signifies Fry Readability Level)

Belpre, Pura. *Rainbow-Colored Horse.* New York: Warner, 1978. IL: 4–6. RL: 6.

Goble, Paul. *Gift of the Sacred Dog.* New York: Bradbury, 1980. IL: 3–5. RL: 6.

———. *The Girl Who Loved Horses.* New York: Bradbury, 1978. IL: 3–6. RL: 4.

Hodges, Margaret. *If You Had a Horse.* New York: Scribner's, 1984. IL: 4–6. RL: 7.

Mayer, Marianna. *Black Horse.* New York: Dial, 1984. IL: 3–5. RL: 6.

Otsuka, Yuzo. *Suho and the White Horse: A Legend of Mongolia.* New York: Viking, 1981. IL: 3–6. RL: 6.

Fiction

Bagnold, Enid. *National Velvet.* New York: Morrow, 1985. IL: 4–7.

Balch, Glenn. *Buck, Wild.* New York: Harper, 1976. IL: 5–8. RL: 6.

Bauer, Marion Dane. *Touch the Moon.* New York: Clarion, 1987. IL: 4–7. RL: 5.

Beatty, Patricia. *I Want My Sunday, Stranger.* New York: Morrow, 1977. IL: 6–8. RL: 7.

Bodker, Cecil. *Silas and Ben-Godik.* New York: Delacorte, 1978. IL: 5–7. RL: 7.

———. *Silas and the Black Mare.* New York: Delacorte, 1978. IL: 5–7. RL: 6.

Braun, P. C. *The Big Book of Favorite Horse Stories.* New York: Putnam, 1982. IL: 7–9.

Byars, Betsy. *The Winged Colt of Casa Mia.* New York: Avon, 1975. IL: 4–7.

Calvert, Patricia. *The Money Creek Mare.* New York: Macmillan, 1981. IL: 7–9.

———. *Snowbird.* New York: Scribner's, 1980. IL: 5–7. RL: 6.

———. *The Stone Pony.* New York: NAL, 1983. IL: 7–9.

Campbell, Barbara. *A Girl Called Bob and a Horse Called Yoki.* New York: Dial, 1982. IL: 4–7. RL: 4.

Cavanna, Betty. *Banner Year.* New York: Morrow, 1987. IL: 7–9.

Chambers, John W. *Colonel and Me.* New York: Atheneum, 1985. IL: 5–8. RL: 5.

Christopher, Matt. *Earthquake.* Boston: Little, Brown, 1975. IL: 4–6. RL: 5.

Clymer, Eleanor. *The Horse in the Attic.* New York: Bradbury, 1983. IL: 4–6. RL: 4.

Corcoran, Barbara. *A Horse Named Sky.* New York: Macmillan, 1986. IL: 4–7.

DeJong, Meindert. *A Horse Came Running.* New York: Macmillan, 1970. IL: 5–7. RL: 6.

Doty, Jean S. *Can I Get There by Candlelight?* New York: Macmillan, 1980. IL: 4–6. RL: 6.

————. *The Crumb.* New York: Greenwillow, 1976. IL: 5–8.

————. *Dark Horse.* New York: Morrow, 1983. IL: 5–7. RL: 4.

————. *If Wishes Were Horses.* New York: Macmillan, 1984. IL: 5–8.

————. *Valley of the Ponies.* New York: Macmillan, 1982. IL: 5–7. RL: 8.

————. *Winter Pony.* New York: Macmillan, 1975. IL: 4–6. RL: 6.

Dryden, Pamela. *A Horse for Betsy.* New York: Bantam, 1988. IL: 4–7.

Dunn, Marylou, and Ardath Mayhar. *The Absolutely Perfect Horse.* New York: Harper, 1983. IL: 5–8. RL: 4.

Ellis, Mel. *Wild Horse Killers.* New York: Scholastic, 1981. IL: 7–9.

Farley, Walter. *The Black Stallion.* New York: Random House, 1982. IL: 4–8. RL: 5.

————. *Black Stallion and Flame.* New York: Random House, 1960. IL: 4–8.

————. *Black Stallion and Satan.* New York: Random House, 1949. IL: 4–8.

————. *The Black Stallion and the Girl.* New York: Random House, 1971. IL: 4–8.

————. *Black Stallion Challenge.* New York: Random House, 1964. IL: 4–8.

————. *The Black Stallion Legend.* New York: Random House, 1983. IL: 4–8.

————. *The Black Stallion Returns.* New York: Random House, 1982. IL: 4–8.

————. *The Black Stallion Revolts.* New York: Random House, 1977. IL: 4–8.

————. *Black Stallion's Courage.* New York: Random House, 1956. IL: 4–8.

————. *Black Stallion's Filly.* New York: Random House, 1952. IL: 4–8.

————. *Black Stallion's Ghost.* New York: Random House, 1969. IL: 4–8.

―――. *Black Stallion's Sulky Colt*. New York: Random House, 1954. IL: 4–8.

―――. *Blood Bay Colt*. New York: Random House, 1950. IL: 4–8.

―――. *The Horse Tamer*. New York: Random House, 1980. IL: 4–8.

―――. *Island Stallion*. New York: Random House, 1948. IL: 4–8.

―――. *Island Stallion Races*. New York: Random House, 1965. IL: 4–8.

―――. *Island Stallion's Fury*. New York: Random House, 1951. IL: 4–8.

―――. *Man O' War*. New York: Random House, 1983. IL: 5–8. RL: 6.

―――. *Son of the Black Stallion*. New York: Random House, 1947. IL: 4–7.

Fleischman, Paul. *Path of the Pale Horse*. New York: Harper, 1983. IL: 6–9.

Gates, Doris. *A Filly for Melinda*. New York: Viking, 1984. IL: 4–7. RL: 4.

―――. *A Morgan for Melinda*. New York: Viking, 1980. IL: 4–7. RL: 4.

Godden, Rumer. *Dark Horse*. New York: Viking, 1981. IL: 5–8. RL: 6.

Greene, Constance C. *Beat the Turtle Drum*. New York: Viking, 1976. IL: 5–7. RL: 4.

Gregory, Diana. *I'm Boo, That's Who*. Philadelphia: J. B. Lippincott, 1979. IL: 5–7. RL: 6.

Griffiths, Helen. *Blackface Stallion*. New York: Holiday, 1980. IL: 5–8.

―――. *The Dancing Horses*. New York: Holiday, 1982. IL: 5–8. RL: 8.

―――. *The Last Summer: Spain 1936*. New York: Holiday, 1979. IL: 5–8. RL: 6.

Haas, Jessie. *Keeping Barney*. New York: Greenwillow, 1982. IL: 5–7. RL: 5.

Hall, Lynn. *Danza!* New York: Scribner's, 1981. IL: 5–9. RL: 5.

―――. *Flowers of Anger*. Chicago: Follett, 1976. IL: 5–7.

―――. *The Horse Trader*. New York: Macmillan, 1981. IL: 5–8.

―――. *Megan's Mare*. New York: Scribner's, 1983. IL: 4–7. RL: 7.

―――. *Ride a Dark Horse*. New York: Morrow, 1987. IL: 7–9.

―――. *Ride a Wild Dream*. New York: Avon, 1978. IL: 5–9.

―――. *The Something Special Horse*. New York: Macmillan, 1985. IL: 5–7.

Haney, Lynn. *Show Rider*. New York: Putnam, 1982. IL: 7–9.

Hanson, Andrea. *The Adventures of Black Beauty: Beauty Finds a Home*. New York: Random House, 1983. IL: 4–7.

————. *Beauty and Vicky.* New York: Random House, 1984. IL: 4–7.

Hanson, June A. *Summer of the Stallion.* New York: Macmillan, 1979. IL: 5–9. RL: 6.

————. *Winter of the Owl.* New York: Scholastic, 1983. IL: 4–6.

Harris, Mark Jonathan. *Last Run.* New York: Lothrop, Lee & Shepard, 1981. IL: 5–7. RL: 7.

Hearne, Betsy Gould. *South Star.* New York: Atheneum, 1977. IL: 4–6. RL: 4.

Heck, Bessie Holland. *Golden Arrow.* New York: Scribner's, 1981. IL: 5–7. RL: 6.

Henry, Marguerite. *Black Gold.* Chicago: Rand McNally, 1957. IL: 4–6.

————. *Born To Trot.* Chicago: Rand McNally, 1950. IL: 4–7.

————. *Justin Morgan Had a Horse.* Chicago: Rand McNally, 1954. IL: 4–6. RL: 6.

————. *King of the Wind.* Chicago: Rand McNally, 1948. IL: 4–6. RL: 5.

————. *Misty of Chincoteague.* Chicago: Rand McNally, 1947. IL: 3–6. RL: 4.

————. *Mustang, Wild Spirit of the West.* Chicago: Rand McNally, 1966. IL: 5–8.

————. *San Domingo: The Medicine Hat Stallion.* Chicago: Rand McNally, 1972. IL: 5–7. RL: 5.

————. *Sea Star: Orphan of Chincoteague.* Chicago: Rand McNally, 1949. IL: 3–6.

————. *Stormy: Misty's Foal.* Chicago: Rand McNally, 1963. IL: 3–6.

Holland, Isabelle. *Horse Named Peaceable.* New York: Lothrop, Lee & Shepard, 1982. IL: 5–8. RL: 6.

————. *Perdita.* Boston: Little, Brown, 1983. IL: 7–9.

Irwin, Hadley. *Moon and Me.* New York: Atheneum, 1981. IL: 5–7. RL: 3.

James, Will. *Smoky the Cow Horse.* New York: Scribner's, 1981. IL: 5–7. RL: 8.

Kennedy, Richard. *Song of the Horse.* New York: Dutton, 1981. IL: 3–6. RL: 5.

Levin, Betty. *Binding Spell.* New York: Lodestar, 1984. IL: 5–7.

Lyons, Dorothy. *Dark Sunshine.* New York: Harcourt, 1951. IL: 6–8.

McHargue, Georgess. *The Horseman's Word.* New York: Delacorte, 1981. IL: 7–9.

Miller, Albert G. *Mystery of the Missing Stallions.* New York: Scholastic, 1981. IL: 4–6.

Morpurgo, Michael. *War Horse*. New York: Greenwillow, 1983. IL: 5–8.

Morrison, Dorothy. *Somebody's Horse*. New York: Macmillan, 1986. IL: 4–7.

Morey, Walt. *Runaway Stallion*. New York: Dutton, 1973. IL: 5–7. RL: 6.

———. *Year of the Black Pony*. New York: Dutton, 1976. IL: 4–6. RL: 3.

O'Hara, Mary. *The Catch Colt*. New York: Harper, 1985. IL: 5–8.

———. *My Friend Flicka*. New York: Harper, 1973. IL: 6–8.

Peck, Robert N. *Spanish Hoof*. New York: Alfred A. Knopf, 1985. IL: 5–8.

Reynolds, Marjorie. *A Horse Called Mystery*. New York: Harper, 1964. IL: 3–6.

Rockwood, Joyce. *Groundhog's Horse*. New York: Holt, Rinehart & Winston, 1978. IL: 4–6. RL: 3.

Rounds, Glen. *Blind Outlaw*. New York: Holiday House, 1980. IL: 4–6. RL: 8.

———. *Stolen Pony*. New York: Holiday House, 1969. IL: 4–6.

———. *Wild Appaloosa*. New York: Holiday House, 1983. IL: 3–6. RL: 8.

Sandoz, Mari. *Horsecatcher*. Philadelphia: Westminster, 1957. IL: 7–9.

Savitt, Sam. *A Horse To Remember*. New York: Penguin, 1984. IL: 5–7. RL: 6.

Sewell, Anna. *Black Beauty: The Autobiography of a Horse*. New York: Messner, 1982. IL: 5–7. RL: 7.

Singer, Marilyn. *Horsemaster*. New York: Macmillan, 1985. IL: 7–9.

Sneve, Virginia Driving Hawk. *High Elk's Treasure*. New York: Holiday House, 1972. IL: 4–6. RL: 6.

Snyder, Zilpha. *A Season of Horses*. New York: Macmillan, 1973. IL: 4–7.

Springer, Nancy. *A Horse To Love*. New York: Harper, 1987. IL: 7–9.

Stanton, Mary. *The Heavenly Horse from the Outermost West*. Riverdale, New York: Baen, 1988. IL: 7–9+.

Steinbeck, John. *The Red Pony*. New York: Bantam, 1936. IL: 5–9+. RL: 4.

Thomas, Joyce. *The Golden Pasture*. New York: Scholastic, 1986. IL: 7–9.

Walker, Diana. *The Year of the Horse*. New York: Abelard, 1975. IL: 5–7.

Wallin, Marie-Louise. *Tangles*. New York: Delacorte, 1977. IL: 6–8.

Whitley, Mary A. *A Circle of Light*. New York: Walker, 1983. IL: 6–9.
Wojciechowska, Maia. *Kingdom in a Horse*. New York: Harper, 1965. IL: 7–9.

Nonfiction

Anderson, C. W. *Twenty Gallant Horses*. New York: Macmillan, 1965. IL: 4–6. RL: 6.
Balch, Glen. *Book of Horses*. New York: Four Winds, 1967. IL: 4–7.
Ball, Charles E. *Saddle Up! The Farm Journal Book of Western Horsemanship*. Philadelphia: J. B. Lippincott, 1970. IL: 5–7. RL: 6.
Brady, Irene. *America's Horses and Ponies*. Boston: Houghton Mifflin, 1969. IL 5–7.
Davidson, Margaret. *Five True Horse Stories*. New York: Scholastic, 1979. IL: 3–6.
Demuth, Jack, and Patricia Demuth. *City Horse*. New York: Dodd, 1979. IL: 4–6. RL: 7.
Henry, Marguerite. *All about Horses*. New York: Random House, 1967. IL: 4–6. RL: 6.
———. *The Pictorial Life Story of Misty*. Chicago: Rand McNally, 1976. IL: 4–6. RL: 5.
Krementz, Jill. *Very Young Rider*. New York: Knopf, 1977. IL: 4–6. RL: 5.
Lavine, Sigmund. *Wonders of the Draft Horse*. New York: Dodd, 1983. IL: 5–7. RL: 8.
———. *Wonders of Ponies*. New York: Dodd, 1980. IL: 5–7. RL: 9.
MacClintock, Dorcas. *Horses as I See Them*. New York: Scribner's, 1980. IL: 4–6. RL: 8.
Patent, Dorothy Hinshaw. *Arabian Horses*. New York: Holiday House, 1982. IL: 4–6. RL: 7.
———. *Draft Horses*. New York: Holiday House, 1986. IL: 3–6.
———. *Horses of America*. New York: Holiday House, 1981. IL: 4–6. RL: 7.
Pervier, Evelyn. *Horsemanship: Basics for Beginners*. New York: Messner, 1984. IL: 4–6. RL: 7.
Sayer, Angela. *Young Rider's Handbook*. New York: Arco, 1984. IL: 5–7. RL: 9.
Van Steenwyk, Elizabeth. *Illustrated Horseback Riding Dictionary for Young People*. Englewood Cliffs, New Jersey: Prentice-Hall, 1980.

Periodical

Horse and Rider Magazine
Rich Publishing Co.
1060 Calle Cordillera, Suite 103
San Clemente, CA 92672

Poetry

Hopkins, Lee B. *My Mane Catches the Wind: Poems about Horses.* New York: Harcourt, 1979. IL: 4–7.

Nonprint

Some of the sources listed here may exist in more than one format, but only one is noted. In some cases, the video distributor has been listed in place of the original producer.

The Adventures of Black Beauty. New York: Sony Video Software, 1972. (50-min. videocassette)
Black Beauty. Los Angeles: Paramount Home Videos, 1971. (109-min. videocassette)
Black Beauty. TC 1322. New York: Caedmon. (52-min. sound recording)
The Black Stallion. Atlanta, Georgia: MGM/UA Home Video, 1979. (118-min. videocassette)
The Black Stallion Returns. Atlanta, Georgia: MGM/UA Home Video, 1983. (103-min. videocassette)
Horse. New York: ABC, 1972. (12-min. 16mm film)
Horse. New York: ABC, 1976. (22-min. 16mm film)
The Horse America Made. Amarillo, Texas: American Quarter Horse Association, 1973. (40-min. 16mm film)
The Horse and Its Relatives. Deerfield, Illinois: Coronet, 1942. (11-min. 16mm film)
Horse Family. Chicago: International Film Bureau, 1965. (10-min. 16mm film)
The Horse in the Gray Flannel Suit. Burbank, California: Walt Disney Home Video, 1968. (113-min. videocassette)
Horse Sense. Washington, D.C.: U.S. Forest Service, 1965. (23-min. 16mm film)
The Horse with the Flying Tail. Burbank, California: Walt Disney Educational Media, 1960. (47-min. 16mm film)

Horsemen of the Pampas: Argentina. Universal City, California: Universal Education and Visual Arts, 1948. (21-min. 16mm film)

Horses. Studio City, California: Film Fair Communications, 1971. (7-min. videocassette)

Horses! Chicago: Encyclopedia Britannica Educational Corporation, 1976. (24-min. 16mm film)

Horses and How They Live. Van Nuys, California: AIMS, 1968. (11-min. 16mm film)

Horses and Their Ancestors. Del Mar, California: McGraw-Hill Films, 1962. (12-min. 16mm film)

The Horses of Appleby Fair. Deerfield, Illinois: Coronet, 1982. (12-min. 16mm film)

International Velvet. Atlanta, Georgia: MGM/UA Home Video, 1978. (126-min. videocassette)

Lightning: The White Stallion. Burbank, California: Walt Disney Home Video, 1986. (93-min. videocassette)

The Magic Pony: A Russian Fairy Tale. Deerfield, Illinois: Coronet, 1980. (11-min. videocassette)

The Man from Snowy River. New York: CBS/Fox, 1982. (104-min. videocassette)

Miracle of the White Stallions. Burbank, California: Walt Disney Home Video, 1963. (92-min. videocassette)

National Velvet. Atlanta, Georgia: MGM/UA Home Video, 1945. (124-min. videocassette)

Phar Lap. New York: CBS/Fox, 1984. (107-min. videocassette)

Ponies. Van Nuys, California: Oxford Film/AIMS, 1972. (15-min. 16mm film)

Ponies of Miklaengi. New York: Phoenix/BFA, 1979. (25-min. videocassette)

Pony. Del Mar, California: McGraw-Hill Films, 1958. (29-min. 16mm film)

The Red Pony. Los Angeles: Republic, 1949. (89-min. videocassette)

The Red Pony. New York: Phoenix/BFA, 1974. (101-min. 16mm film)

Ride a Wild Pony. Burbank, California: Walt Disney Home Video, 1976. (86-min. videocassette)

Method: Bulletin Boards

Bulletin boards are visual display boards on which messages promote events or inform a large group. Bulletin boards can be as simple or as ornate as the creator desires. As such, the boards are used for pleasure and/or instruction. Preparation of a bulletin board involves a number of art techniques, including concept and design, layout, illustration, color, and lettering. Use of these combined techniques can be an effective learning device.

The classroom teacher or art teacher may concentrate on the concept or design first, addressing the message or main idea of what must be communicated. Students should consider their purpose and audience. What would be the best way to catch that audience's eye?

Usually bulletin boards include both pictures and lettering. Students should be encouraged to consider the kinds of illustrations that should be included. They have a wide range of choices, including freehand drawing, clip art, computer art, silhouettes, cutouts, three-dimensional art, painted works, origami, and plaster of paris objects. Each choice involves another technique. Whatever the choice, students should continue thinking about appeal to the audience.

Lettering should complement the drawing so the overall message is unified. After all, the lettering usually provides the theme and helps focus attention on the main idea. There are many forms of lettering, as well as many type styles. Students can be introduced to cutout paper letters, wooden letters, plastic pin-on letters, or letters made from other materials. The styles and types might include calligraphy, clip art, rub-on, computer type, cutout letters, letters hand-drawn with markers and crayons, mechanical letters, or painted or stenciled letters. Whatever the choice, the lettering should be large enough so that the message can be read from a distance. The letters in the message should be spaced so that the words are clear and stand out without being engulfed by the larger space of the bulletin board.

The teacher may present a review of contrasting and complementary colors. The use of color can induce the viewer to look at and comprehend the message on a bulletin board. The background color should be suitable to the topic and enhance the message. It also unifies the board, draws attention to the message, and helps show relationships of pictures or illustrations and the lettered message.

When the students have clarified their message, the layout may be addressed. After considering the space available and the kind of background, the students must decide how the message will be laid out. In the process, they will also consider words and pictures needed to convey the idea. Whatever the background, the materials will be fastened to the board. Some bulletin boards are flat, with designs made up of cut paper, while others include three-dimensional figures. Students must consider how they will attach the materials to the board. The choices will range from tacks, staples, and pins to tape or glue, and even small blocks of wood to provide the third dimension.

As the students try to visualize the positions of pictures and lettering on the board, they may consider the ways in which the eye might focus or come to rest on items on the board. Many individuals use a Z format, in which the eye enters the board about a third of the way from the top by reading the message that begins there. The message zigzags, as a Z does, and exits two-thirds of the way down on the opposite side. Others might place the message in a circular or semicircular design. The message follows that design, with pictures placed accordingly. Books on design may show other options available for producing the most effective layout. Some students may become interested in the design process through exposure to this activity, and may want to pursue this as an interest.

The teacher may share the idea of shapes as methods for creating mood. Angular shapes may be more jarring than more rounded shapes. Spacing of illustrations and lettering can create harmony or disharmony in the design. Sometimes texture can add to the message; for instance, rough or smooth materials can be used.

Depending on the point of interest and the message, the design should deal with balance, which might be symmetrical or asymmetrical. Throughout the process, students should address the question of whether or not all the elements fit together.

In the process of thinking through these elements, the designer of the bulletin board must be sure of the area, total space, message, and so forth. These ideas should be drawn on a planning sheet, preferably a sheet of graph paper drawn to scale of the space available. A pencil and an eraser are the chief tools in this stage, when the individual plays around with ideas and positions the items in the space. When all is drawn, the individual collects the materials and begins to assemble the bulletin board, cutting, pasting, or using whatever other technique has been chosen.

Resources Related to Bulletin Boards

There are many idea books related to preparation of bulletin boards. These may be located in educational supply stores and similar outlets. The following are examples of especially useful volumes.

Canoles, Marian L. *The Creative Copycat.* Littleton, Colorado: Libraries Unlimited, 1982.

———. *The Creative Copycat II.* Littleton, Colorado: Libraries Unlimited, 1985.

Coplan, Kate. *Effective Library Exhibits: How To Prepare and Promote Good Displays.* Dobbs Ferry, New York: Oceana, 1974.

Coplan, Kate, and Constance Rosenthal. *Guide to Better Bulletin Boards.* Dobbs Ferry, New York: Oceana, 1970.

Flores, Anthony. *Instant Borders.* Belmont, California: David S. Lake, 1979.

Franklin, Linda Campbell. *Display and Publicity Ideas for Libraries.* Jefferson, North Carolina: McFarland, 1985.

———. *Library Display Ideas.* Jefferson, North Carolina: McFarland, 1980.

Garvey, Mona. *Library Displays: Their Purpose, Construction, and Use.* New York: H. W. Wilson, 1969.

———. *Teaching Displays, Their Purpose, Construction, and Use.* Hamden, Connecticut: Shoe String, 1972.

Gomberg, Karen Cornell. *Books Appeal: Get Teenagers into the School Library.* Jefferson, North Carolina: McFarland, 1987.

Horn, George F. *How To Prepare Visual Materials for School Use.* Worcester, Massachusetts: Davis, 1963.

Involvement Bulletin Boards. Washington, D.C.: Association for Childhood International, 1970.

Jay, M. Ellen. *Involvement Bulletin Boards and Other Motivational Activities.* Hamden, Connecticut: Linnet, 1976.

Kemp, Herrold. *Planning and Producing Audiovisual Materials.* New York: Crowell, 1980.

Kohn, Rita. *Experiencing Displays*. Metuchen, New Jersey: Scarecrow, 1982.

Lee, Eva M. *Motivate with Bulletin Boards*. Cincinnati, Ohio: Standard, 1982.

————. *Motivate with Bulletin Boards, No. 2*. Cincinnati, Ohio: Standard, 1985.

Marshall, Karen K. *Back to Books: 200 Library Activities To Encourage Reading*. Jefferson, North Carolina: McFarland, 1983.

Schaeffer, Mark. *Library Displays Handbook*. New York: H. W. Wilson, 1991.

Wallick, Clair H. *Looking for Ideas? A Display Manual for Libraries and Bookstores*. Metuchen, New Jersey: Scarecrow, 1970.

Sharks

Many students find sharks as appealing for study as dinosaurs or other animals. What is it about sharks that appeals to students? Is it the powerful aspect of an animal that has survived so long? Is it the fact that many humans fear sharks? Is it their teeth, their reputedly ruthless nature, their control of their environment? The appeal of shark books and materials will be discovered.

Resources Related to the Investigation of Sharks

Boshung, Herbert T. *The Audubon Society Field Guide to North American Fishes, Whales and Dolphins*. New York: Alfred A. Knopf, 1983.

Sharks: Silent Hunters of the Deep. New York: Readers Digest, 1986.

Sample Activity Related to Sharks

Using a video or film about sharks, the students have a chance to look at the animals as they move. This audiovisual experience is used in place of an actual experience.

Older students may watch a selected film and report how they felt while watching. Some imagination may be expected from the older students. For example, if a video showing a skin diver is used, students may complete the language experience activity or approach as if they were the diver.

The classroom teacher tells students that they will be writing their own versions of the story after they have seen the film. They will take on the role of the skin diver. If there is no diver, another role may be taken. For example, students might imagine themselves to be the shark or the shark's prey. They may discuss how the roles they are going to play may affect what they see and remember.

Following the viewing, students work in pairs, each reporting what he or she saw to the other student, who records that information. This report is then be read back to the one who dictated it, and that student may modify or change any points that were left out or incorrectly recorded. Each student should have the opportunity of reporting as well as recording the other student's report.

Finally, the reports are checked for spelling, and then the stories are rewritten and displayed so that students can compare versions of the same viewing experience.

Student Resources Related to Sharks

Fiction

Great Shark Stories. New York: Harper, 1978. IL: 7–9+.

Hemingway, Ernest. *The Old Man and the Sea.* New York: Macmillan, 1977. IL: 8–9+.

Sperry, Armstrong. *Call It Courage.* New York: Macmillan, 1940. IL: 4–7.

Thiele, Colin. *Blue Fin.* New York: Harper, 1974. IL: 6–8.

———. *Shadow Shark.* New York: Harper, 1985. IL: 6–8.

Nonfiction

Albert, Burton. *Sharks and Whales.* New York: Putnam, 1979. IL: 2–6.

Anton, Tina. *Sharks, Sharks, Sharks.* Milwaukee, Wisconsin: Raintree, 1989. IL: 2–5.

Berger, Gilda. *Sharks.* Garden City, New York: Doubleday, 1987. IL: 3–5.

Blassingame, Wyatt. *Wonders of Sharks.* New York: Dodd, 1984. IL: 5–8.

Blumberg, Rhonda. *Sharks.* New York: Watts, 1976. IL: 4–7.

Bunting, Eve. *The Great White Shark.* New York: Messner, 1982. IL: 4–7.

————. *The Sea World Book of Sharks.* New York: Harcourt, 1980. IL: 4–7.

Chinery, Michael. *Shark.* Mahwah, New Jersey: Troll Associates, 1990. IL: 4–7.

Coupe, Sheena, and Robert Coupe. *Sharks.* New York: Facts on File, 1990.

Dingerkus, Guido. *The Shark Watcher's Guide.* New York: Messner, 1985. IL: 7–9.

Freedman, Russell. *Sharks.* New York: Holiday House, 1985. IL: 3–5.

Green, Carl, and William R. Sanford. *The Great White Shark.* Mankato, Minnesota: Crestwood House, 1985. IL: 4–7.

Harris, Margaret. *Sharks and Troubled Waters.* Milwaukee, Wisconsin: Raintree, 1977. IL: 4–7.

Langley, Andrew. *The World of Sharks.* New York: Watts, 1988. IL: 3–6.

McGowen, Tom. *Album of Sharks.* New York: Macmillan, 1977. IL: 5–7.

Penzler, Otto. *Hunting the Killer Shark.* Mahwah, New Jersey: Troll Associates, 1976. IL: 5–8.

Pety, Kate. *Sharks.* New York: Watts, 1985. IL: 2–5.

Reed, Don C. *Sevengill: The Shark and Me.* New York: Alfred A. Knopf, 1986. IL: 5–8.

Sattler, Helen R. *Sharks, the Super Fish.* New York: Lothrop, Lee & Shepard, 1985. IL: 8–9+.

Springer, Victor G., and Joy P. Gold. *Shark in Question: Smithsonian Answer Book.* Washington, D.C.: Smithsonian Institution Press, 1989.

Steele, Rodney. *Sharks of the World.* New York: Facts on File, 1985. IL: 8–9+.

Stevens, John. *Sharks.* New York: Facts on File, 1987. IL: 5–9.

Wheeler, Alwyne. *Sharks.* New York: Watts, 1987. IL: 2–6.

Wildlife Education. *Sharks.* San Diego, California: Wildlife Education, 1983. IL: 5–8.

Poetry

Ciardi, John. "About the Teeth of Sharks." In Ciardi, John. *You Read to Me, I'll Read to You.* Philadelphia: J. B. Lippincott, 1962, p. 9.

Douglas, Lord Alfred. "The Shark." In Prelutsky, Jack. *The Random House Book of Poetry for Children*. New York: Random House, 1983, p. 78.

Irwin, W. "The Rhyme of the Chivalrous Shark." In Cole, William. *Humorous Poetry for Children*. New York: World, 1955, pp. 81–82.

Melville, Herman. "The Maldive Shark." In Smith, J. A. *Looking Glass Book of Verse*. New York: Random House, 1959, p. 275.

Richards, Laura. "The Shark." in Richards, Laura E. *Tirra Lirra*. Boston: Little, Brown, 1932, pp. 63–64.

Periodical Articles (Sampling)

Clark, Eugenie. "Sharks: Magnificent and Misunderstood." *National Geographic Magazine* (August 1981), pp. 138–187.

Howlett, Dave. "My First 'Shark' Encounter." *Skin Diver* 38 (March 1989), p. 47.

McCosker, John E. "Great White Shark." *Science* 81 (July-August 1981), pp. 42–52.

Rudloe, Jack, and Anne Rudloe. "The Shadows of the Sea: People Fear the Shark, but They Are Vital to the Sea." *Sports Illustrated* 71 (December 4, 1989), pp. 97–104.

Rutledge, Archibald. "Death in the Moonlight." *Field and Stream* 85 (March 1981), pp. 112–113.

"Sharks: Getting To Know Them." *National Geographic World* (July 1986), pp. 24–30.

Stutz, Bruce. "Why the Shark Bites." *Natural History* 96 (November 1987), pp. 94–99.

Nonprint

About Sharks. Washington, D.C.: National Geographic Society, 1981. (12-min. 16mm film)

Biology: Sharks, Ancient Mystery of the Sea. New York: Allegro Film Production for National Science Teachers Association and Engineers Council for Professional Development, Counselor Films, 1975. (15-min. 16mm film)

Inside the Shark. Boston: WGBH-TV, 1976. (50-min. 16mm film)

Jaws. Universal City, California: MCA, 1975. (124-min. videocassette; rated PG)

Shark. Deerfield, Illinois: Learning Corporation of America, 1976. (28-min. 16mm film)

The Shark. New York: Heritage Enterprises, 1975. (22-min. 16mm film)

The Shark: Man-Eater or Myth? Chicago: Encyclopedia Britannica Educational Corporation, 1976. (23-min. 16mm film)

Sharks. Irvine, California: Doubleday Multimedia, 1969. (22-min. 16mm film)

Sharks. Los Angeles: Churchill Films, 1970. (24-min. videocassette)

The Sharks. Washington, D.C.: National Geographic Society, 1982. (60-min. videocassette)

Sharks/Dangerous Animals. Paramus, New Jersey: Time/Life Film and Video, 1979. (46-min. 16mm film)

Sharks, Some Facts. New York: Phoenix/BFA, 1978. (17-min. videocassette)

Sharks' Treasure. Culver City, California: MGM/UA Home Video, 1975. (95-min. videocassette; rated PG)

Method: Language Experience Approach

In the language experience method, students are taught how to read by using their own words recorded on chart paper. The process of recording students' experiences on paper to allow them to read them back capitalizes on students' innate language abilities. Although usually this method is used with younger students to begin the process of learning to read, it can be useful in other circumstances as well.

The process is advantageous for showing language relationships. It helps to develop students' sense about their observations as well as their current knowledge and understanding. In other words, by recording what they know about a topic, students can review what they do not know. Using this method allows students to read their products and to identify other areas of information they would like to pursue. It sets up situations for considering other directions in exploring a topic related to the initial experience.

Basically, students are able to observe the content that they have generated. This is written in their own language. As students work on their experience charts, they use all of their language skills. Reading becomes an active process in which students are involved.

The language experience process is a relatively simple one, as seen in the following steps:

1. Provide students with a common experience.
2. Encourage students to discuss the experience.
3. Listen to their ideas and record the key ideas on a chart.
4. Read the ideas recorded on the chart.
5. Isolate elements that need emphasis or elaboration. (Where would you go to find out more about the particular idea?)
6. Reread the story.
7. Type up the story for sharing later. (What other direction would you like to explore based on the story?)

By following this procedure, the library media specialist or classroom teacher and students may explore a number of topics and ready themselves for further reading and research.

Resources Related to the Language Experience Approach

Research on and use of this method have generated many papers and articles. The following may be useful for those working with middle-grade students.

Articles

Hall, Mary Ann. "Focus on Language Experience Learning and Teaching." *Reading* 19:1 (April 1985), pp. 5–12.

Moustafa, Margaret. "Comprehensive Input PLUS the Language Experience Approach: A Longterm Perspective." *Reading Teacher* 41:3 (December 1987), pp. 276–286.

Peterson, Susan, et al. "Using the Language Experience Approach with Precision." *Teaching Exceptional Children* 22:3 (Spring 1990), pp. 28–31.

Sharp, Sidney J. "Using Content Subject Matter with LEA in Middle School." *Journal of Reading* 33:2 (November 1989), pp. 108–112.

Smith, N. J. "The Word-Processing Approach to Language Experience." *Reading Teacher* 38 (1985), pp. 556–559.

Stauffer, Russell, and W. Dorsey Hammond. "The Effectiveness of Language Arts and Basic Reader Approaches to First Grade Reading Instruction Extended into Second Grade." *Reading Teacher* 20 (May 1967), pp. 740–746.

Strickland, Dorothy S., and Lesley Mandel Morrow. "The Daily Journal: Using Language Experience Strategies in an Emergent Literary Curriculum (Emerging Readers and Writers)." *Reading Teacher* 43:6 (February 1990), pp. 422–423.

Sullivan, Joanna. "The Global Method: Language Experience in the Content Areas." *Reading Teacher* 39:7 (March 1986), pp. 664–668.

Books

Bishop, David. *Subject Area Reading in the Middle School: Learning Through Text and Learning Through Experience.* Columbus, Ohio: National Middle School Association, 1982.

Hall, Mary Ann. *Teaching Reading as a Language Experience.* Columbus, Ohio: Charles E. Merrill, 1976.

Nessel, Denise D., and Margaret B. Jones. *The Language Experience Approach to Reading: A Handbook for Teachers.* New York: Teachers College Press, 1981.

Stauffer, Russell. *The Language-Experience Approach to the Teaching of Reading.* New York: Harper, 1980.

Van Allen, Roach. *Language Experiences in Communication.* Boston: Houghton Mifflin, 1976.

Van Allen, Roach, and Claryce Allen. *Language Experience Activities.* Boston: Houghton Mifflin, 1976.

Van Allen, Roach, Richard L. Venezky, and Harry T. Hahn. *Language Experiences in Reading.* Chicago: Encyclopaedia Britannica, 1974.

Venus's-Flytrap

Unusual plant and animal life often can cause students to stop for further investigation. This investigation occurs during quiet walks and visits to nature centers or while watching events in everyday life, such as the Venus's-flytrap.

Resources Related to Venus's-Flytrap

Darwin, Charles. *Insectivorous Plants.* New York: AMS, 1972.
Lloyd, Francis E. *The Carnivorous Plants.* New York: Dover, 1976.
Pietropaolo, James, and Patricia Pietropaolo. *Carnivorous Plants of the World.* Forest Grove, Oregon: Timber, 1986.
Schnell, Donald E. *Carnivorous Plants of the United States and Canada.* Winston-Salem, North Carolina: John F. Blair, 1976.
Slack, Adrian. *Carnivorous Plants.* Cambridge: MIT Press, 1980.
———. *Insect-Eating Plants and How To Grow Them.* Seattle: University of Washington Press, 1988.

Sample Activity Related to Venus's-Flytrap

Following a trip to a nursery or plant store, the classroom teacher or library media specialist displays a Venus's-flytrap for students to observe. Materials about carnivorous plants may be placed nearby.

Students should have time to watch a film about the care and feeding of carnivorous plants before the library media specialist explains that the students will have a chance to observe the plant.

The library media specialist discusses the steps in a scientific method with students before inviting them to watch the plant in action:

Identify problem.
Collect preliminary data.
Hypothesize.
Experiment.
Conclude.
Check conclusions.

The acronym "I CHECC" (I check) can be formed from these shortened statements; students may use this mnemonic device to remember the process.

Basically, students will consider how this kind of plant finds nourishment and the kinds of behaviors involved in the plant's feeding. The students will gather preliminary data before forming their hypotheses. The experiment will involve the plant and some insects. As the students watch the insects, they may keep notes and later draw their own conclusions about this plant and other carnivorous plants.

Although general reference sources explain that the plant, native to North and South Carolina, generally snaps shut on its prey in about half a second, the length of time required for the plant to digest the insect and reopen may vary. Usually it takes about ten days for digestion to take place. Students may also want to find out how many times a leaf or trap can capture an insect before dying and dropping off.

Student Resources Related to Venus's-Flytrap

Print

Dean, Anabel. *Plants That Eat Insects: A Look at Carnivorous Plants.* Minneapolis: Lerner, 1977.

Fortman, Janis L. *Creatures of Mystery.* Milwaukee, Wisconsin: Raintree, 1977. IL: 4–7.

Goldstein, Philip. *Animals and Plants That Trap.* New York: Holiday House, 1974. IL: 4–7.

Lerner, Carol. *Pitcher Plants: The Elegant Insect Traps.* New York: Morrow, 1983.

Overbeck, Cynthia. *Carnivorous Plants.* Minneapolis: Lerner, 1982. IL: 4–7.

Prince, Jack Harvey. *Plants That Eat Animals.* New York: Lodestar, 1979. IL: 7–9.

Rahn, Joan Elma. *Traps and Lures in the Living World.* New York: Atheneum, 1980. IL: 5–8.

"Venus Fly Trap." In Hess, Lilo. *Small Habitats.* New York: Scribner's, 1976, pp. 42–45.

Waters, John Frederick. *Carnivorous Plants.* New York: Watts, 1974. IL: 4–7.

Wexler, Jerome. *Secrets of the Venus's Fly Trap.* New York: Dodd, 1981. IL: 4–7.

Nonprint

Carnivorous Plants. Washington, D.C.: National Geographic Society, 1974. (13-min. 16mm film)

Carnivorous Plants. Redondo Beach, California: Stanton Films, 1979. (11-min. 16mm film)

Method: Scientific Investigation

The scientific method is a way of systematically pursuing knowledge or developing understanding of things and events. It involves several steps: the formulation of a problem, the collection of data through observation or experimentation, the formulation of a hypothesis, the testing of that hypothesis, and confirmation or rejection of that hypothesis.

There are many advantages to such a process. The knowledge gained is usually unique to the individual because the student has some control over what is being questioned, tried, and perceived. It is exciting to explore, whether or not one is successful. Because much of the experience is controlled by the students, their abilities, interests, and strengths figure in the exploration. Such exploration often leads to increased self-confidence.

There can also be some difficulties in using the scientific method. For instance, it is slower than giving information in lecture, because time must be allowed for the process. It may be more difficult to use with large groups because of facilities or materials. Use of the method also involves some assumptions that the students can think divergently and abstractly. Sometimes results are not as might have been planned.

The general process is deceptively simple. Individuals must take the following steps (described previously as the "I CHECC" method): (1) Observe or perceive a problem; (2) Collect preliminary data or information (this may be through preliminary observation or by reading); (3) Form a hypothesis; (4) Experiment; (5) Draw conclusions; and (6) Check conclusions.

The method may be used in a number of situations that are not necessarily traditional science. It certainly is a strong process that can easily become part of a student's repertoire.

Resources Related to Scientific Investigation

Print

Altes, Agustin Salvat, and Magda Medir Merce. "The Scientific Method Used in Physics." *International Journal of Science* 10:1 (January-March 1988), pp. 111–120.

Bicak, Laddie J., and Charles J. Bicak. "Scientific Method: Historical and Contemporary Perspectives." *American Biology Teacher* 50:6 (September 1988), pp. 348–353.

Bookman, Peter A. "An Outdoor Lab Exercise Using Leaf Traps." *American Biology Teacher* 51:7 (October 1989), pp. 432–435.

Cross, Burnett. "A Passion within Reason: The Human Side of Process." *Science and Children* 27:4 (January 1990), pp. 16–20.

Fields, Steve. "The Scientific 'Teaching' Method." *Science and Children* 26:7 (April 1989), pp. 15–17.

Garrison, James W., and Michael L. Bentley. "Teaching the Scientific Method: The Logic of Confirmation and Falsification." *School Science and Mathematics* 90:3 (March 1990), pp. 188–197.

Guerra, Cathy L. "The Scientific Method Helps Secondary Students Read Their Textbooks." *Journal of Reading* 27:6 (March 1984), pp. 487–489.

Halkitis, Perry N. "Activate Your Science Class." *Instructor* 99:1 (August 1989), pp. 34–35, 38.

Kellogg, Ted, and Jon Latson. *Teaching Scientific Methodology Through Microcomputer Simulations in Genetics.* Final Project Report. Cambridge, Massachusetts: Educational Technology Center, 1985. ED 304309.

Lyon, Tom. "A Scientific Method for Teaching Elementary Science." *American Education* 19:2 (March 1983), pp. 19–22.

Martin, Rebecca R. "Library Instruction and the Scientific Method: A Role for Librarians in an Introductory Biology Class." *Research Strategies* 4:3 (Summer 1986), pp. 108–115.

Peters, Richard. "Modeling for Effective Skills Development: A Case Study." *Social Studies Teacher* 8:1 (September-October 1986), pp. 3, 8.

Phillips, D. C. "Can Scientific Method Be Taught?" *Journal of College Science Teaching* 15:2 (November 1985), pp. 95–101.

Rice, Patricia C. "Adventures in the Scientific Method." *Anthropology and Education Quarterly* 16:4 (Winter 1985), pp. 276–279.

Romey, W. D. *Inquiry Techniques for Teaching Science.* Englewood Cliffs, New Jersey: Prentice-Hall, 1968.

Rosenshine, B. V. "Synthesis of Research on Explicit Teaching." *Educational Leadership* 43:7 (1986), pp. 60–68.

Sarinsky, Gary B., and Carol A. Biermann. "Learning How To Observe: It's Not Just the Same Old Shell Game." *American Biology Teacher* 51:7 (September 1989), pp. 366–369.

Ward, Veronica, and John Orbell. "Sherlock Holmes as a Social Scientist." *Political Science Teacher* 1:4 (Fall 1988), pp. 15–18.

Nonprint

Science Skills, No. 1: Observing, Reporting, Mapping, and Graphing. Evanston, Illinois: Journal Films, 1975. (16-min. 16mm film)

Science Skills, No. 2: Controlling Variables, Making Measurements. Evanston, Illinois: Journal Films, 1975. (15-min. 16mm film)

Science Skills, No. 3: Defining, Classifying and Identifying. Evanston, Illinois: Journal Films, 1975. (16-min. 16mm film)

Science Skills, No. 4: Interpreting Data. Evanston, Illinois: Journal Films, 1975. (16-min. 16mm film)

Science Skills, No. 5: Conducting an Experiment. Evanston, Illinois: Journal Films, 1975. (15-min. 16mm film)

Scientific Method. Chicago: Encyclopedia Britannica Educational Corporation, 1954. (12-min. 16mm film)

Scientific Method in Action. Chicago: Visual Educational Films/International Film Bureau, 1960. (20-min. 16mm film)

Imaginary Things

Monsters

What is a monster? Most individuals can conjure up an image when the word is introduced. Although some might argue about the classification of monsters, they have arbitrarily been placed under the classification of thing. Perhaps this is because the concept of a monster often is one of a creature that is without some human characteristics; this nonhumanness is directly related to the fear of monsters.

Over the last 50 years, a fascination has grown around monster movies. However, monsters, or the concept of monsters, are not new. Monsters appear throughout literature and mythology. One need only read Greek and Roman myths to find some of the more frightening images.

It is difficult to understand the psychology behind students' seeming need for monsters. Perhaps in confronting and conquering the fears of the imagination, students find a sense of success. Thus the need for monsters of some kind is embedded in human psychology.

Resources Related to Studying Monsters

Ashley, Michael. *Who's Who in Horror and Fantasy Fiction.* New York: Taplinger, 1977.

Cohen, Daniel. *The Encyclopedia of Monsters.* New York: Dodd, 1982.

Eberhart, George M. *Monsters: A Guide to Information on Unaccounted for Creatures, Including Bigfoot, Many Water Monsters, and Other Irregular Animals.* New York: Garland, 1983.

Frank, Frederick S. *The First Gothics: A Critical Guide to the English Gothic Novel.* New York: Garland, 1987.

Glut, Donald F. *The Frankenstein Catalog: Being a Comprehensive Listing of Novels, Translations, Adaptions, Stories, Critical Works, Popular Articles, Series, Fumetti, Verse, State Plays, Films, Cartoons, Puppetry, Radio and Television Programs, Comics, Satire and Humor, Spoken and Musical Recordings, Tapes and Sheet Music Featuring Frankenstein's Monster and or Descended from Mary Shelley's Novel.* Jefferson, North Carolina: McFarland, 1984.

Justice, Keith L. *Science Fiction, Fantasy and Horror Reference: An Annotated Bibliography of Works about Literature and Film.* Jefferson, North Carolina: McFarland, 1989.

McHargue, Georgess. *The Beasts of Never: A History of Natural and Unnatural of Monsters Mythical and Magical.* New York: Delacorte, 1988.

Page, Michael, and Robert Ingpen. *Encyclopedia of Things That Never Were: Creatures, Places, and People.* New York: Viking, 1987. IL: 7–9+.

Palmer, Robin. *Centaurs, Sirens and Other Classical Creatures; A Dictionary, Tales and Verse from Greek and Roman Mythology.* New York: Walck, 1969.

Powers, Tom. *Movie Monsters.* Minneapolis: Lerner, 1989.

Rovin, Jeff. *Encyclopedia of Monsters.* New York: Facts on File, 1989.

Science Fiction, Fantasy and Horror. Oakland, California: Locus, 1987.

Simpson, Jacqueline. *European Mythology.* New York: Peter Bedrick, 1987.

Tymn, Marshall B. *Horror Literature: A Core Collection and Reference Guide.* New York: Bowker, 1981.

Video Times Magazine. *Your Movie Guide to Horror Video Tapes and Discs.* New York: Signet, 1985.

Willis, Donald C. *Horror and Science Fiction Films: A Checklist.* Metuchen, New Jersey: Scarecrow, 1972.

———. *Horror and Science Fiction Films II*. Metuchen, New Jersey: Scarecrow, 1982.

———. *Horror and Science Fiction Films III*. Metuchen, New Jersey: Scarecrow, 1984.

Sample Activity Related to Monsters

A large bag, preferably as large as a mailbag, is laid on a table and partially filled with newspaper. With the bottom stuffed with newspaper, the top may be stuffed with different kinds of monster books. A large sign is placed on the bag saying "Free Reading Monster Grab Bag." Further instructions may state, "This bag contains remains of monsters past and present. Stick your hand in the bag, grab a book, try it! If you don't like it, try putting it back!"

Students are given time to read the instructions. The classroom teacher or library media specialist may give students some suggestions about free reading and browsing. Depending on the students' experience, they may not have considered some of their own criteria for judging whether or not they want to try a book.

1. Check the cover and blurb on the book jacket if available.
2. Check the title and table of contents if there is one.
3. Try a few pages.
4. If you don't like it, try something else. Free and voluntary reading should be just that.

It is interesting to note differences in students when they are given opportunities for free choice and reading. Some good readers look for books that they might like the most. However, there are those who can never seem to find books they like. It is not unusual for a student to say, "There are no good books in this place." For those students, free reading provides a unique opportunity for them to find the books they think are the worst. In the process, they may find the ones they like the best.

Student Resources Related to Monsters

Print

Asimov, Isaac, Martin Greenberg, and Charles Waugh. *Young Monsters*. New York: Harper, 1985. IL: 5–8.

Aylesworth, Thomas G. *Monsters from the Movies.* Philadelphia: J. B. Lippincott, 1972. IL: 5–8.

———. *Movie Monsters.* Philadelphia: J. B. Lippincott, 1975. IL: 4–7. RL: 6.

———. *Vampires and Other Ghosts.* Reading, Massachusetts: Addison-Wesley, 1972. IL: 5–7.

Bennett, Jack. *The Voyage of the Lucky Dragon.* Englewood Cliffs, New Jersey: Prentice-Hall, 1982. IL: 7–9.

Berenstain, Michael. *Creature Catalog.* New York: Random House, 1982. IL: 5–7. RL: 7.

Blumberg, Rhoda. *Monsters.* New York: Watts, 1983. IL: 6–9. RL: 8.

Carmichael, Carrie. *Bigfoot: Man, Monster, or Myth?* Milwaukee, Wisconsin: Raintree, 1983. IL: 4–7.

Cohen, Daniel. *Bigfoot: America's Number One Monster.* New York: Pocket Books, 1982. IL: 7–9.

———. *Everything You Need To Know about Monsters and Still Be Able To Get to Sleep.* Garden City, New York: Doubleday, 1981. IL: 4–6.

———. *The Greatest Monsters in the World.* New York: Pocket Books, 1986. IL: 4–7.

———. *Monster Hunting Today.* New York: Dodd, 1983. IL: 4–6. RL: 7.

———. *Monsters You Never Heard Of.* New York: Dodd, 1984. IL: 4–7.

———. *Science Fiction's Greatest Monsters.* New York: Dodd, 1980. IL: 4–6. RL: 6.

———. *Supermonsters.* New York: Pocket Books, 1986. IL: 4–7.

Cornell, James. *The Monster of Loch Ness.* New York: Scholastic, 1978. IL: 7–9.

Edelson, Edward. *Great Monsters of the Movies.* New York: Pocket Books, 1973. IL: 7–9.

Farson, Daniel. *Mysterious Monsters.* Angus Hall, New York: Mayflower, 1980. IL: 5–8.

Fisk, Nicholas. *Monster Maker.* New York: Macmillan, 1979. IL: 5–7. RL: 4.

Gaffron, Norma. *Bigfoot: Opposing Viewpoints.* Saint Paul, Minnesota: Greenhaven, 1989. IL: 7–9.

Hitchcock, Alfred. *Alfred Hitchcock's Monster Museum.* New York: Random House, 1982. IL: 5–8.

McHargue, Georgess. *The Beast of Never.* New York: Delacorte, 1987. IL: 7–9.

————. *Meet the Vampire.* New York: Dell, 1979. IL: 7–9.

————. *Meet the Werewolf.* New York: Dell, 1976. IL: 7–9.

Place, Marian T. *Bigfoot All Over the Country.* New York: Dodd, 1978. IL: 4–6. RL: 7.

Protter, Eric. *Monster Festival.* New York: Vanguard, 1965. IL: 4–7. RL: 7.

Quackenbush, Robert M. *Movie Monsters and Their Masters: The Birth of the Horror Movie.* Chicago: Whitman, 1980. IL: 5–8.

Reeves, James. *Heroes and Monsters: Legends of Ancient Greece.* Glasgow, Scotland: Blackie, 1969.

Ross, Dave. *How To Prevent Monster Attacks.* New York: Morrow, 1984. IL: 4–7.

Shelley, Mary Wollstonecraft. *Frankenstein.* Milwaukee, Wisconsin: Raintree, 1983. IL: 4–7.

————. *Frankenstein.* New York: NAL, 1965. IL: 7–9+. RL: 8.

Simon, Seymour. *Space Monsters from the Movies, TV and Books.* New York: Harper, 1977. IL: 4–7.

Stoker, Bram. *Dracula.* New York: Delacorte, 1980. IL: 4–7.

Taylor, David. *Animal Monsters: Fantasies and Facts of the Animal World.* Minneapolis: Lerner, 1989. IL: 4–6.

Thorne, Ian. *Creature from the Black Lagoon.* Mankato, Minnesota: Crestwood House, 1981. IL: 4–7. RL: 4.

————. *The Deadly Mantis.* Mankato, Minnesota: Crestwood House, 1982. IL: 3–6. RL: 4.

————. *Dracula.* Mankato, Minnesota: Crestwood House, 1977. IL: 4–7. RL: 4.

————. *Frankenstein.* Mankato, Minnesota: Crestwood House, 1977. IL: 4–7. RL: 4.

————. *Godzilla.* Mankato, Minnesota: Crestwood House, 1977. IL: 4–7. RL: 4.

————. *It Came from Outer Space.* Mankato, Minnesota: Crestwood House, 1982. IL: 4–7. RL: 4.

————. *King Kong.* Mankato, Minnesota: Crestwood House, 1977. IL: 4–7. RL: 4.

————. *Mad Scientists.* Mankato, Minnesota: Crestwood House, 1977. IL: 4–7. RL: 4.

————. *The Wolf Man.* Mankato, Minnesota: Crestwood House, 1977. IL: 4–7. RL: 4.

Wolf, Leonard. *Monsters: Twenty Terrible and Wonderful Beasts from the Classic Dragon and Colossal Minataur to King Kong and the Great Godzilla.* San Francisco: Straight Arrow, 1974. IL: 5–8.

Yolen, Jane. *Dragon's Blood.* New York: Dell, 1984. IL: 7–9. RL: 7.

Zelazny, Roger. *A Dark Traveling.* New York: Walker, 1987. IL: 7–9.

Nonprint

Because there are so many choices, only a few examples are provided here. Check bibliographies of horror movies for complete information.

Frankenstein. Universal City, California: MCA Home Video, 1931. (71-min. videocassette)

The Monster. Deerfield, Illinois: Centron Educational Films, 1976. (16-min. 16mm film)

Monsters: Mysteries or Myths? Chicago: Films, Inc., 1976. (49-min. 16mm film)

Mysterious Monsters. Stamford, Connecticut: Educational Dimensions, 1979. (2 sound filmstrips)

The Wolf Man. Universal City, California: MCA Home Video, 1941. (70-min. videocassette)

Method: Free Reading

Free reading should be just that—students should be able to try materials with no penalties or strings attached. While the best opportunities occur when students have complete run of the entire library media center, sometimes students need to know that free reading is valued. Such valuing means that one can read at will and by choice. It is also recreational.

Unfortunately, some students have never browsed or begun to develop their own criteria for selecting reading material. It may be helpful for the teacher or library media specialist to narrow the topic for a short period to model a browsing behavior. Browsing suggests random looking at the materials that are available. However, there are varied ways of randomly looking and making choices. Students should be given hints for use of the materials to find something they want. The classroom teacher might provide just such hints by calling attention to behaviors that help:

1. Looking at the cover
2. Reading the blurb on a book jacket

3. Considering the title for hints about the content
4. Considering the author in case other titles by that person have been read and enjoyed
5. Checking the table of contents for what might be included
6. Skimming the first few pages

Some students think that they have to read a book all the way through if they choose it. They should be told that they have the option to stop reading if what they have chosen turns out to be uninteresting. They should understand that recreational reading means they have the right to read or not, depending on whether a book interests them.

One of the problems encountered in establishing free reading among students is time. Many students have so many activities that they have little time left for leisure reading. Many of their parents are also in the same position. It may be helpful to suggest that students make themselves a chart to block out time to read for fun. With their parents, they might go browse for something that might be of interest.

Resources Related to Free Reading

Chisom, Yvette L. "Increasing Literature Appreciation and Recreational Reading Behavior of Intermediate Grade Students." Ed.D. Practicum, Nova University, 1989. ED 308494.

Clench, J. D. "The Voluntary Reading of F. E. Students." *Use of English* 33:1 (Fall 1981), pp. 57–62.

Connor, D. "The Relationship between Reading Achievement and Voluntary Reading of Children." *Educational Research* 6 (1954), pp. 221–227.

Hincks, Tony, and John W. Balding. "On the Relationship Between Television Viewing Time and Book Reading for Pleasure: The Self-Reported Behavior of 11 to 16 Year Olds." *Reading* 22:1 (April 1988), pp. 40–50.

Irving, Ann. *Promoting Voluntary Reading for Children and Young People.* Paris: UNESCO, 1980. ED 207035.

Landy, Sarah. "An Investigation of the Relationship Between Voluntary Reading and Certain Psychological, Environmental, and Socioeconomic Factors in Early Adolescence." Master's Thesis, University of Regina, 1977. ED 145409.

Lawson, H. D. "Effects of Free Reading on the Reading Achievement of Sixth-Grade Pupils." In Figurel, J. A. *Forging Ahead in Reading.* Newark, Delaware: International Reading Association, 1968.

Long, H., and E. H. Henderson. "Children's Uses of Time: Some Personal and Social Correlates." *Elementary School Journal* 73 (1973), pp. 193–199.

Manning, G. I., and M. Manning. "What Models of Recreational Reading Make a Difference?" Reading World 23 (1984), pp. 375–380.

Meisel, Stephen, and Gerald G. Glass. "Voluntary Reading Interests and the Interest Content of Basal Readers." *Reading Teacher* 23:7 (1970), pp. 655–659.

Memory, David M. "Voluntary Reading in Content-Area Classes." *Clearinghouse* 54:7 (March 1981), pp. 313–316.

Monseau, Virginia. *Independent Reading: A Teacher's Tale of Success in a Small, Traditional School.* Paper presented at the Annual Meeting of the National Teachers of English, Cincinnati, Ohio, November 21–26, 1980. ED 195943.

Morrow, Lesley Mandel. "Attitudes of Teachers, Principals, and Parents Toward Promoting Voluntary Reading in the Elementary School." *Reading Research and Instruction* 25:2 (Winter 1986), pp. 116–130.

———. "Developing Young Voluntary Readers: The Home, the Child, the School." *Reading Research and Instruction* 25:1 (Fall 1985), pp. 1–8.

———. "Field-Based Research on Voluntary Reading: A Process for Teachers' Learning and Change." *Reading Teacher* 39:3 (December 1985), pp. 331–337.

———. "Promoting Voluntary Reading: Activities Represented in Basal Reader Manuals." *Reading Research and Instruction* 26:3 (Spring 1987), pp. 189–202.

———. *Promoting Voluntary Reading at School and Home.* Bloomington, Indiana: Phi Delta Kappa Educational Foundation, 1985. ED 261966.

Morrow, Lesley Mandel, and Carol Simon Weinstein. "Encouraging Voluntary Reading: The Impact of a Literature Program on Children's Use of Library Centers." *Reading Research Quarterly* 21:3 (Summer 1986), pp. 330–346.

Roeder, Harold H., and Nancy Lee. "Twenty-Five Teacher-Tested Ways To Encourage Voluntary Reading." *Reading Teacher* 27:1 (1973), pp. 48–50.

Taylor, J. J. "The Voluntary Reading Habits of Secondary School Pupils." *Reading* 7:3 (1973), pp. 11–18.

Yatvin, J. "Recreational Reading for the Whole School." *Reading Teacher* 31 (1977), pp. 185–188.

Unidentified Flying Objects (UFOs)

Unidentified flying objects have occupied the thoughts of people since 1947, when the first highly publicized sighting occurred. Kenneth Arnold officially reported his sighting of nine strange flying objects in Washington's Cascade Mountains. From that time, there has been controversy and speculation about whether or not the earth has been visited by alien beings from other planets.

The interest in such sightings has been recorded in short stories, science fiction novels, poems, newspaper and periodical articles, and movies and television programs. It is a natural area of curiosity for young adults, who seem to enjoy the speculation as much as adults do.

Resources for Collecting Information and Materials about UFOs

Several guides and studies are available for locating articles and information about unidentified flying objects. These are in addition to the general bibliographical sources of children's and young adults' literature. It may also be of benefit to check bibliographic sources in science fiction.

UFOs

Condon, E. U. *Scientific Study of Unidentified Flying Objects.* New York: Bantam, 1969.

Eberhart, George M. *UFOs and the Extraterrestrial Contact Movement: A Bibliography. Volume 1: Unidentified Flying Objects. Volume 2: The Extraterrestrial Contact Movement.* Metuchen, New Jersey: Scarecrow, 1986.

Rasmussen, Richard Michael. *The UFO Literature: A Comprehensive Annotated Bibliography of Works in English.* Jefferson, North Carolina: McFarland, 1985.

Sagan, Carl, and Thornton Page. *UFOs: A Scientific Debate.* Ithaca, New York: Cornell University Press, 1973.

Story, Ronald G., and J. Richard Greenwell. *The Encyclopedia of UFOs.* Garden City, New York: Doubleday, 1980.

Science Fiction—Articles

Antczak, Janice. "Future Tense: Science Fiction Confronts the New Science." *School Library Journal* 36:1 (January 1990), pp. 29–32.

"Fiction for Children, 1970–1982: 3. Science Fiction." *Children's Literature in Education* 14:4 (Winter 1983), pp. 222–236.

Gunn, James. "A Basic Science Fiction Library." *Library Journal* 113 (November 15, 1988), p. 25.

Huntington, John. "Science Fiction and the Future." *College English* 37:4 (1975), pp. 345–352.

Klause, Annette Curtis. "Booktalking Science Fiction to Young Adults." *Journal of Youth Services in Libraries* (Winter 1990), pp. 102–116.

———. "A Hitchhiker's Guide to Science Fiction." *School Library Journal* 35:1 (September 1988), pp. 120–123.

Muller, Al, and C. W. Sullivan III. "Science Fiction and Fantasy Series Books." *English Journal* 69:7 (October 1980), pp. 71–74.

Pohl, Frederick. "Astounding Story: A Leading Science-Fiction Writer Traces the Course of Sci-Fi in America from Its Beginnings When a Few Kids Met in a Drugstore to Its Present State as a Powerful, Worldwide Literary Movement." *American Heritage* 40:6 (September-October 1989), pp. 42–54.

Tymn, Marshall B. "Guide to Resource Materials for Science Fiction and Fantasy Teachers." *English Journal* 68:1 (January 1979), pp. 68–74.

Science Fiction—Books

Allen, L. David. *The Ballantine Teachers' Guide to Science Fiction: A Practical Creative Approach to Science Fiction in the Classroom.* New York: Ballantine, 1975.

———. *Science Fiction: An Introduction.* Lincoln, Nebraska: Cliff Notes, 1973.

Anderson, Craig. *Science Fiction Films of the Seventies.* Jefferson, North Carolina: McFarland, 1985.

Aquino, John. *Science Fiction as Literature.* Washington, D.C.: National Education Association, 1976.

Ash, Brian. *The Visual Encyclopedia of Science Fiction.* New York: Harmony, 1977.

————. *Who's Who in Science Fiction.* New York: Taplinger, 1976.

Barron, Neil. *Anatomy of Wonder: A Critical Guide to Science Fiction.* New York: Bowker, 1987.

Benson, Michael. *Vintage Science Fiction Films, 1896–1949.* Jefferson, North Carolina: McFarland, 1985.

Bleiler, Everett Franklin. *The Checklist of Fantastic Literature: A Bibliography of Fantasy, Weird and Science Fiction Books Published in the English Language.* Redding, California: Shasta, 1948.

Bretnor, Reginald. *The Craft of Science Fiction: A Symposium on Writing Science Fiction and Science Fantasy.* New York: Harper, 1976.

Brown, Charles, and William G. Contento. *Science Fiction, Fantasy, and Horror: 1988.* Oakland, California: Locus, 1989.

Burgess, Michael. *Reference Guide to Science Fiction and Fantasy.* Littleton, Colorado: Libraries Unlimited, 1990.

Careson, Thomas D. *Science Fiction Criticism: An Annotated Checklist.* Kent, Ohio: Kent State University Press, 1972.

Currey, L. W. *Science Fiction and Fantasy Authors: A Bibliography of First Printings of Their Fiction and Selected Non-Fiction.* Boston: G. K. Hall, 1980.

Fletcher, Marilyn. *Reader's Guide to Twentieth Century Science Fiction.* Chicago: American Library Association, 1989.

Frank, Alan. *The Science Fiction and Fantasy Film Handbook.* New York: Barnes & Noble, 1983.

Friend, Beverly. *Science Fiction: The Classroom in Orbit.* Glassboro, New Jersey: Educational Impact, 1974.

Gunn, James. *The Discovery of the Future: The Ways Science Fiction Developed.* College Station: Texas A&M University, 1975.

Hall, H. W. *Science Fiction and Fantasy Reference Index, 1878–1985: An International Author and Subject Index to History and Criticism.* Detroit: Gale Research, 1987.

Hardy, Phil. *The Aurum Film Encyclopedia. Volume 2: Science Fiction.* London: Aurum, 1984.

Hartwell, David. *Age of Wonders: Exploring the World of Science Fiction.* New York: McGraw-Hill, 1984.

Holdstock, Robert. *Encyclopedia of Science Fiction.* London: Octopus, 1978.

Justice, Keith L. *Science Fiction, Fantasy and Horror Reference: An Annotated Bibliography of Works about Literature and Film.* Jefferson, North Carolina: McFarland, 1989.

————. *Science Fiction Master Index of Names.* Jefferson, North Carolina: McFarland, 1986.

Lentz, Harris M. *Science Fiction, Horror and Fantasy Film and Television Credits.* Jefferson, North Carolina: McFarland, 1983.

Nicholls, Peter. *The Science Fiction Encyclopedia.* Garden City, New York: Doubleday, 1979.

Parrinder, Patrick. *Science Fiction: Its Criticism and Teaching.* London: Methuen, 1980.

Reginald, R. *Science Fiction and Fantasy Literature. Volume 1: A Checklist, 1700–1974. Volume 2: Contemporary Scientific Authors. Supplement: 1975–1986.* Detroit: Gale Research, 1990.

Rose, Mark. *Science Fiction: A Collection of Critical Essays.* Englewood Cliffs, New Jersey: Prentice-Hall, 1976.

Searles, Baird, Martin Last, Beth Meacham, and Michael Franklin. *A Reader's Guide to Science Fiction.* New York: Facts on File, 1980.

Tuck, Donald Henry. *The Encyclopedia of Science Fiction and Fantasy through 1968.* Chicago: Advent, 1974.

Twentieth Century Science Fiction Writers. Chicago: St. James, 1986.

Warren, Bill. *Keep Watching the Skies! American Science Fiction Movies of the Fifties, Volume 2.* Jefferson, North Carolina: McFarland, 1986.

Wehmeyer, Lillian Bierman. *Images in a Crystal Ball: World Futures in Novels for Young People.* Littleton, Colorado: Libraries Unlimited, 1981.

Williamson, Jack. *Teaching Science Fiction: Education for Tomorrow.* London: Chiswick, 1980.

Wright, Gene. *The Science Fiction Image: The Illustrated Encyclopedia of Science Fiction in Film, Television, Radio and the Theater.* New York: Facts on File, 1983.

Wymer, Alice Calderonello, Lowell P. Leland, Sara Jayne Steen, and R. Michael Evers. *Intersections: The Elements of Fiction in Science Fiction.* Bowling Green, Ohio: Popular Press, 1978.

Young Adult Services Division. *Science Fiction,* Chicago: American Library Association, 1989.

Sample Activity Related to UFOs

The library media specialist may begin a discussion with a question, "Are there really UFOs?" He or she may then invite a number of students' opinions. The library media specialist can introduce a number of books and suggest that the students discuss the matter on their own after they have conducted their own reading investigation.

Books and other media may be checked out and used before students meet in groups of four or five. The library media specialist should suggest that the students select a discussion leader in order to report the opinion of the group. The group discussion rules should include a requirement about presenting evidence from what one has read to back up one's own opinions or to refute someone else's. In other words, students' opinions must be defended during the discussions with what they have seen and read.

The library media specialist may offer some suggestions for students concerning how to use what they have read in the discussion and in general conversation.

1. They should consider what they have read and how it relates to their own opinions.

2. They should consider how they might share what they have read. They might summarize a story or events, use statistics or facts about what they have read, or quote those who have reported sightings.

3. They should listen to the opinions and reports of other group members and think about how their own readings relate to the speakers' ideas.

4. They should respond to other speakers with courtesy and state their own ideas as clearly as possible.

Students should read and come prepared to discuss their opinions based on the materials they have read or viewed.

Student Resources Related to UFOs

Fiction

Byars, Betsy. *The Computer Nut.* New York: Viking, 1984. IL: 3–6. RL: 5.
Clark, Margaret Goff. *Barney and the UFO.* New York: Dodd, 1979. IL: 3–6. RL: 4.

Fradin, Dennis. *How I Saved the World*. Minneapolis: Dillon, 1986. IL: 4–7.

Pinkwater, Daniel Manus. *The Muffin Friend*. New York: Lothrop, Lee & Shepard, 1986. IL: 3–6. RL: 5.

Sleator, William. *Into the Dream*. New York: Dutton, 1979. IL: 1–6. RL: 2.

Nonfiction

Arvey, Michael. *UFOs: Opposing Viewpoints*. Minneapolis: Greenhaven, 1989. IL: 4–7.

Asimov, Isaac. *Unidentified Flying Objects*. New York: Gareth Stevens, 1989. IL: 7–9+.

Berger, Melvin. *The Supernatural: From ESP to UFOs*. New York: Harper, 1977.

———. *UFOs, ETs and Visitors from Space*. New York: Putnam, 1988. IL: 5–7.

Blumberg, Rhonda. *UFO*. New York: Avon, 1980. IL: 4–7.

Branley, Franklyn M. *A Book of Flying Saucers for You*. New York: Harper, 1973. IL: 3–6.

Butts, Donna, and S. Scott Corder. *UFO Contact, the Four*. Tucson, Arizona: UFO Photo Library, 1989. IL: 8–9+.

Christian, Mary B. *UFOs*. Mankato, Minnesota: Crestwood House, 1984. IL: 5–7.

Cohen, Daniel. *A Close Look at Close Encounters*. New York: Putnam, 1981. IL: 6–8.

———. *Creatures from UFOs*. New York: Dodd, 1978. IL: 4–8.

———. *UFOs: The Third Wave*. New York: Evans, 1988. IL: 7–9.

———. *World of UFOs*. New York: Harper, 1978. IL: 4–6.

Collins, Jim. *Unidentified Flying Objects*. Milwaukee, Wisconsin: Raintree, 1983. IL: 4–7.

Dank, Milton, and Gloria Dank. *A UFO Has Landed*. New York: Dell, 1983. IL: 5–9.

Dolan, Edward F. *Bermuda Triangle and Other Mysteries of Nature*. New York: Watts, 1980. IL: 5–7. RL: 5.

Gallagher, I. J. *The Case of the Ancient Astronauts*. Milwaukee, Wisconsin: Raintree, 1983. IL: 4–7.

Gelman, Rita, and Marcia Seligson. *UFO Encounter*. New York: Scholastic, 1978. IL: 4–6.

Kitamura, Satoshi. *UFO Diary*. New York: Farrar, 1989.

Knight, David C. *Those Mysterious UFOs: The Story of Unidentified Flying Objects.* Hillside, New Jersey: Enslow, 1979.

Larsen, Sherman J. *Close Encounters: A Factual Report on the UFOs.* Milwaukee, Wisconsin: Raintree, 1978. IL: 4–6. RL: 5.

Oleksy, Walter. *UFO Teen Sightings.* New York: Messner, 1984. IL: 7–9.

Riehecky, Janet. *UFOs.* Chicago: Children's Press, 1989. IL: 4–7.

Rutland, Jonathan. *UFOs.* New York: Random House, 1987. IL: 3–6.

Spellman, Linda. *Monsters, Mysteries, UFOs.* Santa Barbara, California: Learning Works, 1984. IL: 4–6.

Stevens, Wendelle C. *UFO: Contact from Reticulum, Update.* Tucson, Arizona: UFO Photo Archives, 1989. IL: 8–9+.

The UFO Phenomena. New York: Time/Life, 1987. IL: 7–9+.

World Almanac Book of the Strange. New York: NAL, 1982. IL: 7–9+.

Nonprint

Close Encounters of the Third Kind. New York: RCA/Columbia, 1977. (135-min. videocassette; rated PG)

The Day the Earth Stood Still. New York: CBS/Fox, 1951. (88-min. videocassette)

Learn about UFOs. Mount Kisco, New York: Guidance Associates, 1978. (4 sound filmstrips)

Mysteries Old and New. Washington, D.C.: National Geographic Society, 1982. (2 sound filmstrips)

Star Monsters. Bedford Hills, New York: Orange Cherry Media, 1978. (4 sound filmstrips)

UFO: Friend, Foe, or Fantasy. New York: CBS, 1966. (60-min. 16mm film)

The War of the Worlds. Van Nuys, California: Paramount, 1953. (85-min. videocassette)

Method: General Discussion

Usually discussion is a small group oral interaction conducted in some systematic order about a given topic. Participants present more than one point of view, listen to the different points of view, and gather more knowledge on the topic. This means that the purposes of discussions are generally to share the knowledge of each individual with others in the group, to develop understanding of complex problems, to analyze proposals or propositions, to stimulate new attitudes and opinions, and to arrive at decisions about issues or problems.

For a discussion to take place, a physical and mental atmosphere conducive to such interactions must be a condition. The participants themselves are likely to gain more from discussion if they are able to show respect for other individuals, are able to be truthful in their responses, can treat others equitably, can maintain responsibility for their actions and words, have a sense of order and organization, are peaceful in their approach to ideas, and believe in the freedom of others to express themselves. Discussions should be open to all individuals, unhindered by arbitrary meeting times. In open discussions, participants are free to come to their own conclusions.

Given these characteristics and the atmosphere that must be developed, it is obvious that the skills of discussion leaders and participants are developed over time. There are many skills that can be honed by the teacher, library media specialist, and student. During a discussion, the individuals involved must be conscious of both the communication skills required in the delivery of ideas and the cognitive skills involved with the content of the discussion. Thus, they must be able to listen to ideas and generalize from other points made, to listen to varying points of view and use those in determining their own, to develop questions or statements for exploration, to identify examples to explain their point of view, and to be sensitive to the needs of the others in the group.

Given the complexities of human interaction, variations in discussions would be expected. These variations include question generation, physical setup, leadership, group members' experience, and group size. Questions may be generated by the teacher, the library media specialist, or the students. The room setup may vary. Circles or semicircles of individuals are favored because the individuals can see each other. The discussion group may be led by the teacher or library media specialist, or it may be student led. The experience of those involved usually dictates these decisions. As the students gain experience in discussion groups, they should begin to feel more at ease in leadership roles. The size of the group can also have an impact on the decisions reached. A small group of four or five individuals provides more freedom than a larger group.

The discussion method has many advantages. It promotes student responsibility and independence in learning, because the teacher or library media specialist relinquishes sole responsibility for teaching a topic. Students must think about the issues or themes for themselves and must practice voicing their ideas. Thus, this method also provides for student participation and the development of students' leadership abilities. For the teacher or library media specialist, the method works well in combination with other teaching methods. The students gain many skills using this method. They must organize their facts, ask discerning questions, listen to others' opinions, integrate ideas about a topic into present thinking, test their ideas to see if the ideas can withstand new evidence, and form opinions. Socially, the students are given an opportunity to solve problems with a group of individuals who may or may not agree with them, to pool the information that they gain as they listen, to become intellectually independent, and to improve their self-concepts in an open atmosphere.

This method can also have some disadvantages. Because discussion is unpredictable, the consensus of the group about a topic may not be the learning intended, and conclusions about a character may not be those favored by the teacher or library media specialist. In some groups, more outspoken members may hamper others, so that quieter individuals might not be heard. If students do not have enough common background, discussion will be more difficult. If a book is going to be discussed, the students must have been motivated enough to read it in the first place. Thus, the discussion method may not be as successful without introduction and preparation. It is not likely to be the only method used with extremely reluctant readers. However, when used in combination with other techniques more suited to introducing an idea or for providing background knowledge, it can become a method for intensifying the appreciation of reading.

Resources Related to General Discussion

Articles

Alvermann, Donna E., and James R. Olson. "Discussing Read-Aloud Fiction: One Approach for Motivating Critical Thinking." *Reading Horizons* 28:4 (Summer 1988), pp. 235–241.

Corpening, Dodie K. "All Right Class, Let's Discuss It! Communication II: Teaching Discussion Skills in the Classroom." *G/C/T*, 35 (November-December 1984), pp. 27–29.

Dillon, J. T. "Research on Questioning and Discussion." *Educational Leadership* 42:3 (November 1984), pp. 50–56.

———. "To Question and Not To Question during Discussion. I: Questioning and Discussion." *Journal of Teacher Education* 32:5–6 (1981), pp. 15–20.

———. "To Question and Not To Question during Discussion. II: Nonquestioning Techniques." *Journal of Teacher Education* 32:5–6 (1981), pp. 51–55.

Francis, E. "Discussion Across the Curriculum." *Teaching English* (Spring 1984), pp. 20–23.

Gall, M. D., and J. P. Gall. "The Discussion Method." In *Psychology of Teaching Methods* (NSSE 75th Yearbook, Part I). Chicago: University of Chicago Press, 1976.

Kahn, Elizabeth, et al. "Making Small Groups Work: Controversy Is the Key." *English Journal* 73:2 (February 1984), pp. 63–65.

Kitagawa, Mary M. "Improving Discussions or How To Get the Students To Ask the Questions." *Reading Teacher* 36:1 (October 1962), pp. 42–45.

Lowe, William T. "Discussion Skills." *Social Science Record* 21:2 (Fall 1984), pp. 10–12.

Nelson, M. A. "Discussion Strategies and Learning Science Principles." *Journal of Research in Science Teaching* 10 (1975), pp. 25–38.

Perez, Samuel A., and Eric V. Strickland. "Teaching Children How To Discuss What They Read." *Reading Horizons* 27:2 (Winter 1986), pp. 89–94.

Schaffer, Jane C. "Improving Discussion Questions: Is Anyone Out There Listening?" *English Journal* 78:4 (April 1989), pp. 40–42.

Books

Alvermann, Donna E. *Discussion, the Forgotten Language Art: Becoming Literate in the Secondary School.* Paper presented at the Annual Meeting of the American Educational Research Association, San Francisco, April 16–20, 1986. ED 269717.

Alvermann, Donna E., et al. *Using Discussion To Promote Reading Comprehension.* Newark, Delaware: International Reading Association, 1987.

Book, Cassandra, and Kathleen Galvin. *Instruction in and about Small Group Discussion*. Urbana, Illinois: ERIC Clearinghouse on Reading and Communication Skills/Speech Communication Association, 1975.

Bormann, Ernest G. *Discussion and Group Methods*. New York: Harper, 1969.

Cazden, Courtney B. *Classroom Discourse: The Language of Teaching and Learning*. Portsmouth, New Hampshire: Heinemann, 1988.

Conduct Group Discussions, Panel Discussions, and Symposiums, Second Edition: Module C-2 of Category C—Instructional Execution. Columbus: Ohio State University, 1982.

Francis, E. *Learning To Discuss*. Edinburgh, Scotland: Moray House College of Education, 1982.

Harnack, Robert Victor. *Group Discussion*. New York: Appleton, 1964.

Hill, W. F. *Learning through Discussion*. Beverly Hills, California: Sage, 1977.

Hyman, R. T. *Improving Discussion Leadership*. New York: Teachers College Press, 1980.

Johnson, M. C. *Discussion Dynamics*. Rowley, Massachusetts: Newbury, 1979.

Miles, M. B. *Learning To Work in Groups: A Program Guide for Educational Leaders*. New York: Teachers College Press, 1959.

Rudduck, J. *Learning To Teach through Discussion*. Norwich, England: Centre for Applied Research in Education, 1979.

Nonprint

Creating an Open Discussion. Bloomington, Indiana: Agency for Instructional Television, 1975. (18-min. 16mm film)

Evaluating Your Discussion. Bloomington, Indiana: Agency for Instructional Television, 1975. (16-min. 16mm film)

Group Discussion. New York: McGraw-Hill, 1954. (12-min. 16mm film)

How To Conduct a Discussion. Chicago: Encyclopedia Britannica Educational Corporation, 1953. (24-min. 16mm film)

INANIMATE THINGS

Resources Related to Inanimate Objects

Buchman, Dian Dincin, and Seli Groves. *What If? Fifty Discoveries That Changed the World.* New York: Scholastic, 1988.

Caney, Steven. *Steven Caney's Invention Book.* New York: Workman, 1985.

Crump, Donald J. *How Things Work.* Washington, D.C.: National Geographic Society, 1983.

Giscard d'Estaing, Valerie-Ann. *The World Almanac Book of Inventions.* New York: World Almanac, 1985.

Growing Up with Science: The Illustrated Encyclopedia of Invention. Freeport, New York: Marshall Cavendish, 1984.

Hawke, David Freeman. *Nut and Bolts of the Past: A History of American Technology, 1776–1860.* New York: Harper, 1988.

Macaulay, David. *The Way Things Work.* Boston: Houghton Mifflin, 1988.

Small Inventions That Make a Big Difference. Washington, D.C.: National Geographic Society, 1984.

Sutton, Caroline. *How Do They Do That? Wonders of the Modern World.* New York: Morrow, 1981.

Vare, Ethlie Ann, and Greg Ptacek. *Mothers of Invention: A History of Forgotten Women and Their Unforgettable Ideas.* New York: Morrow, 1988.

Real Things

Tennis Shoes

Tennis shoes, jeans, and T-shirts are among the clothes that have come to represent the American teenager's costume. Athletic shoes have taken on even greater meaning as some youths have literally killed for certain shoes, and the costs of covering one's feet in style have gone beyond the concept of prestige.

Sample Activity Related to Tennis Shoes

The teacher or library media specialist should begin this exercise by inviting a general discussion of athletic or tennis shoes.

Advertisements from newspapers and magazines can be used to stimulate discussion. Students may be asked to wear their favorite pairs to school, and a mock sneaker fashion show can be held. Following the shoe fashion show, students may discuss why these shoes have become a major source of income for some companies, and why so many are willing to invest in them. Students should be encouraged to look for articles about sneakers and to try to find some books on the subject.

The teacher or library media specialist should explain that at the next meeting the students will have a chance to design their own model sneakers out of papier mache. Before they do, however, they need to read about sneakers and check current shoe ads in periodicals. They may even collect information from stores.

On the sneaker design day, the students must come with their ideas. The teacher will need to collect the paste, paper, and other materials needed to make papier mache.

Each student should draw his or her design on paper and decide on the colors and so forth. Students will first make molds for their sneakers. These may be made using paper that is rolled and scrunched into the shape of a sneaker, with masking tape used to hold the paper in place. Molds could also be made using old sneakers or other shoes, clay, or chicken wire or screen bent into the desired shape.

Following the preparation of the mold or form, the students may gather the paper and begin tearing. For this project, students may wish to use relatively small pieces of torn paper, especially over the rounded portions of the toe and heel. They can then mix the paste and begin the process of dipping the paper in it. The first layer will be important in order to assure a good shape for the sneaker. Some students may make oversized sneakers rather than realistic sizes; this makes the shape easier to mold. Paper may be applied in one or two layers before allowing at least one day for drying.

When the forms are dry, another layer or two of paper may be applied. When these are dry, the students may prepare the surface for painting. Tempera paint is easy to mix and apply; the forms are likely to need more than one coat. When dry, the shoes may be lacquered and displayed.

Student Resources Related to Tennis Shoes

Articles

Many examples are available. Check periodical indexes under such terms as SNEAKERS, ATHLETIC SHOES, FOOTWEAR, and SHOES.

Bosveld, Jane. "The Long Trek to the Perfect Sneaker." *Ms.* 10 (August 1981), pp. 26–28.

"Cool Shoes: What's the Difference Between You and Joe Montana? It's Not the Shoes." *Sport* 81 (September 1990), pp. 90–92.

Cox, James A. "Being Snuck Up On by Sneaker Chic." *Smithsonian Magazine* 16 (January 1986), p. 168.

———. "Sneaker Chic." *Readers Digest* (June 1987), p. 17.

Kaplan, James. "Sneak Attacks." *Vogue* (May 1989), pp. 178–179.

Leo, J. "The Well-Heeled Drug-Runner." *U.S. News & World Report* 108 (April 1990), p. 20.

Osborne, Terry. "Fancy Footwork: Exercise Shoes in the '80s." *Current Health* 2 (April 1987), pp. 19–21.

"Running with the Pack." *Time* 125 (May 27, 1985), p. 62.

Sandmaier, Marian. "Sneaker Attacks." *Mademoiselle* 95 (July 1989), p. 100.

Swift, E. M. "Farewell My Lovely: The Good Ol' All-Purpose Sneaker Is Obsolete in a World of Hyped-Up, High-Tech, High-Priced Athletic Shoes." *Sports Illustrated* 72 (February 19, 1990), p. 74.

Books

Amstutz, Beverly. *Moccasins and Sneakers*. Weston, Missouri: Precious Resources, 1980. IL: 4–7.

Cheskin, Melvyn P., Kel J. Sherkin, and Barry T. Bates. *The Complete Handbook of Athletic Footwear*. New York: Fairchild, 1986. IL: 8–9+.

Cobb, Vicki. *Sneakers Meet Your Feet*. Boston: Little, Brown, 1985. IL: 4–6.

Mackintosh, Prudence. *Thundering Sneakers*. Houston: Pacesetter, 1987. IL: 5–8.

McMillan, Bruce. *Making Sneakers*. Shapleigh, Maine: Apple Island, 1989. IL: 4–7.

Sobol, Donald. *Encyclopedia Brown and the Case of the Disgusting Sneakers.* New York: Morrow, 1990. IL: 3–6.

Nonprint

The Computer Wore Tennis Shoes. Burbank, California: Walt Disney Home Video, 1969. (87-min. videocassette)

Method: Papier Mache

Papier mache is an art method used for making three-dimensional objects. It combines the use of torn pieces of paper applied with paste to a base structure, then painted or otherwise decorated. The base may be constructed from chicken wire, boxes, balloons, cardboard, rolled and bunched newspaper, plastic, or clay. This technique can be used to make baskets, masks, and many other sculpted objects.

Usually old newspaper is used in the process, but other kinds of paper may be used as well. The paper is applied with a paste, usually wheat paste, which is available at stores where wallpaper or arts and crafts materials are sold. The dry paste is sifted into water slowly and mixed until it is smooth and creamy. There are other substances that might be used in place of paste; for example, a newer product called Metylan is often used. In the past, an economical paste was sometimes made of sifted flour.

After the paste material is chosen and prepared, the process of coating the torn pieces of paper with it begins. Torn pieces of paper are dipped in or covered with paste and applied over the base that has been prepared. For round pieces that are molded over other materials, such as bowls, the item used as a mold is covered with petroleum jelly, so that the dried product can be removed from it easily. Torn pieces of paper are overlapped so that there is a smooth surface (unless, of course, a rough surface is desired). Round surfaces are smoother when covered with small pieces of paper. In contrast, flat surfaces can be covered with larger pieces. One or two layers of paste and paper are applied and allowed to dry before one or two more layers are added. Some individuals use different kinds or colors of paper so that they can remember which layer they are working on.

When the object is dry, it is painted or otherwise decorated. For special works, the object may be lightly sanded for smoothness before it is shellacked or varnished. New polymer media may also be used.

Resources Related to the Papier Mache Method

Alkema, Chester Jay. *Starting with Papier Mache*. New York: Sterling, 1974.

Anderson, Mildred. *Original Creations with Papier Mache*. New York: Sterling, 1967.

———. *Papier Mache and How To Use It*. New York: Sterling, 1965.

———. *Papier Mache Crafts*. New York: Sterling, 1975.

Bawden, Juliet. *Art and Craft of Papier Mache*. New York: Grove/Weidenfeld, 1990.

Dawson, Robert, and Joan Dawson. *Sculpture with Simple Materials*. Menlo Park, California: Lane, 1972.

Gottily, Doris R. *Creative Dollmaking: From Papier Mache, Cloth, Clothespins and Appleheads to Yarn, Corn Cob, Bottle and Seashell Dolls*. Watkins Glen, New York: American Life Foundation and Study Institute, 1976.

Henry, Ian. *Pottery from Paper*. New York: State Mutual Book and Periodical Service, 1985.

Johnson, Lillian. *Papier Mache*. New York: McKay, 1958.

Kalina, Sigmund. *How To Make a Dinosaur*. New York: Lothrop, Lee & Shepard, 1976.

Kenny, Carla, and John B. Kenny. *The Art of Papier Mache*. Philadelphia: Chilton, 1968.

Kuykendall, Karen. *Art and Design in Papier Mache*. Great Neck, New York: Hearthside, 1986.

Lorrimar, Betty. *Creative Papier Mache*. New York: Watson-Guptill, 1971.

McGraw, Sheila. *Papier-Mache Today*. Buffalo, New York: Firefly, 1990.

McLaughlin, Terence. *Papier Mache*. New York: Larousse, 1975.

Meilach, Dona Z. *Papier Mache Artistry*. New York: Crown, 1971.

Papier Mache. Van Nuys, California: AIMS Media, 1985. (videocassette)

Papier Mache, Dying and Leatherwork. New York: Watts, 1973.

Romberg, Jenean. *Let's Discover Papier-Mache*. New York: Center for Applied Research in Education, 1974.

Rush, Peter. *Papier Mache*. New York: Farrar, 1980.

Saunders, Everett E. *Papier Mache.* Chicago: Whitman, 1967.

Seidelman, James E., and Grace Mintonye. *Creating with Papier Mache.* New York: Crowell-Collier, 1971.

Shannon, Alice. *Decorative Treasures from Papier Mache.* Great Neck, New York: Hearthside, 1970.

Slade, Richard. *Modeling in Clay, Plaster and Papier-Mache.* New York: Lothrop, Lee & Shepard, 1967.

Starting with Papier Mache. New York: Sterling, 1978.

Computers

Although computers are real, people often ascribe imagined powers to the machines. There are hackers who become absorbed in the pursuit of an answer, locating pathways to sources, finding information, or just figuring out what is going on. Thus, the topic of computers encompasses many possible areas for exploration among potential readers.

Resources Related to Computers

Computer Readable Databases. Detroit: Gale Research, 1991.

Computers and Computing Information Resources Directory. Detroit: Gale Research, 1987.

Connors, Martin, and Janice A. DeMaggio. *Computers and Computing Information Resources Directory: Supplement.* Detroit: Gale Research, 1987.

Directory of Online Databases. Detroit: Gale Research, 1991.

Directory of Portable Databases. Detroit: Gale Research, 1991.

EPIE. *TESS: The Education Software Selector.* Water Mill, New York: Educational Products Information Exchange, 1986.

Kilpatrick, Thomas L. *Microcomputers and Libraries: A Bibliographic Sourcebook.* Metuchen, New Jersey: Scarecrow, 1987.

La Faille, Eugene. "Computers in Science Fiction." *Voice of Youth Advocates* 8:2 (June 1985), pp. 103–106.

Online Database Search Services Directory. Detroit: Gale Research, 1988.

The Software Encyclopedia. New York: Bowker, 1991.

The Software Reviews on File Subscription Service. New York: Facts on File, monthly.

Truett, Carol. *Microcomputer Software Sources: A Guide for Buyers, Librarians, Programmers, Business People, and Educators*. Littleton, Colorado: Libraries Unlimited, 1990.

Young, Sayre Van. *Microsource: Where To Find Answers to Questions about Microcomputers*. Littleton, Colorado: Libraries Unlimited, 1986.

Sample Activity Related to Computers

In this exercise, the classroom teacher and the library media specialist collect as many titles related to computers as possible. The materials may be grouped or classified in different areas—books that deal with programming, computer fiction, and so on.

During a short period of time, about a week or two, everyone is given a chance to select from any of the categories to decide on an area of interest related to computers. At a given time every day, everyone—including the classroom teacher and the library media specialist—will stop, select, and read.

Books may be placed in a mock computer display made out of a large cardboard box. The books may be placed inside the simulated computer terminal so that students reach into the display to get the books that appeal to them. Books may be set up by category, with strings connecting books within a category so that it looks like a branched network. Students can then see some of the books in relationship to ideas or main topics.

Student Resources Related to Computers

The number of computer books on the market has grown so large during the last few years that it is difficult to identify the most current in the area of nonfiction. A sampling of different kinds of books about computers and computing is suggested. For more specific books on particular computer languages, programming, and equipment, *Books in Print* should be consulted.

Fiction

Asimov, Isaac, Patricia S. Warrick, and Martin H. Greensberg. *Machines That Think: The Best Science Fiction Stories about Robots and Computers*. New York: Holt, Rinehart & Winston, 1983. IL: 8–9+.

Bartholomew, Barbara. *The Great Gradepoint Mystery.* New York: Macmillan, 1983. IL: 4–7.

Bethancourt, T. Ernesto. *The Great Computer Dating Caper.* New York: Crown, 1984. IL: 7–9.

Bly, Robert. *Ronald's Dumb Computer.* New York: Dell, 1983. IL: 4–7.

Butterworth, William E. *Next Stop, Earth.* New York: Walker, 1978. IL: 3–6.

Byars, Betsy. *The Computer Nut.* New York: Viking, 1984. IL: 3–7. RL: 3.

Carris, Joan Davenport. *The Revolt of 10-X.* New York: Harcourt, 1980. IL: 5–8.

Chetwin, Grace. *Out of the Dark World.* New York: Lothrop, Lee & Shepard, 1985. IL: 6–9.

Christopher, Matt. *Supercharged Infield.* Boston: Little, Brown, 1985. IL: 5–7.

Clarke, Arthur C. *2001: A Space Odyssey.* New York: NAL/Signet, 1968. IL: 8–9+. RL: 7.

Cross, Gillian. *The Prime Minister's Brain.* New York: Oxford University Press, 1985. IL: 5–8.

Dank, Milton, and Gloria Dank. *The Computer Caper.* New York: Dell, 1986. IL: 5–8.

———. *The Computer Game Murder.* New York: Delacorte, 1985. IL: 5–8.

D'Ignazio, Fred. *Chip Mitchell: The Case of the Chocolate-Covered Bugs.* New York: Dutton, 1985. IL: 5–8.

———. *Chip Mitchell: The Case of the Robot Warriors.* New York: Lodestar, 1984. IL: 5–8.

———. *Chip Mitchell: The Case of the Stolen Computer Brains.* New York: Lodestar, 1982. IL: 5–8.

Francis, Dorothy. *Computer Crime.* New York: Lodestar, 1987. IL: 7–9.

Haas, Dorothy. *The Secret Life of Dilly McBean.* New York: Bradbury, 1986. IL: 5–7.

Harris, LaVinia. *Cover Up.* New York: Scholastic, 1985. IL: 7–9.

———. *A Touch of Madness.* New York: Scholastic, 1985. IL: 7–9.

Kidd, Ronald. *The Glitch: A Computer Fantasy.* New York: Dutton, 1985. IL: 5–8.

Korman, Gordon. *The War with Mr. Wizzle.* New York: Scholastic, 1982. IL: 4–7.

Landsman, Sandy. *The Gadget Factory.* New York: Macmillan, 1984. IL: 5–8.

Leroe, Ellen W. *Robot Romance*. New York: Harper, 1985. IL: 6–9.

Levy, Elizabeth. *The Computer That Said Steal Me*. New York: Macmillan, 1983. IL: 4–7.

Marney, Dean. *The Computer That Ate My Brother*. Boston: Houghton Mifflin, 1985. IL: 3–6.

Matthews, Ellen. *Debugging Rover*. New York: Dodd, 1985. IL: 4–7.

McGregor, Ellen, and Doris Pantell. *Miss Pickerell Meets Mr. H. U. M.* New York: McGraw-Hill, 1974. IL: 3–6.

McMahan, Ian. *The Fox's Lair*. New York: Macmillan, 1983. IL: 4–7.

———. *Lake Fear*. New York: Macmillan, 1985. IL: 4–7.

———. *The Lost Forest*. New York: Macmillan, 1985. IL: 4–7.

Pantell, Dora. *Miss Pickerell and the War of the Computers*. New York: Watts, 1984. IL: 4–6.

Stone, G. H. *Fatal Error*. New York: McKay, 1991. IL: 5–7.

Strasser, Todd. *The Complete Computer Popularity Program*. New York: Dell, 1986. IL: 5–8.

Nonfiction

See the subject guide to *Books in Print* for specific titles. Some examples of beginning-level titles are listed here. As students become involved with the topic, they are likely to seek more technical sources.

The Chipmakers. Westwood, New Jersey: Silver Burdett, 1990. IL: 7–9+.

Communications. Westwood, New Jersey: Silver Burdett, 1990. IL: 7–9+.

Computer Basics. Westwood, New Jersey: Silver Burdett, 1990. IL: 7–9+.

Computer Languages. Westwood, New Jersey: Silver Burdett, 1990. IL: 7–9+.

Computer Security. Westwood, New Jersey: Silver Burdett, 1990. IL: 7–9+.

Computers and the Cosmos. Westwood, New Jersey: Silver Burdett, 1990. IL: 7–9+.

Darling, David J. *Computers at Home: Today and Tomorrow*. Minneapolis: Dillon, 1986. IL: 4–7+.

———. *Fast, Faster, Fastest: The Story of Supercomputers*. Minneapolis: Dillon, 1986. IL: 4–7.

———. *Inside Computers: Hardware and Software*. Minneapolis: Dillon, 1986. IL: 4–7.

———. *The Microchip Revolution*. Minneapolis: Dillon, 1986. IL: 4–7.

Input/Output. Westwood, New Jersey: Silver Burdett, 1990. IL: 7–9+.

Kettlekamp, Larry. *Computer Graphics: How It Works, What It Does*. New York: Morrow, 1989. IL: 7–9.

Memory and Storage. Westwood, New Jersey: Silver Burdett, 1990. IL: 7–9+.

Pizzey, Steve. *The Computerized Society*. Ann Arbor, Michigan: Bookwright, 1986. IL: 4–7.

Schneiderman, Ron. *Computers: From Babbage to the Fifth Generation*. New York: Watts, 1986. IL: 4–7+.

Schulman, Elayne Engleman. *Databases for Beginners*. New York: Watts, 1987. IL: 7–9.

Software. Westwood, New Jersey: Silver Burdett, 1990. IL: 7–9+.

White, Jack R. *How Computers Really Work*. New York: Dodd, 1986. IL: 4–7.

Nonprint

Computer Wizard. Los Angeles: VCL Home Video, 1977. (91-min. videocassette)

Computers in Your Life. Washington, D.C.: National Geographic Society, 1985. (2 sound filmstrips)

Computers: The Friendly Invasion. Deerfield, Illinois: Walt Disney/Coronet/MTI Film and Video, 1983. (20-min. videocassette)

Computers: The Truth of the Matter. Deerfield, Illinois: Walt Disney/Coronet/MTI Film and Video, 1984. (15-min. videocassette)

Computers: Where They Come from and How They Work. Deerfield, Illinois: Walt Disney/Coronet/MTI Film and Video, 1989. (9-min. videocassette)

Ethics in the Computer Age. Deerfield, Illinois: Walt Disney/Coronet/MTI Film and Video, 1985. (23-min. videocassette)

War Games. Atlanta, Georgia: MGM/UA Home Video, 1983. (112-min. videocassette)

Method: Sustained Silent Reading

Ruth Cline and George Kretke (1980) found that junior high students improved significantly in reading when they were involved in sustained silent reading programs. The students were happier about going to the school library, reading books, and doing assigned readings. Many other studies have reported similar results.

Basically a technique for modeling, a sustained silent reading program requires that time be set aside regularly for reading. Usually this involves a daily period of 15 to 30 minutes. During this time, everyone reads, including adults. Everyone is encouraged to read in quantity and to read widely to gain confidence and information. To start such a program it is helpful to use high-interest material.

Resources Related to Sustained Silent Reading

Berglund, Roberta L., and Jerry L. Johns. "A Primer on Uninterrupted Sustained Silent Reading." *Reading Teacher* 36:6 (February 1983), pp. 534–539.

Campbell, Robin. "The Teacher as a Role Model during Sustained Silent Reading (SSR)." *Reading* 23:3 (November 1989), pp. 179–183.

Cline, Ruth J. K., and George L. Kretke. "An Evaluation of Long-Term SSR in the Junior High School." *Journal of Reading* (March 1980), p. 505.

Dully, Melanie. "The Relation between Sustained Silent Reading to Reading Achievement and Attitude of the At-Risk Student." Master's Thesis, Kean College, 1989. ED 312631.

Dwyer, Edward J., and Valda Reed. "Effects of Sustained Silent Reading on Attitudes toward Reading." *Reading Horizons* 29:4 (Summer 1989), pp. 283–293.

Farrell, Ellen. "SSR as the Core of a Junior High Reading Program." *Journal of Reading* 26:1 (October 1982), pp. 48–51.

Grubaugh, Steven. "Initiating Sustained Silent Reading in Your School: Ask, 'What Can SSR Do for Them?'" *Clearinghouse* 60:4 (December 1986), pp. 169–174.

Hanson, R. A. "A Study of the Effects of Sustained Silent Reading on the Reading Attitudes and Habits of Second-, Third-, and Fourth-Grade Students in a Low-Income Area School." Doctoral Dissertation, University of North Dakota, Grand Forks, 1972.

Hobbs, Marcee. "Enhancing SSR." *Reading Teacher* 42:7 (March 1989), pp. 548–549.

Holt, Sondra B., and Frances S. O'Tuel. "The Effect of Sustained Silent Reading and Writing on Achievement and Attitudes of Seventh and Eighth Grade Students Reading Two Years Below Grade Level." *Reading Improvement* 26:4 (Winter 1979), pp. 290–297.

Langford, J. C. "The Effects of Uninterrupted Sustained Silent Reading on the Attitudes of Students Toward Reading and Their Achievement in Reading." Doctoral Dissertation, Auburn University, Auburn, Alabama, 1978.

Manning-Dowd, Alice. *The Effectiveness of SSR: A Review of Research.* 1985. ED 276970.

McHugh, Caroline. "A Study of the Effects of Sustained Silent Reading and Oral Reading on Reading Attitudes and Interests." Master's Thesis, Kean College, 1989. ED 315723.

Pyle, Valerie S. "SSRW: Beyond Silent Reading (Open to Suggestion)." *Journal of Reading* 33:5 (February 1990), pp. 379–380.

Reed, K. "An Investigation of the Effect of Sustained Silent Reading on Reading Comprehension Skills and Attitude Toward Reading of Urban Secondary School Students." Doctoral Dissertation, University of Connecticut, Storrs, 1977.

Sadoski, Mark C. "SSR, Accountability and Effective Reading Instruction." *Reading Horizons* 24:2 (Winter 1984), pp. 119–123.

Smith, Patricia K. "SSR: What To Do When the Interest Is Gone." *Reading Horizons* 24:1 (Fall 1983), pp. 24–26.

Trelease, Jim. *The Read Aloud Handbook.* New York: Penguin, 1985.

Weisendanger, Katherine D., and Lois Bader. "SSR: Its Effects on Students' Reading Habits After They Complete the Program." *Reading Horizons* 29:3 (Spring 1989), pp. 162–166.

Weisendanger, Katherine D., and Ellen D. Birlem. "The Effectiveness of SSR: An Overview of the Research." *Reading Horizons* 24:3 (Spring 1984), pp. 197–201.

Imaginary Things

Time Machines

Time machines are devices that allow human beings, in physical body or in consciousness, to travel into the past or future. The idea of time travel is often connected with the idea of parallel universes. For this particular activity, the focus is on writings that include an actual time-travel device.

Resources Related to Imaginary Things—Time Machines

Barron, Neil. *Anatomy of Wonder: A Critical Guide to Science Fiction.* New York: Bowker, 1987.

Elleman, Barbara. "Popular Reading: Time Fantasy Update." *Booklist* 81:19 (June 1, 1985), pp. 1407–1408.

Hall, H. W. *Science Fiction and Fantasy Reference Index, 1878–1985: An International Author and Subject Index to History and Criticism.* Detroit: Gale Research, 1987.

Jakiel, S. J., and P. E. Levinthal. "The Laws of Time Travel." *Extrapolation* 21:2 (Summer 1980), pp. 130–138.

Lynn, Ruth Nadelman. *Fantasy for Children: An Annotated Checklist and Reference Guide.* New York: Bowker, 1988.

Schlobin, Roger C. *The Literature of Fantasy: A Comprehensive, Annotated Bibliography of Modern Fantasy Fiction.* New York: Garland, 1979.

The Science Fiction Encyclopedia. Garden City, New York: Doubleday, 1979.

Wingrave, David. *The Science Fiction Source Book.* New York: Van Nostrand, 1984.

Sample Activity Related to Time Machines

Time travel has fascinated many authors of fiction. To give students a sense of what might happen if they traveled back in time, the classroom teacher can set up a writing activity for fun. The students use word processing to simulate the changes that might occur if they went back in time.

Before beginning the short exercise, the students may browse through books about time travel and watch some of the video programs that deal with time machines.

For the purpose of the exercise, the classroom teacher asks students to collect in groups of no more than five. Three may be an optimum number for this exercise, however. The students are then given a scenario. Each student in a group draws a number to see who will write about the scenario first, second, third, and so forth.

Each student is given the name of a character about whom he or she will write.

The first person begins the story. A scenario beginning might include the characters who come upon a machine. The characters discover that the machine will allow them to travel back in time. The first person takes the story from when his or her character travels back in time. The plot actions are typed into the computer and the program is saved on a disk in a separate file. The first person then tells the second person where the story leaves off.

Without reading the first person's story, the second person begins with his or her character and writes the next part of the story. When that section has been typed in, the second person reads what the first person wrote and adds his or her part to the first person's story on a separate disk. Based on the events in the segment the second student wrote, changes are made in the first segment so that the combined first and second segments make one tale. At this point there should be one disk containing the version written originally by the first student and a second disk containing the revised version that includes the first and second students' versions.

This process continues until the students finish their additions. All versions are then printed out and placed on the bulletin board. Students may compare the differences and discuss what happened as they added their parts and changed the versions that had preceded them. They may compare this process with what happened to some of the characters who became involved in time travel with a time machine.

Student Resources Related to Time Machines and Time Travel

Fiction

Anderson, Margaret Jean. *The Ghost Inside the Monitor*. New York: Alfred A. Knopf, 1990. IL: 7–9.

Anderson, Pohl. *The Corridors of Time*. New York: Berkeley, 1978. IL: 8–9+.

———. "Time Patrolmen." In *Guardians of Time*. New York: Ballantine, 1960. IL: 8–9+.

———. *The Year of the Ransom*. New York: Walker, 1988. IL: 8–9+.

Asimov, Isaac. *The End of Eternity.* Garden City, New York: Doubleday, 1955.

Benford, Gregory. *Timescape.* New York: Pocket Books, 1980. IL: 7–9+.

Bond, Nancy. *Another Shore.* New York: Macmillan, 1988. IL: 8–9+.

Bosse, Malcolm. *Cave beyond Time.* New York: Crowell, 1980. IL: 7–9.

De Camp, L. Sprague. *Lest Darkness Fall.* New York: Holt, 1939. IL: 8–9+.

Dexter, Catherine. *Mazemaker.* New York: Morrow, 1989. IL: 7–9.

Greer, Gery, and Bob Ruddick. *Max and Me and the Time Machine.* New York: Harcourt, 1983. IL: 5–7. RL: 4.

Harrison, Harry. *Rebel in Time.* New York: Tor, 1989. IL: 8–9+.

———. *The Technicolor Time Machine.* New York: Tor, 1985. IL: 8–9+.

Henderich, Paula. *The Girl Who Slipped through Time.* New York: Lothrop, Lee & Shepard, 1978. IL: 5–8.

Hurmence, Belinda. *A Girl Called Boy.* New York: Clarion, 1982. IL: 5–8.

Jakes, John. *Time Gate.* Philadelphia: Westminster, 1972. IL: 7–9.

L'Engle, Madeline. *Many Waters.* New York: Farrar, 1986. IL: 7–9+.

Mooney, Bel. *The Stove Haunting.* Boston: Houghton Mifflin, 1988. IL: 5–8.

Ormondroyd, Edward. *Time at the Top.* Boston: Houghton Mifflin, 1963. IL: 5–8.

Pfeffer, Susan Beth. *Future Forward.* New York: Delacorte, 1989. IL: 6–8.

———. *Rewind to Yesterday.* New York: Delacorte, 1988. IL: 6–8.

Service, Pamela. *The Reluctant God.* New York: Atheneum, 1988. IL: 7–9+.

Silverberg, Robert. *Hawksbill Station.* Garden City, New York: Doubleday, 1968. IL: 8–9+.

———. *Letters from Atlantis.* New York: Atheneum, 1990. IL: 8–9+

———. *The Masks of Time.* New York: Ballantine, 1968. IL: 8–9+.

———. *Project Pendulum.* New York: Walker, 1987. IL: 7–9.

———. *Up the Line.* New York: Ballantine, 1969. IL: 8–9+.

Simak, Clifford. *The Goblin Reservation.* New York: Putnam, 1968. IL: 7–9.

———. *Time and Again.* New York: Simon & Schuster, 1951. IL: 8–9+.

———. *Time Is the Simplest Thing.* New York: Garden City, Doubleday, 1961. IL: 8–9+.

Sleator, William. *Strange Attractors.* New York: Dillon, 1990. IL: 7–9.

Swigart, Rob. *Portal: A Dataspace Retrieval.* New York: St. Martin's, 1988. IL: 8–9+.

Thomas, Jane Resh. *The Princess in the Pigpen.* New York: Clarion, 1989. IL: 7–9.

Townsend, John Rowe. *The Visitors.* Philadelphia: J. B. Lippincott, 1977. IL: 7–9.

Weldrick, Valerie. *Time Sweep.* New York: Lothrop, Lee & Shepard, 1978. IL: 5–7.

Wells, H. G. *The Time Machine: An Invention.* London: Heinemann, 1949. IL: 8–9+.

Westall, Robert. *The Wind Eye.* New York: Greenwillow, 1977. IL: 7–9.

Wibberley, Leonard. *The Crime of Martin Coverley.* New York: Farrar, 1980. IL: 7–9+.

Wiseman, David. *Jeremy Visick.* Boston: Houghton Mifflin, 1981. IL: 5–8.

Yolen, Jane. *The Devil's Arithmetic.* New York: Viking, 1988. IL: 7–10.

Nonfiction

The Definitive Time Machine: A Critical Edition of H. G. Wells Scientific Romance with Introduction and Notes. Bloomington: Indiana University Press, 1987. (professional)

Macvey, John W. *Time Travel.* Chelsea, Michigan: Scarborough House, 1990.

Nonprint

Back to the Future. Universal City, California: MCA Home Video, 1986. (116-min. videocassette)

Quantum Leap. Current weekly television program.

Star Trek television episode, "All Our Yesterdays." Los Angeles: Paramount Home Video, 1967. (51-min. videocassette)

Star Trek television episode, "The Alternative Factor." Los Angeles: Paramount Home Video, 1967. (51-min. videocassette)

Star Trek television episode, "The City on the Edge of Forever." Los Angeles: Paramount Home Video, 1967. (51-min. videocassette)

Time Bandits. Los Angeles: Paramount, 1981. (116-min. videocassette)

The Time Machine. Atlanta, Georgia: MGM/UA Home Video, 1982. (103-min. videocassette)

The Time Machine. LFP 7044. Niagara Falls, New York: Listen for Pleasure, 1981. (2 60-min. sound cassettes)

The Time Machine. Glenview, Illinois: National Recording Company, 1947. (60-min. sound recording)

The Time Travelers. New York: HBO Home Video, 1964. (82-min. videocassette)

The Time Tunnel. Television program; some episodes available on videocassette.

The Voyagers. Television program; some episodes available on videocassette.

Resources Related to the Word Processing Method

The companies listed below produce word processing programs for the identified computers. Catalogs from these companies are useful in identifying what may be appropriate to individual needs. Word processing programs for Apple II have not been included, but may be located using computer software review sources.

Software for Apple Macintosh Computers

Appleworks
Claris Corporation
5201 Patrick Henry Drive
Santa Clara, CA 95052
(408) 727-8207

FullWrite Professional
Ashton-Tate Corporation
20101 Hamilton Avenue
Torrance, CA 90502-1319
(213) 329-8000

MacWrite
Claris Corporation
5201 Patrick Henry Drive
Santa Clara, CA 95052
(408) 727-8207

Microsoft Word
Microsoft Corporation
1 Microsoft Way
Redmond, WA 98052-6399
(800) 426-9400

Microsoft Works
Claris Corporation
5201 Patrick Henry Drive
Santa Clara, CA 95052
(408) 727-8207

Write Now
T/Maker Company
1390 Villa Street
Mountain View, CA 94041
(415) 962-0195

Software for IBM PCs and Compatibles

Lotus Manuscript
Lotus Development Corporation
55 Cambridge Parkway
Cambridge, MA 02142
(800) 345-1043

Microsoft Word
Microsoft Corporation
1 Microsoft Way
Redmond, WA 98052-6399
(800) 426-9400

WordPerfect
WordPerfect Corporation
1555 North Technology Way
Orem, UT 84057
(800) 321-4566

Wordstar 2000 Plus
MicroPro International Corporation
33 San Pablo Avenue
San Rafael, CA 94903
(800) 227-5609

6

Events

HISTORICAL EVENTS

Real events often far surpass the fictional events reported in novels and other imaginative literary forms. Evidence of this interest can be seen each night in television "reality" programs. Our fascination with unsolved mysteries causes continued searches for information on the strange and unusual. Cinematic reenactments of events real or purported to be based on fact have become quite popular with many viewers.

Recorded history provides many possible events in which students might show an interest. For example, reading preference studies cited in Chapter 2 show that war is an area of interest for boys. The desires to know about events that really happened and to gain a sense of what came before one's own life are evident in the questions of students. Whether it is the action, the pathos, the violence, the chance to understand or know heroes, or a combination of all of these, a plethora of literature is available in this area.

Touching the past, finding out about the real people who endured and made life-and-death decisions, motivates reading of historical sources.

Resources Related to Real Historical Events

A number of general bibliographic sources are useful for locating materials about historical events, including subject indexes and historical chronologies. The following bibliographies and materials will be helpful in locating materials for students interested in reading about historic events.

The American Presidency: A Historical Bibliography. Santa Barbara, California: ABC-CLIO, 1984.

Anderson, Jay. *The Living History Sourcebook.* Nashville, Tennessee: American Association for State and Local History, 1985.

Beers, Henry P. *Bibliographies in American History: Guide to Materials for Research.* Woodbridge, Connecticut: Research Publications, 1982.

Bibliographic Guide to North American History. Boston: G. K. Hall, annual.

Blanco, Richard L. *The War of the American Revolution: A Selected Annotated Bibliography of Published Sources.* New York: Garland, 1984.

Book of Days 1987: An Encyclopedia of Information Sources on Historical Figures and Events, Keyed to Calendar Dates. Ann Arbor, Michigan: Pierian, 1987.

Book of Days 1988: An Encyclopedia of Information Sources on Historical Figures and Events, Keyed to Calendar Dates. Ann Arbor, Michigan: Pierian, 1988.

Campbell, Craig. *Reel America and World War I: A Comprehensive Filmography and History of Motion Pictures in the United States, 1914–1920.* Jefferson City, North Carolina: McFarland, 1985.

Children's Catalog. New York: H. W. Wilson, 1909–present.

Cole, Garold. *Travels in America from the Voyages of Discovery to the Present: An Annotated Bibliography of Travel Articles in Periodicals.* Norman: University of Oklahoma Press, 1984.

Coletta, Paola E. *Bibliography of American Naval History.* Annapolis, Maryland: Naval Institute Press, 1981.

Conway, Jill. *The Female Experience in Eighteenth– and Nineteenth–Century America: A Guide to the History of American Women.* Princeton, New Jersey: Princeton University Press, 1985.

Cordier, Mary Hurlbut, and Maria A. Perez-Stable. *Peoples of the American West: Historical Perspectives through Children's Literature.* Metuchen, New Jersey: Scarecrow, 1989.

Coughlan, Margaret N. *Creating Independence, 1763–1789; Background Reading for Young People; A Selected Annotated Bibliography.* Washington, D.C.: Library of Congress, 1972.

Deane, Paul. *Mirrors of American Culture: Children's Fiction Series in the Twentieth Century.* Metuchen, New Jersey: Scarecrow, 1991.

Eiss, Harry. *Literature for Young People on War and Peace.* New York: Greenwood, 1989.

Farish, Terry. "If You Knew Him, Please Write Me: Novels about War in Vietnam." *School Library Journal* 35:3 (November 1988), pp. 52–53.

Fitzgerald, Carol B. *American History: A Bibliographic Review.* Westport, Connecticut: Meckler, 1985–present.

Gephard, Ronald M. *Revolutionary America 1763–1789: A Bibliography.* Washington, D.C.: Government Printing Office, 1984.

Gerhardstein, Virginia B. *Dickinson's American Historical Fiction.* Metuchen, New Jersey: Scarecrow, 1986.

The Great Depression: A Historic Bibliography. Santa Barbara, California: ABC-CLIO, 1984.

Hathaway, Milton G. "The Second World War." *School Library Journal* 30:6 (February 1984), pp. 36–37.

Hotchkiss, Jeanette. *American Historical Fiction and Biography for Children and Young People.* Metuchen, New Jersey: Scarecrow, 1973.

———. *European Historical Fiction and Biography for Children and Young People.* Metuchen, New Jersey: Scarecrow, 1972.

Indochina Curriculum Group. *Vietnam Era: A Guide to Teaching Resources.* Cambridge, Massachusetts: Indochina Curriculum Group, 1978.

Junior High School Library Catalog. New York: H. W. Wilson, annual.

Kellogg, Jefferson B., and Robert H. Walker. *Sources for American Studies.* Westport, Connecticut: Greenwood, 1983.

Kinnell, Susan K., and Suzanne R. Ontiveros. *American Maritime History: A Bibliography.* Santa Barbara, California: ABC-CLIO, 1986.

Lane, Jack C. *America's Military Past: A Guide to Information Sources.* Detroit: Gale Research, 1980.

Link, Arthur. *The American Colonies in the Eighteenth Century.* Arlington Heights, Illinois: Harlan Davidson, 1969.

———. *The American Colonies in the Seventeenth Century.* Arlington Heights, Illinois: Harlan Davidson, 1971.

———. *American Diplomatic History before 1860.* Arlington Heights, Illinois: Harlan Davidson, 1971.

————. *American Economic History before 1860.* Arlington Heights, Illinois: Harlan Davidson, 1971.

————. *The American Revolution.* Arlington Heights, Illinois: Harlan Davidson, 1973.

————. *American Social History before 1860.* Arlington Heights, Illinois: Harlan Davidson, 1970.

————. *The Progressive Era and the Great War.* Arlington Heights, Illinois: Harlan Davidson, 1978.

Loeb, Catherine R., Susan E. Searing, and Esther F. Stineman. *Women's Studies: A Recommended Core Bibliography.* Littleton, Colorado: Libraries Unlimited, 1987.

Masterson, James R. *Writings on American History: A Subject Bibliography of Books and Monographs.* White Plains, New York: Kraus International, 1985.

Metzner, Seymour. *World History in Juvenile Books: A Geographical and Chronological Guide.* New York: H. W. Wilson, 1973.

Mittering, Philip I. *U.S. Cultural History: A Guide to Information Sources.* Detroit: Gale Research, 1980.

Morehead, Joe. *Introduction to United States Documents.* Littleton, Colorado: Libraries Unlimited, 1983.

Nevins, Allan, James I. Robertson, and Bell I. Wiley. *Civil War Books: A Critical Bibliography.* Wilmington, North Carolina: Broadfoot, 1984.

Newman, John. *Vietnam War Literature: An Annotated Bibliography of Imaginative Works about Americans Fighting in Vietnam.* Metuchen, New Jersey: Scarecrow, 1988.

Noffsinger, James Philip. *World War I Aviation Books in English: An Annotated Bibliography.* Metuchen, New Jersey: Scarecrow, 1987.

Peake, Louis A. *United States in the Vietnam War, 1954–1975: A Selected, Annotated Bibliography.* New York: Garland, 1986.

Read More about It: An Encyclopedia of Information Sources on Historical Figures and Events, Volume 3. Ann Arbor, Michigan: Pierian, 1989.

Reese, Lyn, and Jean Wilkinson. *Women in the World.: Annotated History Resources for the Secondary Student.* Metuchen, New Jersey: Scarecrow, 1987.

Senior High School Library Catalog. New York: H. W. Wilson, annual.

Smith, Myron J. *American Naval Bibliography, Volumes 1, 2, 4, 5.* Metuchen, New Jersey: Scarecrow, 1974.

———. *War Story Guide: An Annotated Bibliography of Military Fiction*. Metuchen, New Jersey: Scarecrow, 1980.

———. *World War II at Sea, Volumes 1–3*. Metuchen, New Jersey: Scarecrow, 1976.

Those Who Were There: Eyewitness Accounts of the War in Southeast Asia 1956–1975, and Aftermath; Annotated Bibliography of Books, Articles and Topical Magazines, Covering Writing Both Factual and Imaginative. Paradise, California: Dustbooks, 1984.

Van Meter, Vandelia. *American History for Children and Young Adults: An Annotated Bibliographic Index*. Littleton, Colorado: Libraries Unlimited, 1990.

———. *World History for Children and Young Adults: An Annotated Bibliographic Index*. Littleton, Colorado: Libraries Unlimited, 1991.

Wellner, Cathryn J. *Witness to War: A Thematic Guide to Young Adult Literature on World War II, 1965–1981*. Metuchen, New Jersey: Scarecrow, 1982.

Sample Activity Related to Real Historical Events: War

Reenactments of skirmishes and battles occur regularly at historical national battlefields around the United States. Groups and clubs form around interest in particular events, and individual group members costume themselves and engage in these reenactments to learn more. In general, there seems to be an interest in the historically accurate reconstruction of events that took place in the past. National park rangers retell stories about events that took place in the parks so that present-day visitors can understand the human significance of these places.

Many middle-grade students become interested in what happened before their lifetimes. Developmentally, these students are beginning to leave the isolation of self and emotional dependence on parents in order to venture into peer relationships. With this venturing comes a sense that there was a period before their own existence and that there is likely to be a future that they may help form.

Reenactments may be a perfect way to engage this interest. The classroom teacher and library media specialist may identify interested volunteers to help reenact some aspects of U.S. history. Reenactments can be simple retellings of what happened at a local historic place or more complicated re-creations of battles that took place during a given period of history. With the use of video cameras, students may participate in reenactments and then replay the tapes so they can see themselves in the roles that they have chosen.

This example involves a reenactment of a simple event that took place during the American Revolutionary War. The library media specialist collects a number of general materials about events during wartime, particularly the Revolutionary War. Students choose the period of time that they find interesting and participate in a reenactment specific to that period. In order to make their choices, the students need to read and discuss what they have read.

Following the first introduction to the idea, students are given time to browse through the general history sources and discuss areas of interest. At this time, the students talk in small groups and make choices about their areas of interest.

Next, the library media specialist introduces the students to a time line specifically related to the period of interest, using an outline from a general encyclopedia or another source. For this activity, a list of major events that took place during the Revolutionary War is presented because of the interest expressed by these particular students. A list of books and nonprint media is introduced and shared, using short teasers about each item. The library media specialist is careful to note the fiction versus nonfiction versions of stories. Students check the list so that they can begin reading and viewing some of the audiovisual programs.

In the meantime, the students are introduced to the videotape camera. In this case, a camcorder is chosen because it will be easy to carry while taping the reenactment. Some of the students are familiar with the use of the camera because their parents have such equipment at home. The library media specialist reviews camera operation for the students, and they practice operating the camera and shooting scenes in school. As they practice, they critique the results among themselves and with the library media specialist, who gives them hints about simple camera shots, such as zooming and panning. Students also have an opportunity to talk about the techniques for following action, moving with the camera, problems of sound while moving and recording the action, keeping the camera steady, and deciding on the interest point in the action.

The students meet with the classroom teacher to discuss the event they are interested in reenacting. Based on interests, the students group themselves to begin planning how they might do a reenactment. The classroom teacher provides them with an outline for planning that includes the things they must consider:

1. Description of event (sequence)
2. Setting
3. Time of day
4. Costumes
5. Equipment
6. Staging requirements
7. Actors/actresses and roles
8. Sources of information available about the event

The teacher may also point out that there may be some events that would be impossible to reenact, given available resources, actors, and time; the setting or staging required; and possible danger to students. (See Figure 7 for a sample planning considerations handout for students.)

As the students plan, they comprehend what is necessary. They carefully outline the event, the number of characters, the movements and actions of the characters, the time of day, the costumes and props needed, and the practice needed for staging the event to help them clarify what might be required. They also begin to feel the reality and impact of the event. After students outline the plan and, together with the library media specialist and classroom teacher, decide that it is feasible with the resources available, they begin sketching their script. The script will require a column for the actions of the people in the reenactment as well as a column for the camera operator(s). As the script is blocked out, the students will become more and more conscious of each element of the overall event they selected. The script will help them identify how to complete the reenactment safely.

Students will need to decide on the roles of individuals involved. For example, if a battle is selected, a director of the action must be selected as well as the camera operator, the actors in the event, and so on. Using the script, the students will need to practice their actions. Depending on the event chosen, there may or may

Planning Considerations

Description of Event (Sequence):

Setting:

Time of Day:

Costumes:

Equipment:

Staging Requirements:

Actors/Actresses and Roles:

Sources of Information Available about the Event:

Figure 7. Sample Planning Considerations Handout for Students

not be specific dialogue. If there is, the students must research this as closely as possible.

As the script is drafted, the students begin research to make the various elements of the reenactment as authentic as possible. Sources that give the exact movements of the event will be most helpful. Pictures or illustrations should be identified. Other works that have portrayed the event should be viewed for authenticity and accuracy as well as for ideas on how the students might stage the event. Students may talk about what makes something seem real in films. Books on costumes, architecture, scenery, music, food, and so on may be used with the library media specialist's help. Parent volunteers may help the students if desired in collecting materials and making the necessary props.

Practice and refinement will be required before the final event. The camera operator may sketch out and refine how the scene will be taped, although what originally may be considered the best angle or position is often changed during actual taping. Finally the materials are gathered, places are set, and the reenactment is staged. When the taping is completed, the students may make title frames and do some editing, if necessary.

Student Resources Related to War

The following list of books related to wars fought in or by the United States represents a wide range in interest, age level, and reading ability. A subject approach suggests that there should be an even wider readability range allowed than usual. Students may explore materials that are difficult, because their interest often transcends the difficulty of the material. Also, as the students expand their background knowledge, they look for more details about the topic with which they are unfamiliar. This motivates them to search for more difficult material to add factual information to their mental databases. Films and other nonprint materials are suggested here for support of the reading materials.

Because this is such a large topic, the materials suggested here represent only some of the available items. Other sources should be selected as students search for more specific information.

General

Professional

Dougall, Lucy. *War and Peace in Literature: Prose, Drama and Poetry Which Illuminate the Problem of War*. Chicago: World without War, 1982.

Dowling, John. *War/Peace: Film Guide*. Chicago: World without War, 1980.

Gregory, Donna. *The Nuclear Predicament: A Sourcebook*. New York: St. Martin's, 1986.

Greiner, Rosemarie. *Peace Education: A Bibliography Focusing on Young Children*. Santa Cruz, California: Peace Education/Eschaton Foundation, 1983.

Fiction

(IL Signifies Interest Level; RL Signifies Fry Readability Level)

Davies, Andrew. *Conrad's War*. New York: Crown, 1980. IL: 5–8.

Nonfiction

Ardley, Neil. *Future War and Weapons*. New York: Watts, 1982. IL: 6–8.

Cohen, Daniel. *The Ghosts of War*. New York: Putnam, 1990. IL: 6–8.

Dunnigan, James F., and William Martel. *How To Stop a War: Lessons of Two Hundred Years of War and Peace*. Garden City, New York: Doubleday, 1987. IL: 5–8.

Forman, James D. *That Mad Game: War and the Chances for Peace*. New York: Macmillan, 1980. IL: 7–9.

U.S. French and Indian War, 1755–1763

Fiction

Cassel, Virginia C. *Juniata Valley*. New York: Viking, 1981. IL: 6–9.

Edmonds, Walter D. *The Matchlock Gun*. New York: Dodd, 1941. IL: 4–6. RL: 6.

Field, Rachel. *Calico Bush*. New York: Macmillan, 1931. IL: 4–7. RL: 7.

Henty, G. A. *With Wolfe in Canada: Winning of a Continent*. New York: Walker, 1963. IL: 6–9.

Peck, Robert Newton. *Fawn*. Boston: Little, Brown, 1975. IL: 7–9.

Speare, Elizabeth George. *Calico Captive*. Boston: Houghton Mifflin, 1957. IL: 4–7. RL: 7.

Nonfiction

Gauch, Patricia Lee. *The Impossible Major Rogers*. New York: Putnam, 1977. IL: 4–6.

Marrin, Albert. *Struggle for a Continent: The French and Indian Wars*. New York: Atheneum, 1987. IL: 5–8.

Nonprint

The American Story: War for Empire. Dallas: Dallas Community College, 1985. (Distributed by GPN.) (30-min. videocassette)

The Matchlock Gun. Hightstown, New Jersey: Newbery Medal Award/American School, 1971. (2 sound filmstrips)

U.S. Revolutionary War

Fiction

Avi. *The Fighting Gourd*. Philadelphia: J. B. Lippincott, 1984. IL: 4–8. RL: 5.

Beatty, John. *Who Comes to King's Mountain*. New York: Morrow, 1975. IL: 6–9+.

Brady, Esther W. *Toliver's Secret*. New York: Crown, 1976. IL: 4–6. RL: 4.

Butters, Dorothy Gilman. *The Bells of Freedom*. Magnolia, Massachusetts: Peter Smith, 1984. IL: 8–9+.

Cavanna, Betty. *Ruffles and Drums*. New York: Morrow, 1975. IL: 6–8.

Cheney, Cora. *Christmas Tree Hessian*. New York: Holt, 1976. IL: 4–6.

Clapp, Patricia. *I'm Deborah Sampson: A Soldier in the War of the Revolution*. New York: Lothrop, Lee & Shepard, 1977. IL: 5–8.

Collier, James Lincoln, and Christopher Collier. *The Bloody Country*. New York: Scholastic, 1976. IL: 7–9. RL: 6.

———. *My Brother Sam Is Dead*. New York: Four Winds, 1974. IL: 6–9. RL: 6.

———. *War Comes to Willy Freeman.* New York: Delacorte, 1984. IL: 5–7. RL: 6.

Cornwell, Bernard. *Redcoat.* New York: Viking, 1988. IL: 8–9+.

Cover, Arthur Byron. *American Revolutionary.* New York: Bantam, 1985. IL: 5–9.

DeFord, Deborah H. *An Enemy Among Them.* Boston: Houghton Mifflin, 1987. IL: 6–9.

Edwards, Sally. *George Midgett's War.* New York: Scribner's, 1985. IL: 5–8. RL: 4.

Epstein, Samuel. *Change for a Penny.* New York: Coward, 1959. IL: 5–8.

Fast, Howard. *April Morning.* New York: Crown, 1961. IL: 6–8. RL: 5.

———. *The Hessian.* New York: Morrow, 1972. IL: 7–9.

Finlayson, Anne. *Rebecca's War.* New York: Warner, 1972. IL: 5–7. RL: 7.

Forbes, Esther. *Johnny Tremain: A Novel for Old and Young.* Boston: Houghton Mifflin, 1943. IL: 5–8. RL: 5.

Fritz, Jean. *Early Thunder.* New York: Putnam, 1967. IL: 5–8. RL: 6.

Gauch, Patricia Lee. *This Time, Tempe Wick?* New York: Coward, 1974. IL: 3–6. RL: 7.

Haugaard, Erik Christian. *A Boy's Will.* Boston: Houghton Mifflin, 1983. IL: 5–7.

Hones, Peter. *Rebel in the Night.* New York: Dial, 1971. IL: 7–9.

Lawrence, Mildred. *Touchmark.* New York: Harcourt, 1975. IL: 6–8. RL: 7.

Lawson, Robert. *Mr. Revere and I.* Boston: Little, Brown, 1953. IL: 5–7. RL: 7.

Marko, Katherine McGlade. *Away to Fundy Bay.* New York: Walker, 1985. IL: 5–8.

O'Dell, Scott. *Sarah Bishop.* Boston: Houghton Mifflin, 1980. IL: 5–8. RL: 7.

Pope, E. M. *The Sherwood Ring.* Boston: Houghton Mifflin, 1985. IL: 6–9+.

Rinaldi, Ann. *Time Enough for Drums.* New York: Holiday, 1986. IL: 6–8. RL: 6.

Steele, William O. *Man with the Silver Eyes.* New York: Harcourt, 1976. IL: 4–7. RL: 5.

Wibberley, Leonard. *John Treegate's Musket.* New York: Farrar, 1959. IL: 5–8.

Nonfiction

Alderman, Clifford Lindsay. *The Dark Eagle: The Story of Benedict Arnold.* New York: Macmillan, 1976. IL: 5–8.

Birnbaum, Louis. *Red Dawn at Lexington: "If They Mean To Have a War, Let It Begin Here!"* Boston: Houghton Mifflin, 1986. IL: 8–9+.

Bliven, Bruce. *The American Revolution, 1760–1783.* New York: Random House, 1981. IL: 5–8. RL: 5.

Carmer, Carl. *The Boy Drummer of Vincennes.* New York: Harvey House, 1972. IL: 4–8.

Chidsey, Donald Barr. *The World of Samuel Adams.* New York: Elsevier/Nelson, 1974. IL: 5–8.

Clinton, Susan. *The Story of the Green Mountain Boys.* Chicago: Children's Press, 1988. IL: 4–6.

Colby, Jean Poindexter. *Lexington and Concord, 1775: What Really Happened.* New York: Hastings House, 1975. IL: 5–7.

Davis, Burke. *Black Heroes of the American Revolution.* New York: Harcourt, 1976. IL: 5–8.

———. *Heroes of the American Revolution.* New York: Random House, 1971. IL: 5–7.

Ford, Barbara. *Underwater Dig: The Excavation of a Revolutionary War Privateer.* New York: Morrow, 1982. IL: 5–9.

Fritz, Jean. *Traitor: The Case of Benedict Arnold.* New York: Putnam, 1981. IL: 5–8. RL: 5.

Holbrook, Stewart. *America's Ethan Allen.* Boston: Houghton Mifflin, 1949. IL: 4–6.

Holley, Erica. *The American Revolution.* Washington, D.C.: Dryad, 1986. IL: 7–9.

Lomask, Milton. *The First American Revolution.* New York: Farrar, 1974. IL: 6–8.

Marrin, Albert. *The War for Independence.* New York: Atheneum, 1988. IL: 6–8.

Mason, F. Van Dyke. *The Winter at Valley Forge.* New York: Random House, 1953. IL: 5–8.

McGovern, Ann. *Secret Soldier: The Story of Deborah Sampson.* New York: Four Winds, 1975. IL: 5–7. RL: 5.

McPhillips, Martin. *The Battle of Trenton.* New York: Silver Burdett, 1985. IL: 7–9.

Meltzer, Milton. *American Revolutionaries: A History in Their Words.* New York: Harper, 1987. IL: 6–8.

Middlekauff, Robert. *Glorious Cause: The American Revolution, 1763–1789.* New York: Oxford University Press, 1982. IL: 8–9+.

Mollo, John. *Uniforms of the American Revolution.* New York: Sterling, 1985. IL: 7–9+.

Morris, Richard B. *The American Revolution.* Minneapolis: Lerner, 1985. IL: 4–6.

Nelson, Paul David. *Anthony Wayne: Soldier of the Early Republic.* Bloomington: Indiana University Press, 1985. IL: 8–9+.

Pearson, Michael. *Those Yankee Rebels.* New York: Putnam, 1974. IL: 7–9.

Phelan, Mary Kay. *Midnight Alarm: The Story of Paul Revere's Ride.* New York: Crowell, 1968. IL: 4–6.

———. *The Story of the Boston Massacre.* New York: Crowell, 1976. IL: 6–8.

Stein, R. Conrad. *The Story of Lexington and Concord.* Chicago: Children's Press, 1983. IL: 4–6.

———. *The Story of Valley Forge.* Chicago: Children's Press, 1985. IL: 4–6.

Tuchman, Barbara. *The First Salute.* New York: Alfred A. Knopf, 1988. IL: 9+.

Nonprint

The American Revolution: 1770–1773, A Conversation with Lord North. New York: CBS, 1971. (33-min. 16mm film)

The American Revolution: The Impossible War. Deerfield, Illinois: Learning Corporation of America, 1972. (25-min. videocassette)

The American Revolution: The War Years. Deerfield, Illinois: Coronet Instructional Films, 1975. (10-min. videocassette)

American Scrapbook: The World Turned Upside Down. Cleveland, Ohio: WVIZ, 1976. (Distributed by GPN.) (15-min. videocassette)

The American Story: Colonials and Redcoats. Dallas: Dallas Community College, 1985. (Distributed by GPN.) (30-min. videocassette)

The American Story: Declaring Independence. Dallas: Dallas Community College, 1985. (Distributed by GPN.) (30-min. videocassette)

The American Story: Road to Revolution. Dallas: Dallas Community College, 1985. (Distributed by GPN.) (30-min. videocassette)

The American Story: Victory at Yorktown. Dallas: Dallas Community College, 1985. (Distributed by GPN.) (30-min. videocassette)

Battle of Yorktown. New York: BFA Educational Media, 1983. (30-min. videocassette)

Hard Winter. Morristown, New Jersey: Morris County Historical Society, 1984. (Distributed by GPN.) (59-min. videocassette)

Johnny Tremain and the Sons of Liberty. Deerfield, Illinois: Walt Disney/Coronet/MTI Film and Video, 1958. (85-min. videocassette)

Making a Revolution. Paramus, New Jersey: Time/Life, 1972. (52-min. videocassette)

My Brother Sam Is Dead. Hightstown, New Jersey: Newbery Award Media/American School Publishers, 1976. (26-min. videocassette)

Stories and Poems from Long Ago: Heroes and Heroines of the American Revolution. New York: Children's Television International, 1990. (Distributed by GPN.) (15-min. videocassette)

Stories and Poems from Long Ago: The War for Independence. New York: Children's Television International, 1990. (Distributed by GPN.) (15-min. videocassette)

U.S. War of 1812

Fiction

Brady, Esther W. *The Toad on Capitol Hill.* New York: Crown, 1978. IL: 4–6. RL: 4.

Forester, C. S. *The Captain from Connecticut.* Boston: Little, Brown, 1941. IL: 7–9.

Wibberley, Leonard. *Leopard's Prey.* New York: Farrar, 1971. IL: 6–9.

Nonfiction

Marrin, Albert. *1812: The War Nobody Won.* New York: Atheneum, 1985. IL: 5–9.

Morris, Richard B. *The War of 1812.* Minneapolis: Lerner, 1985. IL: 4–7.

Orlob, Helen. *The Commodores's Boys: Naval Campaigns of the War of 1812.* Philadelphia: Westminster, 1967. IL: 6–8.

Phelan, Mary Kay. *The Burning of Washington: August 1814.* New York: Crowell, 1975. IL: 5–7.

Richards, Norman. *The Story of Old Ironsides.* Chicago: Children's Press, 1967. IL: 5–8.

Stein, R. Conrad. *The Story of the Burning of Washington.* Chicago: Children's Press, 1985. IL: 4–6.

Nonprint

The American Story: War of 1812. Dallas: Dallas Community College, 1985. (Distributed by GPN.) (30-min. videocassette)

The Defense of Fort McHenry. Culver City, California: Zenger Video, 1985. (17-min. videocassette)

War of 1812. Deerfield, Illinois: Coronet Films, 1982. (14-min. videocassette)

War of 1812. Washington, D.C.: Creative Arts Studio for the U.S. Government, 1960. (20-min. 16mm film)

War of 1812. Del Mar, California: McGraw-Hill, 1960. (15-min. 16mm film)

U.S. Civil War

Fiction

Beatty, Patricia. *Charley Skedaddle.* New York: Morrow, 1987. IL: 5–8. RL: 5.

——. *Turn Homeward, Hannalee.* New York: Morrow, 1984. IL: 5–8.

Brenner, Barbara. *Saving the President: What If Lincoln Had Lived?* New York: Messner, 1988. IL: 5–8. RL: 5.

Brown, Dee Alexander. *Conspiracy of Knaves.* New York: Holt, 1987. IL: 8–9+.

Burchard, Peter. *The Deserter: A Spy Story of the Civil War.* New York: Crowell, 1973. IL: 5–8.

Clapp, Patricia. *Tamarack Tree: A Novel of the Siege of Vicksburg.* New York: Lothrop, Lee & Shepard, 1986. IL: 7–9.

Climo, Shirley. *A Month of Seven Days.* New York: Harper, 1987. IL: 5–7.

Crane, Stephen. *The Red Badge of Courage.* New York: Dodd, 1979. IL: 7–9+. RL: 6.

Cummings, Betty Sue. *Hew against the Grain.* New York: Atheneum, 1977. IL: 6–9.

Davis, Paxton. *Three Days*. New York: Atheneum, 1980. IL: 7–9.

Forman, James. *Song of Jubilee*. New York: Farrar, 1971. IL: 7–9.

Gauch, Patricia. *Thunder at Gettysburg*. New York: Crowell, 1975. IL: 5–7.

Hansen, Joyce. *Which Way Freedom*. New York: Walker, 1986. IL: 5–8.

Haugaard, Erik. *Orphans of the Wind*. Boston: Houghton Mifflin, 1966. IL: 6–8.

Hunt, Irene. *Across Five Aprils*. Chicago: Follett, 1964. IL: 5–8.

Jones, Douglas C. *Barefoot Brigade*. New York: Holt, 1982. IL: 7–9.

Keith, Harold. *Rifles for Watie*. New York: Harper, 1987. IL: 6–8. RL: 7.

O'Dell, Scott. *Sarah Bishop*. Boston: Houghton Mifflin, 1980. IL: 7–9. RL: 7.

———. *The 290*. Boston: Houghton Mifflin, 1976. IL: 6–8. RL: 7.

Shore, Laura Jan. *Sacred Moon Tree: Being the True Account of the Trials and Adventures of Phoebe Sands in the Great War between the States, 1861–1865*. New York: Bradbury, 1986. IL: 6–8.

Steele, William O. *The Perilous Road*. New York: Harcourt, 1958. IL: 5–8.

Wisner, G. Clifton. *Thunder on the Tennessee*. New York: Lodestar, 1983. IL: 4–7.

Yep, Laurence. *Mark Twain Murders*. New York: Four Winds, 1982. IL: 6–9.

———. *The Tom Sawyer Files*. New York: Morrow, 1984. IL: 5–8.

Nonfiction

Altsheler, J. A. *The Guns of Shiloh*. New York: Appleton, 1976. IL: 7–9.

———. *The Rock of Chickamauga*. New York: Appleton, 1976. IL: 7–9.

———. *The Scouts of Stonewall*. New York: Appleton, 1976. IL: 7–9.

———. *The Shades of the Wilderness*. New York: Appleton, 1976. IL: 7–9.

———. *The Star of Gettysburg*. New York: Appleton, 1976. IL: 7–9.

———. *The Sword of Antietam*. New York: Appleton, 1976. IL: 7–9.

———. *The Tree of Appomattox*. New York: Appleton, 1976. IL: 7–9.

Batty, Peter. *Divided Union: The Story of the Great American War, 1861–65*. Englewood Cliffs, New Jersey: Salem, 1987. IL: 8–9+.

Boylston, Helen. *Clara Barton, Founder of the American Red Cross*. New York: Random House, 1955. IL: 4–7.

Bruns, Roger. *Abraham Lincoln*. New York: Chelsea House, 1986. IL: 6–9.

Catton, Bruce. *The American Heritage Picture History of the Civil War*. Garden City, New York: Doubleday, 1960. IL: 5–9+.

———. *The Battle of Gettysburg*. New York: American Heritage, 1963. IL: 7–9+.

———. *Reflections on the Civil War*. Garden City, New York: Doubleday, 1981. IL: 8–9+.

———. *Stillness at Appomattox*. Garden City, New York: Doubleday, 1953. IL: 8–9+. RL: 8.

The Civil War Series. New York: Time/Life. (Check for individual titles.)

Civil War: Soldiers and Civilians. Boca Raton, Florida: Social Issues Resources Series, 1982. IL: 7–9+.

Clara Barton. Washington, D.C.: National Park Service, 1981. IL: 8–9+.

Coffey, Vincent J. *The Battle of Gettysburg*. New York: Silver Burdett, 1985. IL: 4–6.

Commager, Henry Steele. *America's Robert E. Lee*. Boston: Houghton Mifflin, 1951. IL: 5–7.

Davis, Burke. *Appomattox: Closing Struggle of the Civil War*. New York: Harper, 1963. IL: 6–9.

DeGrummond, L. Y. *Jeb Stewart*. Philadelphia: J. B. Lippincott, 1979. IL: 5–7.

Donovan, Timothy H. *The American Civil War*. Wayne, New Jersey: Avery, 1987. IL: 8–9+.

Faust, Patricia L. *Historical Times Illustrated Encyclopedia of the Civil War*. New York: Harper, 1986. IL: 8–9+.

Fleming, Thomas. *Band of Brothers: West Point in the Civil War*. New York: Walker, 1988. IL: 6–8.

Fritz, Jean. *Stonewall*. New York: Putnam, 1979. IL: 5–8. RL: 8.

Garrison, Webb. *The Treasury of Civil War Tales*. New York: Rutledge Hill, 1988. IL: 8–9+.

Hamilton, Leni. *Clara Barton*. New York: Chelsea House, 1987. IL: 5–8.

Hattaway, Herman. *How the North Won: A Military History of the Civil War*. Urbana: University of Illinois Press, 1983. IL: 8–9+.

Haythornthwaite, Philip. *Uniforms of the American Civil War*. New York: Blandford, 1985. IL: 8–9+.

Kent, Zachary. *The Story of Clara Barton*. Chicago: Children's Press, 1987. IL: 3–6.

————. *The Story of Sherman's March to the Sea*. Chicago: Children's Press, 1987. IL: 4–6.

————. *The Story of the Surrender at Appomattox Court House*. Chicago: Children's Press, 1988. IL: 3–6.

Lee, Susan Dye. *Jefferson Davis*. Chicago: Children's Press, 1978. IL: 3–6.

McDonough, James L. *War So Terrible: Sherman and Atlanta*. New York: W. W. Norton, 1987. IL: 8–9+.

McNeer, May. *America's Abraham Lincoln*. Boston: Houghton Mifflin, 1957. IL: 5–7.

McPherson, James M. *Ordeal by Fire: The Civil War and Reconstruction*. New York: Alfred A. Knopf, 1982. IL: 8–9+.

Miers, Earl Schenck. *Lincoln in Peace and War*. New York: American Heritage, 1964. IL: 7–9+.

North, Sterling. *Abe Lincoln, Log Cabin to the White House*. New York: Random House, 1956. IL: 5–7.

Perez, N. A. *The Slopes of War*. Boston: Houghton Mifflin, 1984. IL: 5–7.

Phelan, Mary Kay. *Mr. Lincoln's Inaugural Journey*. New York: Crowell, 1972. IL: 5–8.

Reit, Seymour. *Behind Rebel Lines: The Incredible Story of Emma Edmonds, Civil War Spy*. New York: Harcourt, 1988. IL: 5–8.

————. *Ironclad! A True Story of the Civil War*. New York: Dodd, 1977. IL: 4–6.

Sifakis, Stewart. *Who Was Who in the Civil War*. New York: Facts on File, 1988. IL: 8–9+.

Smith, Page. *Trial by Fire: A People's History of the Civil War and Reconstruction*. New York: McGraw-Hill, 1982. IL: 8–9+.

Stein, R. Conrad. *The Story of the Monitor and the Merrimack*. Chicago: Children's Press, 1983. IL: 4–7.

Straubing, Harold Elk. *Civil War Eyewitness Reports*. Hamden, Connecticut: Shoe String, 1985. IL: 8–9+.

Warner, Ezra J. *Generals in Blue: Lives of the Union Commanders*. Baton Rouge: Louisiana State University Press, 1964. IL: 8–9+.

Weidhorn, Manfred. *Robert E. Lee*. New York: Atheneum, 1988. IL: 5–8.

Windrow, Martin. *The Civil War Rifleman*. New York: Watts, 1986. IL: 5–8.

Nonprint

Across Five Aprils. Hightstown, New Jersey: Miller-Brody Productions/American School, 1974. (30-min. videocassette)

America Divided: The Civil War and Reconstruction. Chicago: Encyclopedia Britannica Educational Corporation, 1984. (4 15-min. sound filmstrips)

American Scrapbook: Appomattox Courthouse, August 1865. Cleveland, Ohio: WVIZ, 1976. (Distributed by GPN.) (15-min. videocassette)

The American Story: The Blue and the Grey. Dallas: Dallas Community College, 1985. (Distributed by GPN.) (30-min. videocassette)

The American Story: Eve of Conflict. Dallas: Dallas Community College, 1985. (Distributed by GPN.) (30-min. videocassette)

The American Story: Road to Appomattox. Dallas: Dallas Community College, 1985. (Distributed by GPN.) (30-min. videocassette)

The Blue and the Gray. Burbank, California: Columbia, 1982. (2 95-min. videocassettes)

Carl Sandburg at Gettysburg. New York: Carousel, 1961. (28-min. 16mm film)

Civil War Series. Deerfield, Illinois: Coronet Films, 1983. (4 20-min. videocassettes)

Civil War: The Anguish of Emancipation. Deerfield, Illinois: Learning Corporation of America, 1983. (27-min. videocassette)

The Civil War: Two Views. Pleasantville, New York: Educational Audio Visual, 1986. (75-min. videocassette)

Classic Short Stories: "An Occurrence at Owl Creek Bridge." New York: Children's Television International, 1989. (Distributed by GPN.) (30-min. videocassette)

The Confederacy. XLP 30159-1BB. Burbank, California: Columbia. (60-min. sound recording)

Different Drummers: Blacks in the Military. Chicago: Films Incorporated, 1984. (3 58-min. videocassettes)

Down to the Monitor. Culver City, California: Zenger Videos, 1980. (24-min. videocassette)

The Fall of Fort Sumter. Mount Kisco, New York: Guidance Associates, 1987. (30-min. videocassette)

Fredericksburg and Chancellorsville: The Bloody Road to Richmond. Culver City, California: Zenger Videos, 1982. (12-min. videocassette)

From These Honored Dead. Culver City, California: Zenger Videos, 1969. (Distributed by National Audio Visual Center.) (13-min. videocassette)

Gettysburg: The Video History of the Civil War. Culver City, California: Zenger Video, 1987. (27-min. videocassette)

Gone with the Wind. New York: MGM, 1939. (231-min. videocassette)

Lincoln's Gettysburg Address. Van Nuys, California: Oxford Films/AIMS Media. (15-min. videocassette)

The Union. XLP 39101-LB. New York: Columbia. (60-min. sound recording)

Visit in the Past with Robert E. Lee. New York: BFA Educational Media, 1990. (20-min. 16mm film)

Walt Whitman's Civil War. Los Angeles: Churchill Films, 1972. (15-min. videocassette)

Wilson's Creek. Capital Heights, Maryland: National Audio Visual Center, 1985. (15-min. videocassette)

Native American Wars

Fiction

Gall, Grant. *Apache: The Long Ride Home.* Santa Fe, New Mexico: Sunstone, 1988. IL: 7–9.

Jones, Douglas. *Arrest Sitting Bull.* New York: Scribner's, 1977. IL: 8–9+.

Jones, Weyman. *Edge of Two Worlds.* New York: Dial, 1968. IL: 5–8. RL: 5.

Lampman, Evelyn Sibley. *White Captives.* New York: Atheneum, 1975. IL: 5–7.

Nonfiction

Benchley, Nathaniel. *Only Earth and Sky Last Forever.* New York: Harper, 1972. IL: 7–9.

Boring, Mel. *Wovoka.* New York: Dillon, 1981. IL: 4–7.

Brown, Dee Alexander. *Bury My Heart at Wounded Knee: An Indian History of the American West.* New York: Holt, 1971. IL: 8–9+.

Forman, James D. *The Life and Death of Yellow Bird.* New York: Farrar, 1973. IL: 6–9.

Hilts, Len. *Quanah Parker.* New York: Gulliver, 1987. IL: 5–9.

Marrin, Albert. *War Clouds in the West: Indians and Cavalrymen, 1860–1890.* New York: Atheneum, 1984. IL: 6–8.

McGaw, Jessie Brewer. *Chief Red Horse Tells about Custer: The Battle of the Little Big Horn—An Eyewitness Account Told in Indian Sign Language.* New York: Elsevier/Nelson, 1981. IL: 5–8.

Nabokov, Peter. *Native American Testimony: An Anthology of Indian and White Relations.* New York: Harper, 1979. IL: 6–9. RL: 7.

Pollock, Dean. *Joseph, Chief of the Nez Perce.* Portland, Oregon: Binfords, 1950. IL: 5–7.

Stein, R. Conrad. *The Story of Little Bighorn.* Chicago: Children's Press, 1983. IL: 3–6.

———. *The Story of Wounded Knee.* Chicago: Children's Press, 1983. IL: 3–6.

Nonprint

There are many films and videotapes available that are related to conflicts with Native Americans. It should be noted that many are biased toward one side or the other. Introduction of these materials might include discussion of point of view, bias, and stereotyping. This is an excellent way of encouraging students to document and compare ideas presented.

Great Plains Experience: Clash of Cultures. Lincoln, Nebraska: University of Mid-America, 1976. (Distributed by GPN.) (30-min. videocassette)

History Recovered: The Custer Battlefield Archaeological Survey of 1984. Culver City, California: Zenger Video, 1985. (58-min. videocassette)

The Indian Wars. Dimondale, Michigan: Hartley Courseware. (computer simulation for Apple or IBM)

Spanish-American War

Nonfiction

Azoy, Anastasio Carlos Mariano. *Charge! The Story of the Battle of San Juan Hill.* New York: Longman, 1961. IL: 8–9+.

Brown, Charles Henry. *The Correspondent's War–Journalism in the Spanish American War.* New York: Scribner's, 1967. IL: 8–9+.

Kent, Zachary. *The Story of the Sinking of the Battleship Maine.* Chicago: Children's Press, 1988. IL: 3–6.

Lawson, Don. *The United States in the Spanish-American War.* New York: Abelard-Schuman, 1976. IL: 8–9+.

Roosevelt, Theodore. *The Rough Riders.* New York: Scribner's, 1899. IL: 8–9+.

Trask, David F. *The War with Spain in 1898.* New York: Macmillan, 1981. IL: 8–9+.

Nonprint

The Spanish American War. Santa Clara, California: History Simulations. (simulation game)

World War I

Fiction

Cameron, Eleanor. *The Private Worlds of Julia Redfern.* New York: Dutton, 1988. IL: 6–8.

———. *That Julia Redfern.* New York: Dutton, 1982. IL: 6–8.

Hemingway, Ernest. *A Farewell to Arms.* New York: Scribner's, 1929. IL: 8–9+.

Rostkowski, Margaret I. *After the Dancing Days.* New York: Harper, 1986. IL: 6–9.

Voight, Cynthia. *Tree by Leaf.* New York: Atheneum, 1988. IL: 6–8.

Nonfiction

Barnett, Correlli. *The Great War.* New York: Putnam, 1980. IL: 8–9+.

Bowen, Ezra. *Knights of the Air.* New York: Time/Life, 1980. IL: 8–9+.

Colby, C. B. *Fighting Gear of World War I: Equipment and Weapons of the American Doughboy.* New York: Coward, 1961. IL: 4–7.

Cowley, Robert. *1918: Gamble for Victory; The Greatest Attack of World War I.* New York: Macmillan, 1964. IL: 5–7.

Everett, Susan. *World War I: An Illustrated History.* New York: Rand McNally, 1980. IL: 8–9+.

Gilchrist, Cherry. *Finding Out about Britain in World War One.* North Pomfret, Vermont: David & Charles, 1985. IL: 6–8.

Hoobler, Dorothy, and Thomas Hoobler. *An Album of World War I.* New York: Watts, 1976. IL: 5–8. RL: 7.

————. *The Trenches: Fighting on the Western Front in World War I.* New York: Putnam, 1978. IL: 6–9.

Huggett, Renee. *Growing Up in the First World War.* North Pomfret, Vermont: David & Charles, 1985. IL: 6–8.

Marrin, Albert. *The Yanks Are Coming: The United States in the First World War.* New York: Atheneum, 1986. IL: 6–8.

Maynard, Christopher. *Aces: Pilots and Planes of World War I.* New York: Watts, 1987. IL: 8–9+.

Mee, Charles. *End of Order: Versailles 1919.* New York: Elsevier/Dutton, 1980. IL: 8–9+.

Miguel, Pierre. *World War I.* New York: Silver Burdett, 1986. IL: 5–7.

Nordhoff, C. B. *Falcons of France: A Tale of Youth and Air.* Boston: Little, Brown, 1929. IL: 7–9.

Pimlott, John. *The First World War.* New York: Watts, 1986. IL: 6–9.

Snyder, Louis Leo. *World War I.* New York: Watts, 1981. IL: 4–7.

Stein, R. Conrad. *The Story of the Lafayette Escadrilles.* Chicago: Children's Press, 1983. IL: 4–6.

Stokesbury, James L. *A Short History of World War I.* New York: Morrow, 1981. IL: 8–9+.

Tames, Richard. *The Great War.* North Pomfret, Vermont: David & Charles, 1984. IL: 7–9.

Wright, Nicholas. *Red Baron.* New York: McGraw-Hill, 1977. IL: 6–8. RL: 8.

Nonprint

Goodbye Billy: America Goes to War, 1917–1918. Los Angeles: Churchill Films, 1972. (25-min. videocassette)

Witness to History Series. Mount Kisco, New York: Associated Press, 1987. (4 20-min. videocassettes)

World War II

Fiction

Arnold, Elliott. *A Kind of Secret Weapon.* New York: Scribner's, 1969. IL: 6–8.

Arnothy, Christine. *I Am Fifteen and I Don't Want To Die.* New York: Scholastic, 1986. IL: 7–9.

Baklanov, G. *Forever Nineteen.* New York: Harper, 1989. IL: 7–9.

Balderson, Margaret. *When Jays Fly to Barbmo.* Boston: Gregg, 1980. IL: 5–7. RL: 7.

Benary-Isbert, M. *The Ark.* New York: Harcourt, 1958. IL: 6–8.

———. *Castle on the Border.* New York: Harcourt, 1956. IL: 6–8.

———. *Dangerous Spring.* New York: Harcourt, 1961. IL: 6–8.

Benchley, Nathaniel. *Bright Candles: A Novel of the Danish Resistance.* New York: Harper, 1974. IL: 6–8.

———. *A Necessary End: A Novel of World War II.* New York: Harper, 1976. IL: 6–8.

Bishop, Claire. *Twenty and Ten.* New York: Viking, 1961. IL: 5–7.

Bloch, Marie. *Displaced Person.* New York: Lothrop, Lee & Shepard, 1978. IL: 5–7. RL: 7.

Bonham, Frank. *Burma Rifles.* New York: Crowell, 1960. IL: 5–7.

Brancato, Robin. *Don't Sit Under the Apple Tree.* New York: Random House, 1975. IL: 5–7. RL: 5.

Bruckner, Karl. *The Day of the Bomb.* New York: Van Nostrand, 1962. IL: 6–8.

Chaikin, Miriam. *Friends Forever.* New York: Harper, 1988. IL: 5–7.

Chalker, Jack L. *Devil's Voyage: A Novel about Treachery, Heroism, Sharks and the Bomb.* Garden City, New York: Doubleday, 1981. IL: 8–9+.

Coerr, Eleanor. *Sadako and the Thousand Cranes.* New York: Putnam, 1977. IL: 4–6.

Cooper, Susan. *Dawn of Fear.* New York: Macmillan, 1989. IL: 6–8.

Cowan, Lore. *Children of the Resistance.* Des Moines, Iowa: Meredith, 1969. IL: 6–8.

Dank, Milton. *The Dangerous Game.* Philadelphia: J. B. Lippincott, 1981. IL: 7–9.

Degens, T. *Transport 7-41-R.* New York: Viking, 1976. IL: 6–8.

DeJong, Meindert. *House of Sixty Fathers.* New York: Harper, 1956. IL: 4–6. RL: 7.

Ferry, Charles. *One More Time.* Boston: Houghton Mifflin, 1985. IL: 7–9.

———. *Raspberry One.* Boston: Houghton Mifflin, 1983. IL: 7–9.

Forman, James. *Ceremony of Innocence.* New York: Hawthorne, 1970. IL: 7–9.

———. *The Traitors.* New York: Farrar, 1968. IL: 7–9.

Green, Wayne L. *Allegiance.* New York: Crown, 1983. IL: 8–9+.

Greene, Bette. *Morning Is a Long Time Coming*. New York: Dial, 1978.
IL: 6–8. RL: 6.

———. *Summer of My German Soldier*. New York: Dial, 1973. IL: 6–8.
RL: 7.

Haugaard, Erik. *The Little Fishes*. Boston: Houghton Mifflin, 1967.
IL: 6–8.

Hickman, Janet. *The Stones*. New York: Macmillan, 1976. IL: 4–6.
RL: 4.

Kaminsky, Stuart M. *The Fala Factor*. New York: St. Martin's, 1984.
IL: 8–9+.

———. *Smart Moves*. New York: St. Martin's, 1987. IL: 8–9+.

Kerr, M. E. *Gentlehands*. New York: Harper, 1979. IL: 8–9+. RL: 5.

———. *When Hitler Stole Pink Rabbit*. New York: Putnam, 1972.
IL: 5–8. RL: 7.

Leffland, Ella. *Rumors of Peace*. New York: Harper, 1979. IL: 8–9+.

Levoy, Myron. *Alan and Naomi*. New York: Harper, 1977. IL: 5–8.
RL: 6.

Lisle, Janet Taylor. *Sirens and Spies*. New York: Bradbury, 1985.
IL: 7–9.

Lowry, Lois. *Autumn Street*. Boston: Houghton Mifflin, 1980.
IL: 5–8. RL: 5.

———. *Number the Stars*. Boston: Houghton Mifflin, 1989. IL: 5–8.
RL: 5.

Maclean, Allistair. *The Guns of Navarone*. Garden City, New York:
Doubleday, 1957. IL: 8–9+.

Magorian, Michelle. *Good Night, Mr. Tom*. New York: Harper, 1982.
IL: 6–9. RL: 6.

Mazer, Harry. *The Last Mission*. New York: Delacorte, 1979. IL: 5–7.
RL: 4.

McSwigan, Marie. *Snow Treasure*. New York: Dutton, 1967. IL: 4–7.
RL: 4.

Ossowski, Leonie. *Star without a Sky*. Minneapolis: Lerner, 1985.
IL: 4–7.

Piercy, Marge. *Gone to Soldiers*. New York: Summit, 1987. IL: 8–9+.

Richter, Hans Peter. *Friedrich*. New York: Holt, 1970. IL: 5–8.
RL: 6.

Rydberg, Lou, and Ernie Rydberg. *The Shadow Army*. New York:
Elsevier-Nelson, 1976. IL: 5–8.

Sachs, Marilyn. *A Pocketful of Seeds*. Garden City, New York: Doubleday, 1973. IL: 4–6. RL: 5.

Serraillier, Ian. *The Silver Sword*. New York: Philips, 1959. IL: 5–7. RL: 6.

Smith, Doris Buchanan. *Salted Lemons*. New York: Four Lemons, 1980. IL: 4–7.

Streatfield, Noel. *When the Sirens Wailed*. New York: Random House, 1976. IL: 5–8.

Taylor, Theodore. *The Cay*. Garden City, New York: Doubleday, 1969. IL: 5–8. RL: 6.

———. *The Children's War*. Garden City, New York: Doubleday, 1971. IL: 5–8.

Terlouw, James. *Winter in Wartime*. New York: McGraw-Hill, 1976. IL: 5–8.

Todd, Leonard. *The Best Kept Secret of the War*. New York: Alfred A. Knopf, 1984. IL: 5–8.

Toland, John. *Gods of War*. Garden City, New York: Doubleday, 1985. IL: 8–9+.

Tunis, John. *His Enemy, His Friend*. New York: Morrow, 1975. IL: 7–9.

Van Stockum, Hilda. *The Borrowed House*. New York: Farrar, 1975. IL: 5–7.

———. *The Winged Watchman*. New York: Farrar, 1962. IL: 5–7.

Walsh, Jill. *Fireweed*. New York: Farrar, 1970. IL: 7–9.

Werstein, Irving. *The Long Escape*. New York: Scribner's, 1964. IL: 7–9.

Westall, Robert. *Blitzcat*. New York: Scholastic, 1989. IL: 5–7.

———. *The Machine Gunners*. New York: Greenwillow, 1976. IL: 5–7. RL: 6.

Wojciechowska, Maia. *Till the Break of Day*. New York: Dutton, 1972. IL: 5–8.

Nonfiction

Adams, Henry H. *Italy at War*. New York: Time/Life, 1982.

Archer, Jules. *Jungle Fighters: A GI Correspondent's Experiences in the New Guinea Campaign*. New York: Messner, 1985. IL: 7–9.

Armor, John. *Manzanar*. New York: Times Books, 1988. IL: 8–9+.

Bachrach, Deborah. *Pearl Harbor: Opposing Views*. Minneapolis: Greenhaven, 1989. IL: 7–9.

Benford, Timothy B. *The World War II Quiz and Fact Book*. New York: Harper, 1982. IL: 8–9+.

Bliven, Bruce. *From Pearl Harbor to Okinawa: The War in the Pacific: 1941–1945.* New York: Random House, 1960. IL: 7–9.

———. *The Story of D-Day: June 6, 1944.* New York: Random House, 1981. IL: 7–9.

Breuer, William B. *Devil Boats: The PT War Against Japan.* San Rafael, California: Presidio, 1987. IL: 8–9+.

———. *Retaking the Philippines: America's Return to Corregidor and Bataan, July 1944-March 1945.* New York: St. Martin's, 1986. IL: 8–9+.

Campbell, Barbara. *A Girl Called Bob and a Horse Called Yoki.* New York: Dial, 1982. IL: 4–6.

Casewit, Curtis W. *Saga of the Mountain Soldiers: The Story of the 10th Mountain Division.* New York: Messner, 1981. IL: 6–9. RL: 7.

Chaikin, Miriam. *A Nightmare in History: The Holocaust, 1933–1945.* New York: Clarion, 1987. IL: 7–9.

Coffey, Thomas M. *Hap: The Story of the U.S. Air Force and the Man Who Built It, General Henry "Hap" Arnold.* New York: Viking, 1982. IL: 8–9+.

Colby, C. B. *Fighting Gear of World War II: Equipment and Weapons of the American GI.* New York: Coward, 1961. IL: 4–7.

Costello, John. *The Pacific War.* New York: Rawson/Atheneum, 1981. IL: 8–9+.

Crookenden, Napier. *The Battle of the Bulge 1944.* New York: Scribner's, 1980. IL: 8–9+.

Dank, Milton. *D-Day.* New York: Watts, 1984. IL: 6–8.

Davis, Daniel S. *Behind Barbed Wire: The Imprisonment of Japanese Americans during World War II.* New York: Dutton, 1982. IL: 5–8.

Devaney, John. *Blood and Guts: The True Story of General George S. Patton.* New York: Messner, 1982. IL: 4–6.

Dolan, Edward. *Victory in Europe: The Fall of Hitler's Germany.* New York: Watts, 1988. IL: 7–9.

Forman, James. *The Survivor.* New York: Farrar, 1976. IL: 7–9.

Frank, Anne. *The Diary of a Young Girl.* Garden City, New York: Doubleday, 1947. IL: 5–7.

Glines, Carrol V. *Doolittle Raid: America's First Strike Against Japan.* New York: Crown, 1988. IL: 8–9+.

Goldston, Robert. *The Life and Death of Nazi Germany.* New York: Fawcett, 1978. IL: 7–9+.

Graff, Stewart. *The Story of World War II*. New York: Dutton, 1978. IL: 4–6. RL: 5.

Gray, Ronald D. *Hitler and the Germans*. Minneapolis: Lerner, 1983. IL: 6–8.

Hamilton, John. *War at Sea, 1939–1945*. New York: Blandford/Sterling, 1986. IL: 8–9+.

Hammel, Eric. *Guadalcanal: The Carrier Battles: The Pivotal Aircraft Carrier Battles of the Eastern Solomons and Santa Cruz*. New York: Crown, 1987. IL: 8–9+.

Harris, Mark Jonathan. *Homefront: America During World War II*. New York: Putnam, 1984. IL: 6–8.

Harris, Nathaniel. *Pearl Harbor*. North Pomfret, Vermont: David & Charles, 1986. IL: 6–8.

Hastings, Max. *Overlord: D-Day and the Battle for Normandy*. New York: Simon & Schuster, 1984. IL: 8–9+.

Hautzig, Esther. *The Endless Steppe*. New York: Crowell, 1968. IL: 5–8.

Hellman, Peter, and Lili Meier. *Auschwitz Album: A Book Based upon an Album Discovered by a Concentration Camp Survivor, Lili Meier*. New York: Random, 1982. IL: 7–9+.

Hills, C. A. R. *The Second World War*. McMinnville, Oregon: Batsford, 1986. IL: 7–9+.

Hoare, Stephen. *Hiroshima*. Washington, D.C.: Dryad, 1987. IL: 3–6.

Hough, Richard. *The Battle of Britain: The Triumph of R.A.F. Fighter Pilots*. New York: Macmillan, 1971. IL: 5–8. RL: 8.

Houston, Jeanne Wakatsuki. *Farewell to Manzanar: A True Story of Japanese American Experience During and After World War II*. New York: Bantam, 1974. IL: 7–9. RL: 6.

Hoyt, Edwin P. *Invasion before Normandy: The Secret Battle of Slapton Sands*. Briarcliff Manor, New York: Stein & Day, 1985. IL: 8–9+.

———. *McCampbell's Heroes*. New York: Avon, 1983. IL: 7–9.

James, D. Clayton. *Time for Giants: Politics of the American High Command in World War II*. New York: Watts, 1987. IL: 8–9+.

Johnson, Frank D. *United States PT Boats of World War II in Action*. New York: Blandford/Sterling, 1980. IL: 8–9+.

Kenneth, Lee. *G.I.: The American Soldier in World War II*. New York: Scribner's, 1987. IL: 8–9+.

Koehn, Ilse. *Mischling, Second Degree: My Childhood in Nazi Germany*. New York: Greenwillow, 1977. IL: 7–9+. RL: 6.

Kotwoski, Monika. *The Bridge to the Other Side*. Garden City, New York: Doubleday, 1970. IL: 7–9.

Lawson, Don. *An Album of World War II Home Fronts*. New York: Watts, 1980. IL: 7–9.

Leckie, Robert. *Delivered from Evil: The Saga of World War II*. New York: Harper, 1987. IL: 8–9+.

————. *The Story of World War II*. New York: Random House, 1964. IL: 6–8. RL: 7.

Lidz, Richard. *Many Kinds of Courage: An Oral History of World War II*. New York: Putnam, 1980. IL: 7–9.

Lowder, Hughston E. *Batfish: The Champion "Submarine-Killer" Submarine of World War II*. Englewood Cliffs, New Jersey: Prentice-Hall, 1980. IL: 8–9+.

Macksey, Kenneth. *Military Errors of World War Two*. New York: Sterling, 1987. IL: 8–9+.

MacPherson, Malcolm C. *Time Bomb: Fermi, Heisenberg, and the Race for the Atomic Bomb*. New York: Dutton, 1986. IL: 7–9.

MacVane, John. *On the Air in World War II*. New York: Morrow, 1979. IL: 8–9+.

Manvell, Roger. *Goering*. New York: Simon & Schuster, 1962.

Marrin, Albert. *Airmen's War: World War II in the Sky*. New York: Atheneum, 1982. IL: 6–9. RL: 9.

————. *Hitler*. New York: Viking, 1987. IL: 6–9.

————. *Overlord: D-Day and the Invasion of Europe*. New York: Atheneum, 1982. IL: 6–9. RL: 6.

————. *Secret Armies: Spies, Counterspies and Saboteurs in World War II*. New York: Atheneum, 1985. IL: 7–9.

————. *Victory in the Pacific*. New York: Atheneum, 1983. IL: 5–8.

Maruki, Toshi. *Hiroshima No Pika*. New York: Lothrop, Lee & Shepard, 1982. IL: 4–6. RL: 5.

Maynard, Christopher. *Air Battles: Air Combat in World War II*. New York: Watts, 1987. IL: 5–8.

McCombs, Don. *World War II Super Facts*. New York: Warner, 1983. IL: 8–9+.

McGowan, Tom. *Midway and Guadalcanal*. New York: Watts, 1984. IL: 7–9.

McKay, Ernest A. *Carrier Strike Force: Pacific Air Combat in World War II*. New York: Messner, 1981. IL: 7–9.

Messenger, Charles. *The Second World War*. New York: Watts, 1987. IL: 6–9.

Miller, Marilyn. *D-Day*. New York: Silver Burdett, 1987. IL: 5–8.

Morrison, Wilbur H. *Above and Beyond: 1941–1945*. New York: St. Martin's, 1983. IL: 8–9+.

Moskin, Marietta. *I Am Rosemarie*. Garden City, New York: Doubleday, 1972. IL: 8–9+.

Moskovitz, Sarah. *Love Despite Hate: Child Survivors of the Holocaust and Their Adult Lives*. New York: Schocken, 1982.

Mowat, Farley. *And No Birds Sang*. Boston: Little, Brown, 1980. IL: 7–9. RL: 7.

Muirhead, John. *Those Who Fall*. New York: Random House, 1987. IL: 8–9+.

Munson, Kenneth George. *American Aircraft of World War II in Color*. New York: Sterling, 1982. IL: 8–9+.

O'Leary, Michael. *United States Naval Fighters of World War II in Action*. New York: Sterling, 1980. IL: 8–9+.

Pape, Richard. *Boldness Be My Friend*. New York: St. Martin's, 1985. IL: 8–9+.

Pierre, Michel. *The Second World War*. New York: Silver Burdett, 1987. IL: 7–9.

Prange, Gordon W. *December 7, 1941: The Day the Japanese Attacked Pearl Harbor*. New York: McGraw-Hill, 1987. IL: 8–9+.

———. *Miracle at Midway*. New York: McGraw-Hill, 1982. IL: 8–9+.

Pyle, Ernie. *Ernie's War: The Best of Ernie Pyle's World War II Dispatches*. New York: Random House, 1986. IL: 8–9+.

Reiss, Johanna. *The Journey Back*. New York: Crowell, 1976. IL: 4–7.

———. *The Upstairs Room*. New York: Crowell, 1972. IL: 4–7.

Richter, Hans Peter. *I Was There*. New York: Holt, 1972. IL: 6–9.

Rubenstein, Joshua. *Adolf Hitler*. New York: Watts. 1982. IL: 5–7.

Ryan, Cornelius. *Longest Day: June 6, 1944*. New York: Simon & Schuster, 1959. IL: 8–9+.

Samson, Jack. *Chennault*. Garden City, New York: Doubleday, 1987. IL: 8–9+.

Schultz, Duane. *Chennault and the Flying Tigers*. New York: St. Martin's, 1987. IL: 8–9+.

———. *The Doolittle Raid*. New York: St. Martin's, 1988. IL: 8–9+.

———. *The Hero of Bataan: The Story of General Wainwright*. New York: St. Martin's, 1981. IL: 8–9+.

———. *Last Battle Station: The Story of the U.S.S. Houston*. New York: St. Martin's, 1985. IL: 8–9+.

Shapiro, Milton J. *Ranger Battalion: American Rangers in World War II.* New York: Messner, 1979. IL: 7–9.

———. *Tank Command: General George S. Patton's 4th Armored Division.* New York: McKay, 1979. IL: 6–8.

———. *Undersea Raiders: U.S. Submarines in World War II.* New York: McKay, 1979. IL: 6–8.

Shapiro, William E. *Pearl Harbor.* New York: Watts, 1984. IL: 6–9.

Shirer, William L. *The Rise and Fall of Adolf Hitler.* New York: Random House, 1961. IL: 5–7.

———. *The Sinking of the Bismarck.* New York: Random House, 1962. IL: 5–7.

Siegel, Aranka. *Upon the Head of a Goat: A Childhood in Hungary, 1939–1944.* New York: Farrar, 1981. IL: 5–8.

Skipper, G. C. *Battle of Leyte Gulf.* Chicago: Children's Press, 1981. IL: 3–6.

———. *Battle of Midway.* Chicago: Children's Press, 1980. IL: 3–7.

———. *Battle of the Coral Sea.* Chicago: Children's Press, 1981. IL: 3–7.

———. *Invasion of Sicily.* Chicago: Children's Press, 1981. IL: 3–7.

———. *Mussolini: A Dictator Dies.* Chicago: Children's Press, 1981.

———. *Pearl Harbor.* Chicago: Children's Press, 1983. IL: 4–7.

———. *Submarines in the Pacific.* Chicago: Children's Press, 1980. IL: 4–7.

Smith, Peter C. *Dive Bombers in Action.* New York: Sterling, 1988. IL: 8–9+.

Snyder, Louis Leo. *Hitler and Nazism.* New York: Watts, 1961. RL: 4–7.

———. *World War II.* New York: Watts, 1981. IL: 4–6. RL: 7.

Stein, R. Conrad. *Battle of Guadalcanal.* Chicago: Children's Press, 1983. IL: 4–6.

———. *Battle of Okinawa.* Chicago: Children's Press, 1985. IL: 4–6.

———. *Hiroshima.* Chicago: Children's Press, 1982. IL: 4–7.

———. *The Home Front.* Chicago: Children's Press, 1986. IL: 4–7.

———. *Nisei Regiment.* Chicago: Children's Press, 1985. IL: 4–7.

———. *Prisoners of War.* Chicago: Children's Press, 1987. IL: 4–7.

———. *Road to Rome.* Chicago: Children's Press, 1984. IL: 4–7.

Sullivan, George. *Strange but True Stories of World War II.* New York: Walker, 1983. IL: 6–9.

Sweeney, James B. *Army Leaders of World War II.* New York: Watts, 1984. IL: 4–6.

———. *Famous Aviators of World War II*. New York: Watts, 1987. IL: 5–8.

Tateishi, John. *And Justice for All*. New York: Random House, 1984. IL: 8–9+.

Taylor, Theodore. *Air Raid: Pearl Harbor! The Story of December 7, 1941*. New York: Crowell, 1971. IL: 5–7.

———. *The Battle in the Arctic Seas: The Story of Convoy PQ 17*. New York: Crowell, 1976. IL: 6–9. RL: 9.

———. *The Battle Off Midway Island*. New York: Avon, 1981. IL: 6–8.

Toland, John. *The Flying Tigers*. New York: Random House, 1963. IL: 6–8.

Tregaskis, Richard. *Guadalcanal Diary*. New York: Random House, 1955. IL: 6–8. RL: 6.

———. *Invasion Diary*. New York: Random House, 1944.

———. *John F. Kennedy and the PT-109*. New York: Random House, 1962. IL: 5–7.

Uchida, Yoshiko. *Desert Exile: The Uprooting of a Japanese-American Family*. Seattle: University of Washington Press, 1984. IL: 7–9.

———. *Journey to Topaz: A Story of the Japanese American Evacuation*. Berkeley, California: Creative Arts, 1985. IL: 4–7.

Wheeler, Richard S. *Iwo*. Philadelphia: J. B. Lippincott, 1980. IL: 8–9+.

Windrow, Martin. *The World War II GI*. New York: Watts, 1986. IL: 5–7.

Wright, Nicolas. *The Red Baron*. New York: McGraw-Hill, 1976. IL: 5–8.

Wolf, Jacqueline. *Take Care of Josette: Memoir in Defense of Occupied France*. New York: Watts, 1981.

Wootton, Angela M. *The Second World War*. New York: Larousse, 1985. IL: 8–9+.

Young, Peter. *World Almanac Book of World War II: The Complete and Comprehensive Documentary of World War II*. New York: Ballantine, 1986. IL: 8–9+.

Nonprint

America at War: World Wars I and II. Chicago: Society for Visual Education, 1986. (40-min. videocassette)

America's Twentieth-Century Wars: The International Challenge. Hightstown, New Jersey: Random House/American School, 1979. (6 20-min. sound filmstrips)

American Heritage Media Collection. Culver City, California: Zenger Video, 1985. (5 35-min. videocassettes)

Appointment in Tokyo. Washington, D.C.: U.S. Government, 1950. (Distributed by National Audio Visual Center.) (56-min. 16mm film)

The Big Red One. Burbank, California: Lorimar Productions, 1980. (113-min. videocassette)

Causes of World War II. Culver City, California: Social Studies School Service. (simulation game)

From D-Day to Victory in Europe. Oak Forest, Illinois: MPI Home Video, 1985. (112-min. videocassette)

Fuhrer! Rise of a Madman. Oak Forest, Illinois: MPI Home Video, 1985. (108-min. videocassette)

Hitler: Revenge to Ruin. Deerfield, Illinois: Learning Corporation of America, 1980. (24-min. videocassette)

Hitler: The Road to Revenge. Deerfield, Illinois: Learning Corporation of America, 1980. (24-min. videocassette)

Hitler's Henchmen. Oak Forest, Illinois: MPI Home Video, 1985. (60-min. videocassette)

The Homefront. Los Angeles: Churchill Films, 1985. (90-min. videocassette)

Luftwaffe. New York: CBS, 1956. (27-min. 16mm film)

Mussolini: The Decline and Fall of Il Duce. Atlanta, Georgia: HBO, 1985. (112-min. videocassette)

Mussolini: The Untold Story. New York: NBC, 1985. (videocassette)

Patton: A Salute to a Rebel. Los Angeles: Twentieth Century Fox, 1970. (171-min. videocassette)

The Road to War. Oak Forest, Illinois: MPI Home Video, 1982. (75-min. videocassette)

Sands of Iwo Jima. Los Angeles: Republic, 1949. (Distributed by RCA.) (109-min. videocassette)

Storybound: Escape from Warsaw. New York: Children's Television International, 1980. (Distributed by GPN.) (15-min. videocassette)

Triumph of the Will. Rye, New York: Images, 1934. (110-min. videocassette)

Twisted Cross. New York: NBC, 1956. (53-min. videocassette)

Victory at Sea. New York: NBC, 1952. (Distributed by Embassy Home Entertainment.) (26 30-min. videocassettes).

World War I and World War II. Hightstown, New Jersey: Random House/American School, 1986. (10 20-min. sound filmstrips)

World War II Series. Deerfield, Illinois: Coronet, 1985. (5 11–16-min. videocassettes)

World War II with Walter Cronkite. New York: CBS, 1981. (59-min. videocassette)

Korean Conflict

Fiction

Michener, James. *Bridges at Toko-ri.* New York: Random House, 1953. IL: 8–9+.

Nonfiction

Fincher, Ernest Barksdale. *The War in Korea.* New York: Watts, 1981. IL: 4–7.

Gardella, Lawrence. *Sing a Song to Jenny Next.* New York: Dutton, 1981. IL: 8–9+.

Hastings, Max. *The Korean War.* New York: Simon & Schuster, 1987. IL: 8–9+.

Hayman, LeRoy. *Harry S Truman: A Biography.* New York: Crowell, 1969.

Hopkins, William B. *One Bugle No Drums: The Marines at Chosin Reservoir.* Chapel Hill, North Carolina: Algonquin, 1986. IL: 8–9+.

Leckie, Robert. *The War in Korea, 1950–1953.* New York: Random House, 1963. IL: 6–8.

Stokesbury, James L. *A Short History of the Korean War.* New York: Morrow, 1988. IL: 8–9+.

Wolfson, Victor. *The Man Who Cared: A Life of Harry S Truman.* New York: Farrar, 1966. IL: 6–8.

Nonprint

Korea: The Forgotten War. New York: Lou Reda Productions, 1987. (120-min. 16mm film)

Pork Chop Hill. New York: MGM, 1959. (97-min. 16mm film)

That War in Korea. New York: NBC, 1966. (77-min. videocassette)

Vietnam War

Fiction

Anderson, Rachel. *The War Orphan*. New York: Oxford University Press, 1986. IL: 7–9.

Anderson, Robert A. *Cooks and Bakers: A Novel of the Vietnam War*. New York: Avon, 1982. IL: 8–9+.

Boyd, Candy Dawson. *Charlie Pippin*. New York: Macmillan, 1987. IL: 5–7.

Degens, T. *Friends*. New York: Viking, 1981. IL: 5–7.

Hahn, Mary Downing. *December Stillness*. New York: Clarion, 1988. IL: 5–9.

Paterson, Katherine. *Park's Quest*. New York: Dutton, 1988. IL: 5–8. RL: 6.

Wolitzer, Meg. *Caribou*. New York: Greenwillow, 1984. IL: 4–7.

Nonfiction

Edwards, Richard. *The Vietnam War*. Vero Beach, Florida: Rourke, 1987. IL: 7–9.

Fincher, Ernest Barksdale. *The Vietnam War*. New York: Watts, 1980. IL: 6–8.

Griffiths, John. *The Last Day in Saigon*. North Pomfret, Vermont: David & Charles, 1987. IL: 6–9.

Hauptly, Denis J. *In Vietnam*. New York: Atheneum, 1985. IL: 6–9.

Lawson, Don. *An Album of the Vietnam War*. New York: Watts, 1986. IL: 5–8.

———. *The United States in the Vietnam War*. New York: Crowell, 1981. IL: 6–8.

———. *The War in Vietnam*. New York: Watts, 1981. IL: 6–8.

Mabie, Margot C. J. *Vietnam: There and Here*. New York: Holt, 1985. IL: 6–8.

Marshall, Kathryn. *In the Combat Zone*. Boston: Little, Brown, 1987. IL: 7–9.

Myers, Walter Dean. *Fallen Angels*. New York: Scholastic, 1988. IL: 8–9+.

Walker, Keith. *A Piece of My Heart*. San Rafael, California: Presidio, 1986. IL: 8–9+. RL: 6.

Nonprint

European Theater and Pacific Theater. Dimondale, Michigan: Hartley Courseware. (computer simulation for Apple or IBM)

Vietnam: A Case Study for Critical Thinking. Pleasantville, New York: Educational Audio Visual, 1987. (40-min. videocassette)

Vietnam: Chronicle of a War. New York: CBS, 1981. (88-min. videocassette)

Vietnam: In the Year of a Pig. Oak Forest, Illinois: MPI, 1968. (115-min. videocassette)

Vietnam: Lessons of a Lost War. Chicago: Films Incorporated, 1985. (50-min. videocassette)

Vietnam: A Television History. Chicago: Society for Visual Education, 1987. (7 90–120-min. videocassettes)

Vietnam: The Ten Thousand Day War. Toronto: Information Teleproductions, 1980. (Distributed by Embassy Home Video.) (13 50-min. videocassettes)

Why Vietnam? Los Angeles: Churchill Films, 1986. (2 40–55-min. videocassettes)

Method: Videotaping a Reenactment

Videotaping has become a successful method of sharing visual and audio information in the classroom and at home. As the prices of videotape cameras and recorders have come down, many families have acquired simple equipment. Schools can afford to have these machines also, and can make use of them in the classroom with minimal disruption. For effective use of video in the classroom and the library media center, prior planning, production experience, and continuous evaluation are still the most important elements in the process.

Planning for videotaping a reenactment requires that the students carefully consider what must be re-created. In this process, they must complete extensive research to identify the persons involved, the sequence of events, and the setting. What were the people like? What was the setting? What happened first, second, third, and so forth, in which part of the setting? In order to re-create a scene or event, students must also consider the time period covered, especially the time of day or lighting, for the videotaping later.

Students must learn to use the equipment available. Each piece of equipment has a set of working instructions. There are some general camera movements, such as panning and zooming, that the students must master. Lighting will be important, whether the taping is done indoors or out. Sometimes extra lights will be required for scenes shot indoors. And for those involved in videotaping movement, there will be the problem of audio, or sound. Depending on the simplicity of the camera, audio recording may or may not be built in.

Students must map out the scene and identify how the actors must walk through each element in the sequence of events. The actors will need to become involved in every movement so that they can follow through during videotaping without too much interruption.

Finally, props and costumes may be required. In the case of reenacting battles, often uniforms and military equipment are required for the scenes to be realistic. Students must plan for sufficient time to make or borrow the materials.

Given these considerations, a script may be drafted. A simple script may be completed using a form similar to the one included in Figure 8.

Following the completion of the script, the students establish the roles all will play. Using the instructions appropriate to the type or make of the camera they have, students will set up the scenery and practice the videotaping of the sequences. During the replay, they may evaluate the videotape first for content and second for the skill involved in use of the camera.

Resources Related to Videotaping

Bensinger, Charles. *The Home Video Handbook.* Santa Fe, New Mexico: Video-Info, 1979.
———. *The Video Book.* New York: Scribner's, 1982.
Caiati, Carl. *Video Production: The Professional Way.* Blue Ridge Summit, Pennsylvania: Tab, 1985.
Cooper, Carolyn E. *VCRs.* New York: Watts, 1987.
Costello, Marjorie. *The Video Camcorder Handbook.* Tucson, Arizona: HP, 1987.
Dunton, Mark, and David Owen. *The Complete Home Video Handbook.* New York: Random House, 1982.

Visual	Audio

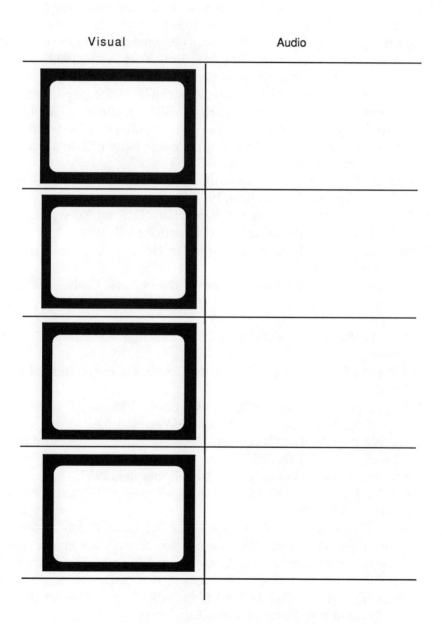

Figure 8. Reenactment Script

Friedberg, Andy. *The Complete Video-Cassette Recorder Book: How To Buy It; How To Get the Most from It.* New York: Pinnacle, 1984.

Hanson, Jarice. *Understanding Video: Applications, Impact, and Theory.* Beverly Hills, California: Sage, 1987.

Harwood, Don. *Everything You Always Wanted To Know about Portable Videotape Recording.* Bayside, New York: VTR, 1983.

Hirshman, Robert. *How To Shoot Better Video: Especially VHS, Beta, and 8mm Cameras.* Milwaukee, Wisconsin: H. Leonard, 1985.

Jobe, Holly, Glenn Cannon, and Ron Miller. *A Guide to Planning, Preparing, and Producing a Videotape.* Scranton: Northeastern Educational Intermediate Unit, Pennsylvania State Department of Education, 1978. ED 171315.

Langman, Larry, and Paul Spinelli. *The Complete Video Book.* Boulder, Colorado: Kensington, 1984.

LeBaron, John. *Portable Video: A Production Guide for Young People.* Englewood Cliffs, New Jersey: Prentice-Hall, 1982.

Maltin, Leonard. *The Complete Guide to Home Video.* New York: Harmony, 1981.

McNitt, Jim. *The Home Video Sourcebook.* New York: Collier, 1982.

Millerson, Gerald. *Video Production Handbook.* New York: Focal, 1987.

Olesky, Walter G. *The Video Revolution.* Chicago: Children's Press, 1986.

On-Camera: The BBC Video Production Course. Chicago: Films, Inc., 1983.

Quick, John, and Herbert Wolff. *Small-Studio Videotape Production.* Reading, Massachusetts: Addison-Wesley, 1976.

Quinn, Gerald V. *The Camcorder Handbook.* Blue Ridge Summit, Pennsylvania: Tab, 1987.

Renowden, Gareth. *Video.* New York: Gloucester, 1983.

Robinson, Joseph F. *Videotape Recording: Theory and Practice.* New York: Focal, 1983.

Stanton, Eileen. *Cash in Your Camcorder: 102 Ways To Make Money (and Have Fun) with Your Camcorder: Shoot Your Family and Friends for Fun and Profit.* Albuquerque, New Mexico: Sandia, 1989.

Thomas, Erwin K. *Make Better Videos with Your Camcorder.* Blue Ridge Summit, Pennsylvania: Tab, 1991.

Video Encyclopedia of Media Education. New York: Telmar Communications, 1985. (5 30-min. videocassettes)

The Video Learning Library. Indianapolis: Kartes Video Communications, 1985. (5 30-min. videocassettes)

Wezel, Ru Van. *Video Handbook.* New York: Heinemann, 1987.

White, Gordon. *Video Techniques.* Woburn, Massachusetts: Butterworth, 1982.

CURRENT EVENTS

Sports Events

Whether one is an active sports enthusiast actually engaged in playing or a more passive "couch potato," there is an excitement about the interaction involved in sports of various kinds. This may relate to the chance of winning or the fear of losing. The emphasis on the individual and the focus on the heroics or skills required to win certainly contribute to this interest. Whether or not arising from the student's own understanding of and involvement in the skill required in most games, a generic understanding or interest in sports is prevalent in the reading practices of the middle-grade student.

Interest in different games varies, of course. Some games stress the mental requirements of strategy, while others stress particular skills or sets of controls on the body, such as hand-eye coordination or brute strength. Whatever skill is emphasized, there is certainly a sense of mastery to be gained during a game or a test of skill. Perhaps that is the motivational force behind the subject of sports. Whatever the cause for the interest, many students enjoy the pursuit of sports. Reading about sports and sports figures can be inspiring to many youngsters.

Resources Related to Sports Events

For those interested in identifying materials and reading motivation activities centered on sports, the following references will be useful.

Articles and Pamphlets

Bachner, Saul. "Sports Literature and the Teaching of Reading: Grab Them and Move Them." *Clearinghouse* 57:7 (March 1984), pp. 313–314.

Brown, Ron. "Coming of Age: Sports Fiction for YAs." *School Library Journal* 29:4 (December 1982), pp. 28–29.

Danielson, Kathy Everts. "Put Reading in Shape with Sports." *Reading Horizons* 28:2 (Winter 1978), pp. 146–152.

Forman, Jack. "Young Adult Sports Novels: Playing for Real." *Horn Book Magazine* 63:4 (July-August 1987), pp. 500–502.

Heitzman, William Ray, and Kathleen Esnes Heitzman. "Sports Literature and the Librarian: Opportunities To Mend, Mold and Motivate—Part I." *Catholic Library World* 48:5 (1976), pp. 207–213.

Lamb, Donald K. *Summer Splash: 1988 Wisconsin Summer Library Program Manual*. Bulletin No. 8230. Madison: Wisconsin State Department of Public Instruction, 1988. ED 297760.

McKinney, Caroline S. "A Natural High: YA Books about Sports, Horses, Music." *English Journal* 78:4 (April 1989), pp. 27–30.

"Playing the Game: Sports Fiction." *Booklist* 83:13 (March 1, 1987), pp. 1009–1010.

Rubenstein, Bob. "Sports History: Motivation for Reluctant Readers." *Elementary English* 52:4 (1975), pp. 591–592.

Unsworth, Robert. "Tunis Goes Down Swinging: Who'll Keep the Ball Rolling." *School Library Journal* 24:9 (May 1978), pp. 38–39.

Waddle, Linda. "School Media Matters." *Wilson Library Bulletin* 63 (April 1989), p. 82.

Books

Blickle, Calvin, and Frances Corcoran. *Sports: A Multimedia Guide for Children and Young Adults*. New York: Neal-Schuman, 1980.

Burns, Grant. *The Sports Pages: A Critical Bibliography of Twentieth-Century American Novels and Stories Featuring Baseball, Basketball, Football, and Other Athletic Pursuits*. Metuchen, New Jersey: Scarecrow, 1987.

The Comprehensive Directory of Sports Addresses. Santa Monica, California: Global Sports Productions, 1989.

Gentile, Lance. *Using Sports for Reading and Writing Activities: Elementary and Middle School Years—A Fun with Reading Book.* Phoenix, Arizona: Oryx, 1983.

———. *Using Sports for Reading and Writing Activities: Middle and High School Years—A Fun with Reading Book.* Phoenix, Arizona: Oryx, 1983.

Harrah, Barbara K. *Sports Books for Children: An Annotated Bibliography.* Metuchen, New Jersey: Scarecrow, 1978.

MacZucker, Harvey, and Lawrence J. Babich. *Sports Films: A Complete Reference.* Jefferson, North Carolina: McFarland, 1987.

New York Times Encyclopedia of Sports. New York: New York Times, 1979.

Remley, Mary L. *Women in Sport: An Annotated Bibliography and Resource Guide, 1900–1990.* Boston: G. K. Hall, 1991.

Shannon, Mike. *Diamond Classics: Essays on 100 of the Best Baseball Books Ever Published.* Jefferson, North Carolina: McFarland, 1989.

Smith, Myron J. *Baseball: A Comprehensive Bibliography.* Jefferson, North Carolina: McFarland, 1986.

Thomas, James L., and Carol H. Thomas. *"Sports Splash"1980: A Librarian's Planning Handbook.* Austin: Texas State Library, 1980. ED 188639.

Wischnia, Bob, and Marty Post. *Running: A Guide to Literature.* New York: Garland, 1983.

Wise, Suzanne. *Sports Fiction for Adults: An Annotated Bibliography of Novels, Plays, Short Stories and Poetry with Sporting Settings.* New York: Garland, 1985.

Woolum, Janet. *Outstanding Women Athletes; Who They Are and How They Influenced Sports in America.* Phoenix, Arizona: Oryx, 1992.

Young Adult Services Division. *Sports.* Chicago: American Library Association, 1989.

Sample Activity Related to Sports Events

The use of magazines to promote sports reading is simple. It is based on access to a large quantity of materials. In this case, comfort while reading and browsing is helpful. For the reader of magazines, the activity may take place anywhere. Like paperback books, magazines are appealing to those who are active, who want to read wherever they are, and who often dislike the stigma of "books."

The library media specialist can try a two-pronged strategy to introduce the use of magazines. Students will more than likely be interested in the most current issues. However, past issues may also be suggested. Using a large display of the most current titles, the library media specialist introduces sports magazine titles for students' perusal. A list of games and events that occurred during the last month may be highlighted with shared glimpses and quotes from articles within the magazines.

In a second meeting or session, the library media specialist can try introducing back issues of sports periodicals to students in some more creative ways, depending on the season of the year. For example, past football games might be listed with questions challenging students to find out about a particular game and come back with full details about what happened. A set of baseball cards of players from the past may be displayed with questions asking students to find out about a particular game, the life of one of the players, or details on a particular team shown on the cards.

Students will be challenged to think about how they might find out about these players from reports made at the time—that is, from back issues of periodicals. The library media specialist should introduce students to periodical indexes as a way of finding out about past events. Depending on the periodical indexes available, the library media specialist may introduce the use of the print or automated form of an index. For example, the library media specialist might introduce students to the *Readers' Guide to Periodical Literature* in print form, or to the periodical index from InfoTrac. Either way, the emphasis should be on understanding the resource in terms of the need to find an interesting article.

Following this review of indexes, students should locate and peruse the periodicals themselves. They may find that the information they want is no longer available in hard copy. Use of microfiche should present no problem. The form may require reading with the reader, but students may find that printing a copy or obtaining copies of past articles is a different kind of interest.

Each student may select a type of game in which he or she has an interest and then pursue it in indexes and magazines.

Student Resources Related to Sports

Indexes

Abridged Readers' Guide to Periodical Literature. New York: H. W. Wilson. (available in print, online, CD-ROM, and tape)
Children's Magazine Guide. New York: Bowker.
Magazine Index. Menlo Park, California: Information Access. (available in microfilm and CD-ROM)
Readers' Guide Abstracts. New York: H. W. Wilson. (available in microfiche, online, CD-ROM, and tape)
Readers' Guide to Periodical Literature. New York: H. W. Wilson. (available in print, online, CD-ROM, and tape)

Electronic Indexing Systems

Dialog. Includes many databases indexing periodicals and identifying periodicals such as *Ulrich's International Periodical Directory, ERIC*, etc.
Magazine Index Plus+ on InfoTrac. Menlo Park, California: Information Access.
Wilsondisc CD-ROM Retrieval System. New York: H. W. Wilson.
Wilsonline Information System. New York: H. W. Wilson. Includes *Abridged Readers' Guide to Periodical Literature, Readers' Guide to Periodical Literature,* and *Readers' Guide Abstracts.*

Periodicals

Athletic Journal
Backpacker
Baseball Digest
Bicycling
Camping Journal
Car and Driver
Cycle
Cycle World
Field and Stream
Fishing Facts
Flying
Football Digest
Golf Digest

Horseman: The Magazine of Western Riding
Hot Rod Magazine
International Gymnast
Journal of Physical Education and Recreation
Motor Boating and Sailing
Motor Trend
Outdoor Life
Runners World
Skating Magazine
Skiing
Skin Diver
Sport
Sporting News
Sports Afield
Sports Illustrated
Strength and Health
Swimming World and Junior Swimmer
World Tennis
Young Athlete

Nonprint

There are many videotape and film sources about sports or sports figures. Check videotape and nonprint catalogs for specific titles in the areas of interest.

Reading Rainbow: Sports Pages. New York: GPN/WNED-TV, 1983. (Distributed by GPN.) (30-min. videocassette)

Method: Using Periodical Articles and Indexes

Using periodicals to motivate students in reading incorporates the advantages of a portable format with content in order to interest the reader. Periodicals can be found on almost any topic one might want to pursue.

In most cases, the main advantage of using periodicals or magazines is the recency of the information. Magazines are used for locating visual and written information and for personal enjoyment. For example, most sports magazines include in-depth articles about current sports figures, information about games that have recently occurred, and upcoming events that readers might want to follow. If the periodical is indexed, the articles can be retrieved.

Most magazines are simple enough in layout that little instruction is necessary. However, students may benefit from an overview of the magazine's usual format. The classroom teacher or library media specialist might discuss headings, paging, tables of contents, indexing, and general types of articles, columns, or other information included in magazines. Students may also benefit from a discussion of general criteria for making selections of periodicals. Students might consider the accuracy, content, and authority of particular periodicals or magazines.

Resources Related to Using Periodical Articles and Indexes

Katz, William, and Linda Sternberg. *Magazines for Libraries: For the General Reader and Public, School, Junior College, and College Libraries.* New York: Bowker, 1989.

———. *Magazines for Young People: A Children's Magazine Guide Companion Volume.* New York: Bowker, 1991.

Paine, Fred K., and Nancy E. Paine. *Magazines: A Bibliography for Their Analysis, with Annotations and Study Guide.* Metuchen, New Jersey: Scarecrow, 1987.

Richardson, Selma K. *Magazines for Children: A Guide for Parents, Teachers and Librarians.* Chicago: American Library Association, 1991.

Serials for Libraries: An Annotated Guide to Continuations, Annuals, Yearbooks, Almanacs, Transactions, Proceedings, Directories, Services. New York: Neal-Schuman, 1985.

Serials Review. Ann Arbor, Michigan: Pierian, quarterly.

Thomas, James L. *Using Periodicals in School Library Media Centers.* Minneapolis: T. S. Denison, 1980.

Ulrich's International Periodicals Directory: A Classified Guide to Current Periodicals, Foreign and Domestic. New York: Bowker, annual print version. (also available online or in CD-ROM)

Wall, C. Edward. *Index to Free Periodicals.* Ann Arbor, Michigan: Pierian, 1978.

———. "A New Look at Free Magazines." *American Libraries* 8 (February 1977), pp. 85–88.

REGULAR OR ROUTINE EVENTS AND CUSTOMS

Students relate to the events that have become personally meaningful to them, such as birthdays or holidays for which their families make special plans. There are many such events in the United States, in part because of the ethnic and cultural diversity of the country.

Routine or special events become ingrained in the students' memories. Children remember the "fun" things that are done for parties. For example, in the United States, birthday customs often include inventive themes, creative cakes, whimsical food, special decorations, and silly games. Birthday celebrations also bring gifts and cards of greetings and best wishes.

Resources Related to Regular or Routine Events and Customs

There are many resources and craft materials related to special holidays. These materials have not been listed here because they are easily available by checking catalogs in the library under the holiday subject heading. The sources listed here represent materials related to those everyday or routine events in the lives of students special to the individual but not unusual in the general course of events. These events might include birthdays, weddings, graduations, religious ceremonies, major illnesses, and deaths. They are special events in individual lives and often represent sharing of "rites of passage."

Print

Hautzig, Esther. *Make It Special: Cards, Decorations, and Party Favors for Holidays and Other Special Celebrations*. New York: Macmillan, 1986.

Ichikawa, Satomi. *Happy Birthday: A Book of Birthday Celebrations*. New York: Philomel, 1988.

Perl, Lila. *Candles, Cakes, and Donkey Tales*. New York: Clarion, 1984.

Price, Christine. *Happy Days: A UNICEF Book of Birthdays, Name Days and Growing Days*. New York: Dutton, 1970.

Turner, Ann Warren. *Rituals of Birth*. New York: McKay, 1978.

Nonprint

A Birthday in the USA, Japan and the USSR. Irwindale, California: Barr Films, 1976. (12-min. videocassette)

The Birthday Movie. Chicago: Made-to-Order Library Productions, 1984. (16mm film)

Sample Activity Related to Regular or Routine Events and Customs: Birthdays

A collection of birthday greeting cards are collected in a basket for examination. After students examine the cards, they may discuss those that they have received and enjoyed. They may also tell about those that they have seen in card shops and would like to give to someone or receive themselves. Students may be invited to bring in samples of cards that are different from those examined in class. Middle-school students will find many of the humorous cards especially fun to share. They may also be less threatening for sharing feelings.

When the cards have been examined, the students can discuss what materials make up the cards. They also can classify the cards into categories—sentimental, humorous, and so forth. Following these discussions, the students are invited to make their own cards for an identified special event, such as a birthday.

Some students may wish to get fancy and make their own paper. For this exercise, however, the students should consider the types of paper they want to use and find ready-made samples.

Before beginning the project, each student should decide on the event for which he or she will make a card, the individual to whom the card will be given, the message that will be on the card, and the format that best suits the message.

Students may wish to group themselves by the types of cards they are producing in order to share ideas, but this is not necessary. The classroom teacher or library media specialist may wish to identify some appropriate art methods for each type of card and category. For example, thicker paper and water color might be more appropriate for a sentimental message. Some students may wish to take Polaroid pictures and mount them on paper, with handwritten or typed messages inside. Cartoons with silly messages might be completed with pen and ink. Students should discuss form, message, and medium before beginning.

While making these decisions, the library media specialist may also wish to introduce the ideas of using symbols on cards. Useful books about symbols are J. C. Cooper's *An Illustrated Encyclopedia of Traditional Symbols* (New York: W. W. Norton, 1987) and Carl G. Liungman's *Dictionary of Symbols* (Santa Barbara, California: ABC-CLIO, 1991).

As students play around with their ideas, they may examine layouts and types of print. If printing, the students may be introduced to print type and formats. Options for type and printing may vary depending on the availability of computer graphics programs and calligraphy skills. The art teacher may discuss the layout of the card in terms of centering the design and message for pleasing effects. Students should select the type of artwork that would be most appealing to the persons to whom their cards are to be sent. The students may sketch out their work before completing their final products.

Method: Making Greeting Cards

Sending birthday cards has been a social custom for more than a hundred years. Although it is a common practice in the United States, it differs from those in other countries. European children are required to give New Year's greeting cards as proof of their improvement in drawing and penmanship ability. In Japan, all greeting cards are saved by the post office for distribution on New Year's Day. England and Germany both claim to be the first country to initiate sending Christmas cards.

The specific process for making a greeting card will depend on the art medium chosen. However, several general rules may be identified:

1. Decide on the occasion for the card.
2. Select art medium and paper.
3. Gather materials.
4. Lay out materials to be used, allowing plenty of space.
5. Decide on the message.

6. Decide on the illustration.
7. Practice on scrap paper to get the appropriate design in the position desired.
8. Draw the design to be used before applying the medium.
9. Apply the medium.

An advantage to making greeting cards is that the cards can be used. Students are likely to have had some experience with cards, and they are also likely to have someone to whom they may send their cards. The students will be limited by the supplies they can obtain and their own creativity.

Resources Related to Making Greeting Cards

Alkema, Chester Jay. *Greeting Cards You Can Make.* New York: Sterling, 1973.

Barish, Matthew. *The Kid's Book of Cards and Posters.* Englewood Cliffs, New Jersey: Prentice-Hall, 1973.

Bennett, Charles. *The Year-Round All-Occasion Make Your Own Greeting Card Book.* New York: St. Martin's, 1977.

Billeter, Erika. "Greeting Cards." *Graphis* 162:3 (1972–1973), pp. 268–281.

Bridgewater, Alan, and Gill Bridgewater. *Holiday Crafts: Year-Round Projects Kids Can Make.* Blue Ridge Summit, Pennsylvania: Tab, 1990, pp. 21–31, 59–64, 102–106, 160–164.

Buday, Gyorgy. *The History of the Christmas Card.* New York: Tower, 1971.

Carlis, John. *How To Make Your Own Greeting Cards.* New York: Watson-Guptill, 1968.

Chadwick, H. Joseph. *Greeting Card Writer's Handbook.* Cincinnati, Ohio: Writer's Digest, 1975.

Chase, Ernest Dudley. *The Romance of Greeting Cards: An Historical Account of the Origin, Evolution and Development of Christmas Cards, Valentines and Other Forms of Greeting Cards from Earliest Days to Present Time.* Dedham, Massachusetts: Rust Craft, 1956.

Evarts, Susan. *The Art and Craft of Greeting Cards: A Handbook of Methods and Materials for Making and Printing Greetings, Announcements, and Invitations.* New York: Van Nostrand Reinhold, 1975.

Flesher, Irene. *Pressed Flower Art: Greeting Cards, Pictures, and Other Decorative Projects*. New York: New Century, 1984.

Francis, Charles. *Make Your Own Greeting Cards*. New York: Crowell, 1955.

Goeller, Carl G. *Selling Poetry, Verse, and Prose: A Guide to the Greeting Card and Magazine Markets*. Boston: Writer, 1967.

A Guide to Greeting Card Writing. Cincinnati, Ohio: Writer's Digest Books, 1980.

Heller, Steven. *Artists' Christmas Cards*. New York: A&W, 1979.

Hohman, Edward J., and Norma E. Leary. *The Greeting Card Handbook: What To Write, How To Write It, Where To Sell It*. New York: Barnes & Noble, 1981.

Holtje, Adrienne. *Cardcraft: Twenty-Two Techniques for Making Your Own Greeting Cards and Notepaper*. Radnor, Pennsylvania: Chilton, 1978.

Kenneway, Eric. *Making Pop-Up Greeting Cards*. Thorndike, Maine: Mills & Boon, 1972.

Kitagawa, Yoshiko. *Creative Cards: Wrap a Message with a Personal Touch*. New York: Kadansha International, 1987.

Kovash, Emily. *How To Have Fun Making Cards*. Mankato, Minnesota: Creative Education, 1974.

Leeming, Joseph. *Fun with Greeting Cards*. Philadelphia: J. B. Lippincott, 1960.

Lister, Ron. *Designing Greeting Cards and Paper Products: A Complete Guide*. Englewood Cliffs, New Jersey: Prentice-Hall, 1984.

McGowen, Harold. *The Spirit of Christmas in Words and Sculpture: Christmas Cards*. Central Islip, New York: Metaprobe Institute, 1974.

Oden, ViAnn. *A New Approach to Christmas Greetings*. Goleta, California: Anvipa, 1988.

Perry, Margaret Curtis. *Christmas Card Magic: The Art of Making Decorations and Ornaments with Christmas Cards*. Garden City, New York: Doubleday, 1967.

Power, Brenda Miller. "Reading the World and Writing Sympathy Cards." *Language Arts* 66:6 (October 1989), pp. 644–649.

Purdy, Susan. *Holiday Cards for You To Make*. Philadelphia: J. B. Lippincott, 1967.

Snow, Peter, and Maria Snow. *Greetings! How To Make Your Own Cards for Birthdays, Anniversaries, Parties, Holidays, Special Days, Any Days*. New York: Bobbs-Merrill, 1976.

Szela, Eva. *The Complete Guide to Greeting Card Design and Illustration.* Westport, Connecticut: North Light, 1987.

Weiss, Morry. *American Greetings Corporation.* Exton, Pennsylvania: Newcomen Society in North America, 1982.

General
References

Barron, Neil, Wayne Barton, Kristin Ramsdell, and Steven A. Stilwell. *What Do I Read Next?* Detroit: Gale Research, 1990.

Butler, Francelia, and Richard Rotert. *Reflections on Literature for Children.* Hamden, Connecticut: Library Professional, 1984.

Carlsen, R., and A. Sherrill. *Voices of Readers: How We Come To Love Books.* Urbana, Illinois: National Council of Teachers of English, 1988.

Chambers, Aidan. *Introducing Books to Children.* Boston: Horn, 1983.

Chambers, Dewey W. *Children's Literature in the Curriculum.* Chicago: Rand McNally, 1971.

Cott, Jonathan. *Pipers at the Gates of Dawn: The Wisdom of Children's Literature.* New York: Random, 1983.

Cullinan, Bernice E. *Children's Literature in the Reading Program.* Newark, Delaware: International Reading Association, 1987.

Davis, Barbara Kerr. *Read All Your Life: A Subject Guide to Fiction.* Jefferson, North Carolina: McFarland, 1989.

Edwards, Clifford H., Howard G. Getz, Franklin G. Lewis, Michael A. Lorber, and Walter D. Pierce. *Planning, Teaching and Evaluating: A Competency Approach.* Chicago: Nelson-Hall, 1977.

Egoff, Sheila, G. T. Stubbs, and L. F. Ashley. *Only Connect: Readings on Children's Literature.* Toronto: Oxford University Press, 1980.

Ettinger, John R. T., and Diana L. Sprit. *Choosing Books for Young People, Volume 2: A Guide to Criticism and Bibliography 1976–1984.* Phoenix, Arizona: Oryx, 1987.

Fox, Barbara J. *Rx for Reading: How the Schools Teach Your Child To Read and How You Can Help.* New York: Penguin, 1989.

Freeman, Judy. *Books Kids Will Sit Still For.* New York: Bowker, 1990.

Guthrie, John. *Measuring Readership: Rationale and Technique.* New York: UNESCO, 1984.

Helbig, Alethea K., and Agnes Regan Perkins. *Dictionary of Children's Fiction 1859–1959: Books of Recognized Merit.* Westport, Connecticut: Greenwood, 1985.

Hearne, Betsy. "Problems and Possibilities: U.S. Research in Children's Literature." *School Library Journal* 34:11 (August 1988), pp. 27–31.

Huck, Charlotte, Susan Hepler, and Janet Hickman. *Children's Literature in the Elementary School.* New York: Holt, 1987.

Jacobs, Leland B. *Using Literature with Young Children.* New York: Teachers College Press, 1965.

Kimmel, Margaret Mary. *For Reading Outloud!* New York: Delacorte, 1983.

Landsberg, Michele. *Reading for the Love of It: Best Books for Young Readers.* Englewood Cliffs, New Jersey: Prentice-Hall, 1987.

Laughlin, Mildred Knight, and Letty S. Watt. *Developing Learning Skills through Children's Literature: An Idea Book for K–5 Classrooms and Libraries.* Phoenix, Arizona: Oryx, 1986.

Literature for Children Series. Glendale, California: Pied Piper, 1975–present.

Lukens, Rebecca. *A Critical Handbook of Children's Literature.* Glenview, Illinois: Scott, Foresman, 1986.

Mertz, Maia Pank, and David A. England. "The Legitimacy of American Adolescent Fiction." *School Library Journal* 30:2 (October 1983), pp. 119–123.

Moss, Joy F. *Focus Units in Literature: A Handbook for Elementary School Teachers.* Urbana, Illinois: National Council of Teachers of English, 1984.

Nilsen, Alice Pace. "Rating, Ranking, Labeling Adolescent Literature." *School Library Journal* 28:4 (December 1981), pp. 24–27.

Nell, Victor. *Lost in a Book: The Psychology of Reading for Pleasure.* New Haven, Connecticut: Yale University Press, 1988.

Norton, Donna E. *Through the Eyes of a Child: An Introduction to Children's Literature.* Columbus, Ohio: Merrill, 1987.

Paulin, Mary A. *Creative Uses of Children's Literature.* Hamden, Connecticut: Library Professional, 1982.

Polette, Nancy, and Marjorie Hamlin. *Reading Guidance in a Media Age.* Metuchen, New Jersey: Scarecrow, 1975.

Rudman, Masha Kabakow. *Children's Literature: Resource for the Classroom.* Needham Heights, Massachusetts: Christopher-Gordon, 1989.

Shapiro, Lillian. "Quality or Popularity? Selection Criteria for YAs" *School Library Journal* 24:9 (May 1978), pp. 23–27.

Sloan, Glenna Davis. *The Child as Critic: Teaching Literature in Elementary and Middle School.* New York: Teachers College Press, 1984.

Smith, Carl B., and Peggy Gordon Elliott. *Reading Activities for Middle and Secondary Schools.* New York: Teachers College Press, 1986.

Spiegel, Dixie Lee. *Reading for Pleasure: Guidelines.* Newark, Delaware: International Reading Association, 1981.

Spink, John. *Children as Readers.* Chicago: American Library Association, 1989.

Stewig, John Warren. *Read To Write: Using Children's Literature as a Springboard to the Teaching of Writing.* New York: Richard C. Owen, 1980.

Thomas, Earl. *Gosh: 103 Ways To Build Interest in Secondary Reading.* Novato, California: Academic Therapy, 1981.

Weiner, J. Pamela, and Ruth M. Stein. *Adolescents, Literature, and Work with Children.* New York: Haworth, 1985.

Index